The Hawk
and the Dove

Distributed to the trade by National Book Network.

Generous quantity discounts are available from Smith/Kerr Associates LLC (207) 439-2921 or www.SmithKerr.com

Cataloging-in-Publication data is on file at the Library of Congress.

• ISBN13: 978-0-9786899-5-7
• ISBN: 0-9786899-5-7

Cover design by Claire MacMaster, Barefoot Art Graphic Design, text design by Kim Arney, author's photo by Meaghen Schnippert Gaffney, cartography by Cherie Northon, Ph.D, Mapping Solutions

Printed in China through Printworks Int. Ltd.

The Hawk and the Dove

World War II at Okinawa and Korea

Roland Glenn

Smith/Kerr Associates LLC
Publishing
43 Seapoint Road
Kittery Point, ME 03905 USA
Tel/Fax 207 439-2921/bizbks@aol.com/www.SmithKerr.com

*To the memory of
my mother and father,
Iva Myrtle Egner Glenn and
Raymond McCrea Glenn
and to my very alive sister,
Doris Adel Glenn Schnippert,
whose love and support
gave me the strength and confidence
to go to war.*

Contents

Acknowledgements

I AM INDEBTED TO A number of people who encouraged me to write about my life, and particularly my experiences during World War II. Many have read and reread these war stories and have offered suggestions as I went along remembering what took place and trying to set down my own recollections. The other half of these stories belong to the many individuals I encountered during infantry training, combat on Okinawa, and the occupation of Korea following the dropping of the atomic bombs on Hiroshima and Nagasaki.

I must thank Blossom and Alvin Tresselt for their early and consistent encouragement, Barbara Williams for her stiff and fair criticism, Paul Siff for his willingness to read an early manuscript and provide historical detail, Myra Hicks for her copy editing, good humor, and endless supply of jokes, Dr. Mike Wisneskie, Dr. Eugene Glick, Dr. Marie Guay, and Psychologist Thomas Moyer who recognized so clearly the invisible wounds suffered by combat soldiers, Lee Essrig, Steve Fox, Ann Hershfang, Georgie Wixson, Norma and Bob Holmes, Sieglinde Hughes, Michelle and Steve Rowan, Donna and Ed Lanigan and members of my family for their support and encouragement.

I will forever remain indebted to Bill Marvin, my first psychoanalyst for the tremendous support he provided during the five years when I first poured out these stories on his couch following my return from war before Post Traumatic Stress Disorder (PTSD) had been identified.

Jody Woodruff, a good friend of many years, has given time and attention beyond the call of duty in assisting me to sharpen the narrative's flow and has thus helped me to become a better writer. Jody recognized the uniqueness of the stories and the value they could have in achieving a better understanding of the barbaric, absurdity, and insanity of our war history where we send our children off to kill each other.

Digby Diehl, a long-time buddy and accomplished author of best sellers, has given generously of his time to read and evaluate the manuscript.

Joe Mazza, a recent friend and teacher, gave voice to many of the characters in the stories by reading aloud these tales of a country boy so that I could hear them speak and bring these people to life in the narrative. I've also been able to bring them to life during stand-up performances before live audiences in recognition of The Veteran's History Project of the Library of Congress.

My recent friends at the Sentry Hill retirement community in York, Maine have graciously listened to my stories and offered encouragement. I want to thank Nat and Irene Bellantone, Pam Card, Margaret Dixon, Al and Rae Kerr, Arthur Higgins, Adelaide Meskill, Marian Mosteller, Helen Samson, Ralph Sprague, Sally Sulloway, Ida Watson, Pat Welsh and Paul Wentworth for their willingness to sit and listen and to laugh at the antics of this country boy growing up.

Carolyn Wilkenson, a former Wellfleet neighbor, diverted her fond gaze of the North Atlantic from the peace of her Cape Cod home to read my stories and offer her professional editorial advice.

My son, Woody Glenn, devoted many hours of his time reading the stories on his computer and calling Dad with suggestions and questions that were always helpful. My daughters, Robyn Glenn Boccardi and Heather Glenn Wixson helped me to become a better writer by pointing out my tendency to compose run-on sentences and "mispel" words. Robert Boccardi, Bill Schnippert and Joel Glenn Wixson are three great men in my life who can be counted upon to offer sage advice. My niece, Gretchen Schnippert Jacobs, has consistently responded to my stories with valuable suggestions. My cousins, Joan and Corky Wilt, helped me to describe the small town of Ligonier, Pennsylvania where we kids grew up in safety. Nevada Fyock, of Johnstown, Pennsylvania, has read all the stories and still provides suggestions as she approaches 95 years with gusto. Lynn Kraft, also of Johnstown, has offered consistent support.

A special mention is due my mother, Iva Myrtle Egner Glenn, who somehow retained and filed away over 300 letters written to me and by me during the war years. These letters were safely boxed and remained unopened in the closet of our homes for over fifty years. My sister, Dori Adel Glenn Schnippert, I, and other members of our family are gaining insight as to how family and friends at home managed the strength to send me and all the others off to war. The powerful lines written in these letters almost bring back to life a mother, father, grandparents, aunts, uncles, school mates and neighbors whose faith in themselves, their God, their country, and their sons and daughters helped to see them through those terrible years.

This book would not have been printed without the able and professional support of my publishers, Smith/Kerr Associates, LLC. Spencer Smith and Jean Kerr saw the possibility of bringing my war stories to the attention of readers beyond my network of family and friends with the hope that my experiences in combat will alert a wide audience to the medical and psychological needs of returning veterans from the Middle East wars.

I have attempted to use the actual names of people referred to in the stories. In some cases, my memory has failed me in recalling actual names, both American and Japanese personnel, who I encountered. With the exception of Captain Isobe, I have used fictitious names for the other Japanese soldiers who I met during the first U. S. occupation of Korea.

I have a special debt of gratitude to the members of Company "I" in the Seventeenth Infantry Regiment of the Seventh Infantry Division. Many heroic deeds were unselfishly undertaken by these scared but very brave men. And, I wouldn't be here to write these words were it not for the steady gaze on my back by John Garcia who "Followed Me" in combat, became my unofficial body guard, and saved my life more than once.

Finally, to the spirit of my recently deceased wife of 60+ years, Carolyn Taylor Glenn, I offer thanks for her persistence in encouraging me to write, and her past willingness to listen to me read aloud to hear my own voice. For all that and much more, I promise the continuation of a love affair for the rest of my days.

It was a great ride that lasted sixty years, 1947–2007.

Preface: The Invisible Wounds of War

AS THIS BOOK GOES TO PRESS, more than 20,000 combat veterans have returned home from the Iraq and Afghanistan wars with medical and emotional injuries. This number could grow to over 100,000 before these wars come to an end. A large number of these veterans are haunted by the killing and violence they witnessed during their months in combat. Nothing in their military training could have prepared these fine young people for the awful experience of taking the life of another human being or witnessing that. The invisible wounds suffered during combat are not so easily recognized by medical doctors. Suicide rates have become a growing concern among military personnel. It is doubtful that the hospital facilities of the Veterans Administration will be capable of providing adequate care to these individuals, many of whom will need psychological help for the remainder of their lives. This unfolding drama may well become one of the most tragic outcomes of our military campaigns in the Middle East.

One thing I can do in response to this tragic situation is to share with you what happened to me during the battle of Okinawa. After our forces tried to achieve peace during the first occupation of Korea, after the atom bombs were dropped on Hiroshima and Nagasaki, nothing could erase the imprint on my mind and spirit from the carnage I had seen. Returning home, I was able to find psychological help which I so badly needed. It is my hope that today's returning veterans will be as fortunate.

Introduction

Trained to Kill

IT'S ALMOST IMPOSSIBLE to express my feelings about killing, and in particular, my feelings about one human being who seems more real than the many faceless enemy encountered in battle. The decision to kill him still haunts me.

One of the most painful memories, repeated time after time in my dreams, is of a day toward the end of the Okinawa battle. A Japanese soldier ran across the field where my company of the Seventeenth Infantry was on patrol. We'd survived major attacks, and felt confident of our skills as we walked along the top of the southernmost tip of the island. There was no thought of taking prisoners alive as we searched for any remaining enemy we could find. We all fired at once when we saw a Japanese soldier running across the field before us, as though we were shooting at a rabbit during hunting season back home. Our lead scout shouted, "*There he goes, Cricket. The Jap is hiding right behind that outcrop of rocks.*" We found him lying there, face up with his hands folded across his clean uniform, as if he were asleep. I knelt and felt for a pulse detecting a faint beat of his heart. There were no medics nearby. We couldn't carry him down the cliff. I asked my men to leave me alone with him while I thought about what to do. He looked like me, a human being. I couldn't bring myself to leave him there to slowly die alone.

While taking his hand in mine, I fired two bullets into his forehead. They made neat round holes with no spurting blood, just as if I'd taken a red crayon and drawn two dots on his skin. His heartbeat stopped. I remained there with him for a few minutes feeling both love and sadness toward this enemy soldier. Then carefully covering his body with ferns, I walked away to rejoin my men realizing that I'd made a compassionate decision. As we continued our patrol, I felt my strength as an infantry combat commander increase.

That particular scene remains very vivid and resurfaces to this day. I grieve that I didn't find the strength to rescue this young man. Somehow we should have carried him down the cliff where he might have received medical attention. Who was he? Were his parents as loving as mine? Did he plan to marry and have a family?

There were many major attacks on enemy positions on Okinawa when we fired in unison, not knowing whose bullets caused a death. Our anonymity shielded us from guilt. We'd spent many hours during basic training back in the States learning the skills of firing the Army's powerful M-1 rifles. I perfected hitting the targets right between the eyes or into the heart. My skills won me lots of medals to pin to my chest. Sitting behind a sub-machine gun and pulling the trigger sent a surge through my body as hundreds of bullets shredded the human-like targets. What power! What a great shot! At night, while sharpening our bayonets and cleaning our rifles, we bragged about our successes in learning how to kill. "*Did you see the way I gouged out the eyes of that enemy soldier? How about the time I planted my boot right in the balls of that bastard? I knifed him while he screamed.*" But all that infantry training didn't prepare me for killing the Japanese soldier behind the boulder. That decision didn't qualify me for another medal on my chest. It did assure me that I'd never forget. Never. That image still won't leave even after years of therapy.

We were trained to kill but also trained to not express any feelings. I doubt that I could have ever carried out our mission to kill so many enemy soldiers if I'd thought much about how I felt in doing the actual killing. Our basic infantry training deliberately avoided dealing with the feelings associated with killing. We were brainwashed to think of our enemy as inhuman, as animals. At no time prior to combat did I hear about the centuries of Japanese culture and history that we were to experience. Even movie newsreels depicted our future enemy as "monkey runts." Their worship of an Emperor and their brutal methods of killing were unknown to us. Information about Japanese culture that might have made them seem more human wasn't provided. We knew nothing about how they were trained for combat, educated, or if they were intelligent men.

The strenuous infantry training that we received before arriving on Okinawa, just after the invasion on Easter Sunday, 1945, turned us into brutal killers. Our drill instructors were tough. But never were we physically hit, slapped or humiliated into obedience. Much later I learned that Japanese youth being trained for cannon fodder and sacrifice on Okinawa were miserably treated with physical slapping and clubbing to instill blind devotion and utter loyalty to their homeland. The Emperor inspired awe and adoration. There was no questioning of their Empire's mission or of one's duty to suffer and die for it. Instilled in their minds was the belief that killing the enemy, by any means, provided an honorable death to that soldier. To the Japanese, suicide was preferable to being captured. For centuries, Japanese culture honored their warriors of death. We knew little if anything about this culture and history when we fought them on Okinawa.

Telling my war stories upon arriving home didn't help. Indeed, it seemed almost impossible. My family didn't really want to hear the truth about combat. But my cousin, Corky and I would go off by ourselves to share our experiences. Corky had served in combat in the Navy. When together with our families, if the subject of combat came up, the conversation suddenly changed to the weather or how many cans of apple butter our mothers recently put up. I believe Dad wanted to know. But he didn't ask until we took walks in the woods together just before he became very sick. It was too late then to talk with him fully about it. If I went into detail about incidents in combat he would begin to cry. That would bring tears to my eyes as we sat side by side. Finally we would hug and continue our walk in silence through the woods.

An exception to this inability to tell my war stories was Monty Clark, the Headmaster of Kiski School in Saltsburg, Pennsylvania which I had attended before going off to war. Monty became a friend and father figure after I returned from Asia. He was interested and drew out the details of my war experiences. He would find me sitting alone at times gazing into space. Monty liked my story about an enemy artillery shell that nearly blew us to smithereens while I rode in a tank behind enemy lines to locate their positions. He asked me to tell it over and over. Monty helped temporarily, but I didn't realize then the extent of the trauma inflicted upon me during combat.

My nightmares began after Carol and I married. In 1947, we were living in the Tenth Street Studio building in New York City. I'd been accepted as an undergraduate student majoring in anthropology at Columbia College. My vision was to become a scientist and explore ancient cultures.

Still screaming, I heard the Drill Sergeant's voice from Infantry Basic Training in Macon, Georgia. "Now listen up you guys. If you want to stay alive, pay attention. We're gonna show you how to slit the throats of those miserable Jap monkeys. And if you don't get it right the first time, it's your head that'll be sliced off so fast you won't even know you're dead. Now, watch me as I sneak up on the Jap, grab him around the head and slice his neck fast with this bayonet. Blood shoots out of his jugular just like water shooting out of a hose under high pressure. I throw him to the ground and jab my boot into the back of his neck. He squirms for just a few seconds, and is dead just like a headless chicken flopping on the ground. You either get him or he'll get you. And don't give me any of that shit about his being a human being. He's no better than a squirrel that you shoot up in a tree. They're not human! They're animals! And you guys are gonna be the best goddamned killers in this man's army. Now practice this with your buddy. Start right now to remember everyone you ever hated in your entire lives. Remember hate. Let me hear you yell hate. Louder! Hate! Hate! Hate! Feel the sharpness of your bayonet blades. You will only have one chance to slice that throat and you better make it good and deep."

"OK, today you're gonna learn how to drive your bayonet into the guts of a Jap who is running at you. You aim it right under the rib cage and jab it in so deep that the point begins to come out of the bastard's back. This time you scream and yell and scare the shit out of him before he can slice your head right off your shoulders. He's been trained to kill and loves death more than surrender. Giving up his life for that fuckin' Emperor will make his family proud. Now, you're gonna practice charging these dummies. I wanna hear the hate coming out of you. Do it over and over. Drive the knife in deeper. Let me hear your anger. We're gonna do a demonstration tomorrow for Bette Davis who's here on base selling War Bonds. Only Bette Davis won't be in the jungle where you're headed. That place will be infested with Japs and you're going over there to kill every one of them. Take no prisoners! Kill them and let them rot!"

All I can remember is screaming and thrashing around in bed, my body covered in a cold sweat. Someone held my arms down. "Cricket, it's OK. You're here with me. Wake up! No one is after you. It's me, Carol. Don't be afraid. Open your eyes. We're here in bed together in our studio in New York City. You're not in combat on Okinawa. You're safe."

"What's the matter with me?" I asked. "Where am I? How did I get here? Where's the enemy? Carol, what's happening to me? I'm soaked and freezing. Oh, My God! I'm scared! Hold me!"

My nightmares continued. The slide show of combat scenes wrenched my gut and tore at my heart.

. . . Tracer bullets hit the Kamikaze plane just before it crashes into one of our Navy ammunition carriers. Massive explosions rattle my teeth. A red and yellow fireball rises into the sky. Both ship and plane sink. There's a medical tent with row upon row of dead American soldiers. Each body is covered with a rain tarp. They'll eventually be picked up and carried to the army morgue. A truck filled with bodies of dead Americans, stacked like cordwood, pauses beside me. It emits an unbelievable stench of death. I encounter a headless Japanese leaning against a tree. Where is his head? I hold Peter's body in my arms. My tears fall on his ashen face. Ben's bloody head continues to ooze his warm blood over my shoulder. Might I have saved him? The Okinawan mother is severely wounded and lashed to a post. It's connected to a trip-wired bomb just out of reach of her screaming child. No way to save them. I hold the frightened young soldier who sobs in my arms deep in a fox hole. He never recovers from the experience we shared climbing a cliff to meet the enemy eye to eye. The face of the young Japanese officer still has two small bullet holes that I shot into his skull. Three of my men remain in mid-air, as if they are leaping dancers, as a result of a massive machine gunning from the enemy. We are trapped and caught in an open field. The force of the bullets literally blew them off the ground. I hear the bombs going off and see the enemy attempting to escape along the cliff top. The flame throwers blast away. The screams of the Japanese soldiers trapped and incinerating in their caves is still with me. Bloated, roasted and steaming bodies lay everywhere. We pull some around our fox holes to provide more cover . . .

On and on the slide show goes. The invisible wounds of war were deep and complicated. I didn't realize the depth of my fear and guilt.

As a student, I had a fortunate and unexpected encounter one evening in 1947. I was at a lecture given by Willian F. Marvin at the Cooper Union in New York CIty on the subject of early childhood education from his perspective as a practicing psychologist. Teaching young children wasn't on my list of goals, but as I listened to Mr. Marvin talk about his views, I found myself becoming interested in his theory that every child has a strong desire to learn. *"All you need to do to help a child become excited about learning is to custom-make an educational program based upon that child's personal interests."* Seemed simple to me. By the end of his lecture I felt that I wanted to talk with him privately about his theories. He agreed to see me a few days later at his office. I hadn't yet connected the dots between the fact that I frequently awoke screaming from nightmares of combat and my supposed interest in talking with Bill Marvin about teaching.

Bill quickly detected that I had more to talk about than exploring his educational philosophy. Before I recognized or admitted to myself the hidden agenda, his interest in my time in the army drew me into telling stories about my combat experiences. On one occasion when telling him about the Okinawa battles, I broke out into a sweat. He placed a thermometer into my mouth and got a reading of 104 degrees.

The morning after this episode, my wife, Carol, a practicing nurse, took me over to a medical lab on East Tenth Street in Greenwich Village. Blood tests revealed that malaria had invaded my body.

While being treated for malaria, I began to see Bill Marvin three times a week. Paying $5 an hour was a steep fee for me as an unemployed college student. My sessions were increased to five times a week during that first year of therapy. For the next five years of my life, Bill became the first person other than Corky, Carol, and Monty Clark to hear my war stories. Bill and I relived the war several times during that five-year period. Sometimes during therapy, my throat would close as I related the incidences of killing. I couldn't speak about the lingering horrors, feeling afraid of revealing all that I'd experienced. Once I began to shake, sob and vomited in his sink. Bill held me. *"It's OK, Roland. You're safe here. Come back over and rest. I'm with you. You're going to be OK."* The memory of killing the young Japanese soldier behind the boulder caused temporary paralysis of my voice. It felt like I'd had my larynx removed. Bill held me in his arms while I cried. We said very little for the next half-hour. Exhausted, I went to sleep on his couch until he gently nudged me awake and said that it was time to go home.

Bill suggested that I might try drawing pictures of what happened there. I drew them at home and brought them to my therapy sessions. When I looked at a picture that I had drawn of a dead Japanese, I could tell the story of what happened on the battlefield.

My biggest hurdle dealt with the guilt that stemmed from my close-range killing of the young, severely wounded Japanese soldier behind that boulder.

Bill and I struggled with the guilt I felt from this one incident. Finally, my agony was partially lifted through educational work with a young Japanese boy who attended the Heathcote School in Scarsdale, New York. I worked at this progressive public school to craft individualized programs for special children. His father, a diplomat at the United Nations, brought him to me for tutoring. Bill enabled me to see that my efforts at helping this one Japanese boy could release me from the guilt that I carried from the earlier incident. That technique only partially worked. I'm still haunted by the face of the man I killed. His face appears to me in dreams like a piece of modern art, similar to a Picasso drawing with two distinct dots in the middle of the forehead. I'm able to see him as clearly as the moment when I shot him in 1945.

Not all my war memories are haunting, however. A difficult, but positive opportunity presented itself after the dropping of the atom bombs. It proved to be an opportunity for me to further mature in an ancient culture little known or understood at that time by American soldiers. We combat soldiers on Okinawa were abruptly transformed from being killers of the Japanese, to assuming responsibility for Japanese repatriation from Korea. We'd been training for the attack on the Japanese mainland. Now, abruptly, we were told to prepare ourselves to collaborate with the enemy we so recently killed. We were given no special training to undertake this task in Korea. Our emotions swung from feeling apprehensive about how to face the Japanese we hated, to expressing confidence that somehow we'd be able to do the job. The Japanese had occupied Korea from 1910– 1945. They were hated by the Koreans. Our task was to take over tremendous amounts of their supplies, stored all over South Korea, and to move thousands of Japanese troops back to Japan. It would be a major logistical operation involving needed collaboration with their commanders.

We arrived to cheers from thousands of Koreans at Inchon harbor in August, 1945. Little has been written about Korea immediately after the battles of World War II. *The Hawk and the Dove* describes this period of history and offers a strong sense of what that aftermath was like. As liaison officer with the Japanese Army commanders, I found challenges and pleasures in my encounters with my former enemy and the Korean people. I have included these stories along with tales of my interactions with Japanese solders who were so recently my mortal enemy. This experience appeared to have helped mask the psychological shock, at least for a time, resulting from the killing of so many humans on Okinawa.

I often have fantasies about returning to Okinawa, wondering just what I might find there on that semi-tropical island. It now serves as a vacation resort for the Japanese. I feel angry and bitter about the fact that the island has been returned to the Japanese government after our having suffered 49,151 American casualties, of which more than 12,000 were killed or missing during that last battle of World War II.

Peter, Harry, David, Ben and other men who served with me during the battle are buried there. The burial site of the two commanding generals of the Japanese forces is now a tourist stop. This is a modest reminder that 110,000 Japanese were also killed during Operation Iceberg. In addition to these losses, roughly 150,000 Okinawan civilians were killed. I understand that there is a Memorial Garden dedicated to all the men who were killed during the battle, both American and Japanese. The giant boulder behind which I killed the Japanese soldier might still be in place. And, in addition, there are the numerous installations of our armed forces located around the island.

I learned more from a nurse while hospitalized for a cardiac episode in Boston in 1995. She and her husband had just returned from a tour of duty in Okinawa. Since 1945, the United States armed forces have occupied twenty percent of the choicest real estate on this relatively small island. She described the problems of our twenty-eight different bases and the duplication involved in separate Air Force, Navy and Marine Corps airfields that had simply sprouted willy-nilly with the advent of the Cold War. No consideration had been given to equitable land use or the lives of the 1.3 million Okinawans. This nurse went on to remark, "*The Japanese on the island still refer to the Okinawans as Gooks. Both the Japanese and the Americans are hated by the native population.*"

Marriage, raising children and climbing the ladder of success consumed my productive adult life and at times kept my demons at bay. Years later when I retired to a seaside wilderness on Cape Cod as an older man, I'd go to my writing desk early each morning and not concern myself with anything important. Bills to be paid were set aside and not permitted to enter into my consciousness. The transactions of daily life were less important than the realization that, for the most part, life had been good while I enjoyed an interesting and diversified career, a solid marriage, good family and many friends. I had survived a war and a severe heart attack. Now I had more time to reflect and decided to lean toward the light rather than the dark. Nevertheless, fear of death still crept in at times. The memories of being in combat still haunted me and the frightening experience of lying immobilized in the emergency room following my heart attack sent shivers up and down my spine.

In *The Hawk and the Dove* I will tell the same stories that I have related to three therapists who helped me to understand the impact of my experiences in Okinawa combat on my psychological and physical health. I appreciate that I'm one of the fortunate ones who began receiving professional help soon after my return home from Asia in 1946. Even so, at certain times in my life I've tried to forget, thinking that was a safer path to follow, but finding it impossible to forget. I have finally written my book to share my experiences in World War II from 1943-1946 with my family and friends.

I look back on my experiences on Okinawa as a small moment in time, following a long history of American imperialism that began long before I was born in 1924. It continues to this day. The military-industrial complex is so entrenched in our economy that the survival of our democratic society is being threatened by our government which too often follows the path of war, rather than diplomacy, in resolving world problems.

In World War II literature or the literature of any of the wars, very little has been addressed concerning the emotional impact of killing on those individuals who fought. Needless to say, it does not serve those who instigate the wars to emphasize or deal with the impact of actually killing another human being. Perhaps telling my stories will help me put my personal demons to rest. Perhaps telling my stories will help others understand that *The Hawk and the Dove* is more than a personal purging. We are still training our young people to kill. We send them off to fight horrible and insane wars in cultures they little understand, stressing that killing is how to go about solving the issues.

Why are we appalled when we learn of our troops resorting to inhuman and barbaric behavior toward prisoners? What do they see in these prisoners other than the inhuman enemy they were trained to kill? So what if these animals are humiliated. The tens of thousands of soldiers who are physically and emotionally wounded either lie in hospitals or are back home, many untreated for their post-traumatic stress disabilities. In a *New York Times* article by Scott Shane, dated December 15, 2004, it was reported that from the conflicts in Iraq and Afghanistan alone there will be no fewer than 100,000 servicemen and women who will require mental health treatment for the next 35 years. I would ask you to think of them as you read *The Hawk and the Dove.*

Part I

Preparing For War

The Lesson

IN AUGUST, 1943 SHORTLY after I turned eighteen as a newly drafted recruit, the Army sent me to Camp Wheeler, in Macon, Georgia for Infantry Basic Training. I thrived on the organized routine, became physically strong, learned that I was a good shot with a rifle, and had a natural know-how in moving fast over the land. In fact, I had greater awareness of the terrain than most of the GIs. I now attribute this to the early coaching received from my Uncle Ford Wilt who took my cousin, Corky, and me on hunting expeditions in the mountains of western Pennsylvania. He always taught us to observe the slightest rise in terrain which could provide a hiding place from the squirrels, pheasants, and rabbits that we were to shoot and bring home for dinner. Hunting was not only a sport but a necessity during those days of the Great Depression. I respected this strong, handsome woodsman with a mop of flaming red hair. Corky, also a red head and the Huck Finn of our family, and I were buddies and grew up together.

One autumn evening years earlier, when we kids were in our midteens, Uncle Ford, Corky, and I sat around the potbellied coal stove in their Ligonier, Pennsylvania kitchen preparing for a hunting trip early the next morning. We listened to Uncle Ford tell stories about his previous adventures in the forest, and when he shot his first deer. I admired this man who knew how to fix anything at this time when most families lacked money to hire others to do jobs around the house. You fixed what you could with your own hands or it went unfixed. Uncle Ford was also a teacher and passed on something to me which neither he nor I knew at the time would save my life when I was in combat.

Corky had much more experience handling guns and had his own rifle. Being the lowest guy on the totem pole, my assigned job was larding

Ford Franklin Wilt—"Uncle Ford" was an outdoorsman. He and Aunt Lucy, Lucinda Harriet Egner Wilt, standing in front of their house on East Main Street in Ligonier. The house was built in 1937 with considerable help from us kids who cleaned the bricks. (Photo courtesy of Glenn family archives)

Kirkland Ford Wilt, "Corky," and Roland Malone Glenn, "Rollie," shown as teenagers about 1939 at the time when Uncle Ford Wilt took them hunting into the Ligonier mountains and taught them survival skills that would save their lives during combat in the South Pacific a few years later. (Photo courtesy of Glenn family archives.)

the boots and getting the heavy socks and gloves ready and lined up. Uncle Ford permitted him to clean the shotguns and get the shells ready. Mom and Dad had denied my earlier pleading to have such a rifle but interestingly permitted us kids to play with the two pearl-handled pistols that Grandmother Glenn was known to carry in her purse.

We piled out of bed long before dawn and headed off crowded together in the front seat of the pickup truck with guns, ammo, and lunches piled around us. The old Lincoln Highway wound its way up Laurel Mountain, and as daylight began, we could see the Ligonier valley spread out before us as the fog slowly lifted like a curtain on that early November morning. The trees were already bare from having dropped their colorful leaves. In the distance were the lower hills of the Allegheny Mountains where we liked to hike to our favorite swimming hole for skinny dipping and family picnics. What a beautiful sight.

"Now, I want you kids to do exactly as I tell you. Keep your traps shut and follow my hand signals." The great man had spoken and we walked cautiously through the mist into the forest with Uncle Ford pointing here and there to places in the frost covered land where we shouldn't step or trip up. He silently pointed at bumps, rises, and little gullies, and at high trees using his hands and without saying a word, to signal us to look carefully. Suddenly he stopped, pointed out a squirrel's nest very high up in an oak and showed us, without uttering a sound, a depression where the three of us quietly stretched out on the very cold ground. Thankfully Mom Glenn and Aunt Lucy had insisted that we all wear long-johns.

Before long a squirrel came out of the nest and began to walk along the high branches. My body began to tingle all over as Uncle Ford fired the first shot and the body of the little animal came tumbling down crashing through the branches to the ground. "You got'm," Corky and I shouted at the tops of our lungs. We both jumped up and ran to retrieve the dead animal.

"You dumb kids. Didn't I tell you to keep your traps shut? Now, you have signaled to every animal this side of the mountain that we are here. If you had just stayed still, we could have gotten two or maybe three. How many times do I have to knock it into your heads that we were completely hidden behind this little rise in the land and not one single animal could see us? You're never going to make good hunters if you don't watch both the land and your mouths. Damn! We need more meat for supper. Come on. Let's go. No use stay'n here."

It was time to pee. We watched our footing and quietly headed back to the truck. Suddenly, there was a whirring of wings and a pheasant took off right before our eyes. Corky fired this time. One shot bagged him. I ran and retrieved the bird. Now the evening's dinner was looking more promising. My Aunt Lucy had warned us the night before that we were to have either a game stew or fried mush for supper, depending upon the outcome of this expedition.

The next stop was a wide corn field which was still covered with early morning frost. The surrounding leafless trees seemed to float in the distance through the still misty morning. The frozen ground crunched as we moved but our feet were dry from the expert larding I'd given to the boots. Uncle Ford fanned us out and used hand signals, directing me to the far right and Corky to the far left. We moved forward together watching where we stepped. Not a sound was heard except for the occasional rustle of the dried corn husks. It happened quite suddenly. Two rabbits took off. Uncle Ford got one and Corky the other. I did the pick ups. Another pheasant went up, down, and into our bag. The evening meal was now going to be a feast.

Later on, we found a big outcrop of rock to sit on and have our lunch. While we ate, Uncle Ford spun more yarns about hunting trips of the past. I can still hear his deep voice and will never forget him. He kept talking about the importance of the land, rises and falls, brush hideouts, and the need for utter silence. We sat, listened, felt the warm sun on our faces, and then climbed back into the truck and headed home with our bounty. We sat around the kitchen and cleaned the game feeling pretty proud of ourselves. An aroma of baking apple pies filled the room. Aunt Lucy and Mom prepared a grand meal. The large oak table in the dining room, lighted by flickering homemade candles, was laden with a meal fit for royalty. Uncle Ford said grace before we all dug in. A bountiful meal! Who cares about this Great Depression anyway? It seemed to me to be somewhere else. We were doin' pretty good, except I missed my Dad who was out of work and off somewhere looking for a job on a WPA road gang.

Those lessons taught by my Uncle Ford Wilt were to have a different application within a few years. He passed on survival skills that neither he nor I knew at the time would save my life during the long bloody days of hand-to-hand combat on Okinawa, when I hunted down and killed Japanese during the last battle of World War II. Once, being ambushed by a sudden enemy attack, I spotted and dived behind a slight rise in the land and pressed my body deep into the earth as a barrage of enemy bullets slammed into the dirt just a few inches from my lowered head.

The opportunity to fully explain and thank Uncle Ford for how I believed he helped me survive during the war unfortunately never presented itself during his lifetime. The adults didn't want to hear about our experiences in combat. Corky and I would need to get off by ourselves to share our war stories. This past summer, nearly seventy years later, I stood together with Corky and other members of his family by the grave of this wonderful man on a sunny hillside in Ligonier. Overlooking the valley and distant mountains where we hunted together, I told them the story of "The Lesson."

A Marching Father

THE EXPECTED ARMY DRAFT notice arrived in the mail just after my 18th birthday in June. The short and clear instructions directed me to report at 4 P.M. on August 24, 1943 in front of the Ligonier, Pennsylvania Movie Theater carrying nothing but a toothbrush and sweater. A couple of weeks remained for me to prepare myself and, at this point, I can't remember what I did with most of that time. I extracted promises from my parents that they would keep and care for my cocker spaniel, Chiene, and the 1935 Chevy sedan that my father bought me with his huge $300 World War I government bonus, a great vehicle to entice girls into the back seat of. There weren't many, but every one gave me confidence and furthered my education. Boy oh boy, did I ever take care of that car!

My cousin, Corky, and I spent time together during those days visiting our secret shack up on Grandfather Egner's hillside just outside of town. Cut trees leaning against the shack made it a totally secret hideout. We had pinched the lumber and nails needed to build this shack from local merchants in Ligonier. We were quite accomplished small-time thieves. From this hideout, we desperadoes staged battles using slingshots and bows and arrows against Indians as they attacked over the hill. POW! BAM! GOT ONE, BY DAMN! During less hostile times, we leisurely browsed our stored collection of girlie magazines in this safe spot . . . Lana Turner, Betty Grable, Carol Lombard, all those beautiful legs.

On the 24th, Mom prepared a stuffed turkey dinner with all the trimmings in my honor. I can still visualize her busy in the kitchen cooking the food she knew I liked. She bossed Dad around to get this and that for her but he slipped out whenever he could to chat with the growing number of relatives who were arriving at the old Victorian house up on East Main Street to give me a proper send off.

My father, Raymond McCrea Glenn, and Mother, Iva Myrtle Egner Glenn, at Idlewild Park in Ligonier about 1940. This picture is how I remember them appearing as I went off to war. We had many family picnics and reunions at this park during my youth. The Egner family descendents still gather there every few years with several generations present. (Photo courtesy of Glenn family archives)

My maternal grandparents, Grandpa and Grandma Egner (in their upper eighties and looking just like the famous painting of the farmer and his wife), Aunt Lucy, who resembled Lucille Ball, Uncle Ford Wilt, John Denver's replica, my cousin, Corky, Uncle Ted Egner and his daughters, and other Egner family uncles, aunts, and cousins came to the dinner. I remember diminutive Aunt Pearl and big, fat, sweating Uncle Ira. I sometimes believed that his neck would explode right out of his tight collar and frequently it did. He grew huge puss-filled carbuncles on that fat neck and Mom would be called to perform kitchen surgery with a sharp razor while I held a towel to catch all that puss.

Our next door neighbors, Mr. and Mrs. Burkey, came over to wish me well. I had mowed their lawn and weeded their large garden to earn money.

My Glenn grandparents died years earlier before the war began, and had once lived in the grand house with all of us. I still felt their presence. Grandmother Glenn's regal bearing reminded everyone of England's Queen Mary. She wore her snow-white hair high on her head, always dressed for a social occasion, wearing frocks trimmed with white lace at the neck and sleeves. Carrying her handbag, containing the little pistols, she commanded whatever space she occupied. Nobody, but nobody argued with Sarah Katherine Hawksworth Glenn. Grandfather Glenn was a dandy of a man, sporting sideburns and a handlebar mustache, who always dressed in three-piece suits, wore spats and a bowler. A gold chain attached to an engraved

Our Egner Grandparents, standing with Corky and Rollie in the backyard of their Ligonier home on East Main Street, about 1930. Lucinda Hemminger Egner and William Kirkland Egner were the two family elders who encouraged us kids to appreciate the magnificent mysteries of nature. (Photo courtesy of Glenn family Archives)

gold watch stretched across his vest. That antique watch passed to Dad and then to me. Grandfather, a grocery salesman, made friends wherever he went and frequently invited them to our home for meals, often without informing any of the women in the household. They were short-order cooks.

For a time, my parents, baby sister, and I had shared the same house with both sets of my grandparents and a canary named Bill. My grandmother had the unfortunate habit of allowing Bill to sit on a towel by the space heater on the floor after he had taken his daily bath. My first rat terrier dog, Patty, chewed his head off one afternoon when nobody was looking. What a terrible experience! I cried with my grandmother because I loved Bill too. We bought Grandma Egner another bird. It didn't help much.

My four grandparents had celebrated their fiftieth wedding anniversaries during that period of my childhood. Including my parents, these six people, together with a host of aunts and uncles, were strong role models. They all made it very clear that loving a person of the opposite sex was the way that one spent one's entire life. There were a couple of family upheavals that brought that conclusion into question—our family wasn't totally free of scandal. Corky and I did our part to challenge the boundaries of community social decorum, but at least we hadn't been jailed as had one of our older peers.

On this special day, the house was overflowing with relatives spilling over from room to room and onto the front porch and sidewalk. Everyone was talking at once, greeting each other, and slapping me on the back. Uncle Ford's voice rose above the others. "You'll do just fine, Roland. We'll write often. Let us know how you're gettin' along. My, we're so proud of you. Kill as many of those devils as you can. Just pretend you're shootin' rabbits. Japs ain't no better. And remember to keep your trap shut and look out fer the lay of the land."

The large family table was set with the best linen and china used only for very special occasions. The delicate china, passed down from generation to generation, graces our table each year at our holiday feasts.

The cooking and preparation for this family meal kept Mom very busy all day. She probably planned that as her way of dealing with the pain of our impending separation. Dad talked with everyone and told stories about his experiences during W.W. I. His pride in his country became evident to me early in my life. I recalled him years earlier dressed in his army uniform as we marched together around the dining room table. We exchanged glances through this crowd of relatives and smiled at one another possibly wishing we could be alone but resolving that it wouldn't happen with so many people around. I wondered why I hadn't taken the time earlier to be alone with this loving man more frequently.

My three-year-old baby sister, Doris, too young to know about war, clung to me all day. I called her "Sunny Girl" and didn't want to leave her. My parents lost three babies in a row, including her twin brother. The successive deaths of those lost babies were an excruciating experience for me and it now seemed like a miracle to have a real live little sister. She'd been very upset all morning and I sensed we needed to be alone. Hand in hand, we went out through the white picket fence into the vast garden area behind the house, away from the chattering mob.

Granddad Egner's wood catwalk stretched from the rear of the house way out to the barn and chicken coop. A small flock of Rhode Island Reds remained from the one hundred I'd raised from chicks. I'd become a chicken farmer during my teens and made money for myself and the family by selling my birds to neighbors. There were still, however, too many birds remaining for the family to manage and I'd killed some off and sold them during the preceding weeks. My special rooster remained until last;

Doris Adel Glenn, Sunny Girl at age 3, as she appeared when I went to war. She has been a gift of a lifetime to me.

"Dori Glenn Schnippert," now a creative woman with 3 children and 7 grandchildren of her own. She remains a cherished and loving "little sister" in my life.

it was a magnificent bird and not as mean as most roosters. I didn't want to chop off his head, but the neighbors complained about his early morning wake-up calls. Raising animals for food wasn't really in my blood even though I had made money by doing it. I had also entered a few of my favorites into poultry contests at the local fairs and had won ribbons, but they were all pets to me.

I held Doris close as we walked along the garden path. Grandmother's old English garden was to the left with delphinium, holly-hock, phlox, daisies, and a host of other wild-flowers still in full bloom. To the right of the path were vegetable gardens laid out in perfect rows by Granddad. The root vegetables were in full leaf. Ripe beefsteak tomatoes hung from vines and the ears of corn looked promising. I told Sunny Girl about my first garden by the barn and pear tree, remembering how Granddad Egner taught Corky and me to shoot BB guns at pennies he would wedge into the bark of that tree. I spoke to her about planting flowers and how Grandma Egner started me out with zinnias, probably realizing that it takes a real lack of gardening skills to fail with zinnias.

She instilled in me my life-long love of planting. The image of her garden is so clear in my mind that it is like my brain snapped a photo never to be lost.

We walked around to the other side of the gardens and sat in the swing under the grape arbor where our parents had swung on their wedding day. The grapevines were old and heavy with blue and white fruit. A climbing American Beauty rose, planted by our mother as a present to her mother, exploded with a profusion of late summer blooms covering the arbor built by Granddad as a place to sit and eat sandwiches and drink lemonade in the shade on a hot afternoon, with the air heavy with rose scent. Walking further along, we came to the swing with seats opposite each other that went higher and higher when you push with your feet on the ground. Baby Doris always liked to sit there with me and swing while the family dog sprawled on the grass.

This time it didn't work. My story-telling wasn't helping either. Doris couldn't stop crying. I finally picked her up in my arms and cradling her head under my chin as I walked back into the old Victorian house where the family was now sitting down for the meal. Granddad mumbled a short grace and everybody ate and talked at the same time. My Grandmother Glenn always choked and farted about this time during a meal. One of the great talkers and farters of the family, she is sadly no longer with us. She used to cuddle me on her lap when I was a little boy. Once I came in from the garden where I had found a zinnia blossom cut off, probably by a worm. I tried to put it back on the plant to save it. Having failed, I ran to Grandmother Glenn crying about my tragic loss. She soothed me and to this day I can still feel the warmth of her arms embracing me.

After that great meal, the crowd of us left the old house where I'd spent so many years of my youth. This grand family procession slowly made its way under the trees down East Main Street passing Hib Niceley's store where we kids doled out our pennies on candy while listening to the old guys who sat around the potbellied stove during winter afternoons. Toothless Hib stood in the store's doorway and yelled, "Go gittem, Roland. We knowed you can do it." "Take care of that candy for me, Hib. I'll need some when I get back." "Don't you worry. I'll mail you a bag of your favorites if you jest let me know where you are." "So long, Hib, thanks for everything; I'll be seeing ya."

Further along, Leona and Peck Long reached down from their front porch to shake my hand. Peck yelled, "Your car will be waiting for ya when you git home." We kids joked about Peck's name behind his back and wondered if it really was long. He and Leona would invite us to take Sunday drives with them before Dad bought me the Chevy. Those were the days of motoring along country roads. We would end those drives by stopping at the newly opened Howard Johnson's on the Pennsylvania turnpike, a swell place to eat out. Leona blew me a kiss. "So long, Roland. We'll all be here waiting for you to get back." Other neighbors whose lawns I mowed waved good-bye as we passed. Dr. Mary Kinney came out of her office to wish me well. She taught me how to drive and took me on many trips around the Ligonier mountains on dark nights when babies were about to be born. Once I wore her heavy pistol because she feared she might be attacked by the woman's husband who didn't trust a woman doctor. I never shot such a gun in my life but swaggered around the yard that night feeling 10 feet tall. Another time, Dr. Mary permitted me to administer ether while she delivered a baby girl. I learned skills that night that would be used later on. What a miracle! I thought then that I wanted to become a doctor.

Our family procession finally reached "The Diamond," one of the most beautifully preserved public squares anywhere. A wooden plaque held the names of Ligonier boys who'd gone off to war. The four great iron canons that once pointed north, east, south, and west were missing, having been sent off to be melted down to make guns for the armed forces. The band shell in the center reminded me of the times I played the euphonium in the community band on summer Saturday nights and then enjoyed free ice cream cones after the concerts. May Breniser, owner and operator of the Victorian Breniser Hotel, stood on the wide steps and waved. May had hired me as a bus-boy, bellhop, driver, and handy-man who carried soiled linen from hotel rooms to the laundry. Some rooms were rented by the hour and I knew too much about that activity for comfort. In circling The Diamond, we passed the charred remains of the old livery stable where a number of horses had died tragically in a recent inferno.

Passing the police station reminded me of the day a member of the high school band got drunk and broke down all the newly installed parking meters. He was hauled off to jail in the back seat of the police cruiser. Pretty scary stuff. Then came the fire house where Uncle Ford served as a volunteer. The community band practiced there every week and from this point we went off to neighboring towns for the annual Firemen's Carnivals.

A block further on, we reached the front of the movie house. Ligonier's mayor and members of the draft board met us, along with other future soldiers and defenders of freedom. The Color Guards of the American Legion and the Veterans of Foreign Wars were already in position to lead the parade. The high school band played patriotic songs. My previous euphonium playing in that band and a $500 tuition loan from a local bank helped me to get admitted, with a music scholarship for my senior year in high school, to Kiski School in Saltsburg, Pennsylvania. Kiski's reputation as an independent boy's school with high academic standards enabled me to get into an academic setting that promised to help me within the army. Kiski boys were thought to be smart and good material for the services. In my case, the plan didn't work because of my color blindness. I scored very high academically at Kiski, but that didn't impress the recruitment officials who were selecting pilots. My record at Kiski, however, turned out to be a major factor in my military life. It led to my selection to become an Army officer, alas even if in the Infantry.

All of my family members and friends lined the sidewalks as we draftees formed up behind the band. My girlfriend, Virginia Pershing, watching along with Gloria Gallo, Virginia Kirschbaum, and Ruth Shoup were there waving small American flags along with Steve Wuchina, Dan Melville, Tom Donnelley and many other school buddies who joined the growing crowd. Some of the little kids ran out into the street, skipping and dancing around pretending that they were soldiers too.

The big deal time finally arrived, one of those moments when you were expected to become a man. At the very least, I needed to try my best to act like one. The mayor launched into a long speech about how proud he felt of us. "We are sending you to defend this great country of ours. You will be constantly in our thoughts and prayers." I wished that he would get on with it so that we could make our exit. Finally, a trumpeter sounded a fanfare and the band struck up a Sousa march. The parade finally began to move down West Main Street, with family and friends walking along the sidewalks. Front porches were common on most of the houses and they were all filled with waving well wishers.

Unexpectedly, my father stepped out of the crowd and marched beside me. He wore the cap from his W.W. I army uniform. "Dad! No other fathers are marching. What are you doin? I gotta go, Dad! This is it!" I didn't know what to do. Confused . . . embarrassed . . . I was unsure of my feelings. Public displays of affection between men, even between fathers and sons, weren't common. But this quiet, gentle man showed his support and on this occasion, didn't seem to give a damn about what others might think, including me. "Cap, I marched in World War I and I'm goin' to make this march with you. You'll never be alone." I felt his arm slip around my back for a moment and got a free hug or two. We marched silently together the remaining few blocks down the hill to the Ligonier railroad station. No one seemed to pay us much attention. Before I boarded the train, we hugged each other one more time and he whispered, "I love you. You're going to be just fine. Don't worry. I'll be with you all the way and will write every night."

Minutes later, I looked down from the open window in the railway car upon the smiling faces of my family. They were all there except for my Glenn grandparents but somehow I visualized even their faces in the crowd. Also a fleeting memory of that earlier hunting trip crossed my mind as I looked down and saw Uncle Ford with his hand raised toward me. I tried to reach down and touch him but couldn't connect. Everybody was waving except for my baby sister who was screaming for me not to leave. "Rollie! Rollie! Don't go! Don't leave me!" Mom tried to comfort her and also put on a smiling face for me. My attention was drawn to Dad who stood at attention at one side of the crowd saluting me. He was standing in front of a huge poster of Uncle Sam pointing his finger at me above the slogan "Your Country Needs You!" As the train pulled out of the station, with bells ringing and the band playing, it didn't even occur to me that I might never see my Grandmother Egner again or ever return to the old Victorian house up on East Main Street. I suddenly felt very alone.

■ ■ ■

Where did my parents and aunts and uncles get the strength to see their sons go off to war? I've never been able to fully understand that until recently while reading their letters to me, carefully boxed and sealed but unopened for over 50 years. What a discovery! It's as if those words, written so many years ago, are bringing back to life Mom and Dad, my Grandmother Egner, Aunt Lucy, Uncle Ford, Corky, Steve, Gloria, Virginia, and the Kiski faculty and students who were my friends. The letters are mostly humorous, and bring tears to my eyes from all the support they poured out. They help to explain how these family members and friends dealt with their own stresses back home by doing community volunteer work in support of the war. They also help me to better understand the deep love that has always existed between my sister and me, a brother-sister love that is a once-in-a-lifetime gift.

Thanks to the spirits who looked over me, I've never needed to see one of my own children go off to learn how to kill other human beings. I realize that the entire world was then involved in a global conflict with the Allies and had a common objective to defend all that the civilized world gained over thousands of years of history. But I still don't think that I could've mustered the kind of quiet strength communicated to me by the various members of my family and friends on that day in August 1943, and during the years of intensive training and horrible combat that followed.

Frankie

THE WHISTLE BLEW. The band played on. Train began rolling slowly. I reached far out the window to touch the raised hands. My focus on individual faces blurred as the distance between us grew. The group looked like one body with many waving arms. Trees finally blotted out the entire scene. I felt suddenly alone, scared, without all the warmth of the previous hours wrapped around me. Not like going off to Scout Camp in summer. That always left me feeling homesick and ready to get the hell out of Camp Echo. Couldn't wait for the family to show up and take me back to my garden, chickens, rabbits, and dog which is where I wanted to be in the first place. Christ! I was going off to war wondering what the hell I had taken along besides my toothbrush that would help me out of this mess.

I was a country boy from western Pennsylvania. Going off to Akron, Ohio a number of years ago in a Greyhound bus with Mom and Dad to visit my Dad's relatives, had taken me to the outer limits of my universe. We were a family that hung close together during good and bad times. Aunts, uncles, and more cousins than you could count lived just 15 minutes away in their Ligonier homes. In times of illness, death, or scarcity of food, everyone mobilized to rescue and prop up the family in trouble.

My mother and father, openly affectionate to one another, found it easy to say, "I love you." Dad showed me the way to love. We had just marched together arm in arm down Ligonier's Main Street. I thought about him and some of the things he had taught me as the train rolled along near Grandfather Egner's hillside where Corky and I had built our secret shack. An important memory that I carried with me on the rickety train popped up like a flashback of another lesson Dad taught me when I was a little kid. The lesson served me well during and following my Army life. Not as tangible as the toothbrush in my pocket, but nevertheless part of what I carried with me to basic training.

Frankie, the only black kid in my first grade class in Greensburg, Pennsylvania had a hard time of it, seemed sad and didn't smile much. Our teacher, Miss Blakely, and many of the kids didn't appear to like him. Nasty lady. She unfortunately lived in the apartment below us at that time. I drove her mad by driving my dump trucks across our wood floors. This poor soul couldn't stand the noise I made. There had been some great fights between my mother and my teacher. I would listen to the shouting below by putting my ear to the floor. My Mom could have been in the boxing ring.

One evening at the supper table, with Mom, Dad, and Grandpap and Grandma Glenn, I giggled out a story about how the other kids teased and chased Frankie and yelled "nigger" at him. Dad dropped his fork; blood seemed to drain from his face. His voice trembled. "That's awful! Terrible! I hope and pray that you were not one of those ignorant kids."

His gasp hit my face like a strong wind. Surprised and bewildered by his reaction, I felt like I had done something terrible. Granddad said, "You're being too hard on the boy." My face flushed. Felt like I had a fever. Dad's heavy breathing reached across the table. Silence! I ran and hid in the dark pantry.

I had a different story to tell the family at supper several days later. (Dinner was served at noon in those days.) "Frankie asked me to come over to his house to play." Dad responded quickly again. "I hope you said you would like to do that. It would be very nice for you boys to get together and come to know one another better. I suggest you accept his invitation."

Honestly, I didn't know just what to say because I suspected that the other kids might turn on me if I became Frankie's friend. I was scared and confused again. His skin was so black and he lived on the other side of Fourth Street just beside the cemetery.

The next day at school, I met up with Frankie in the coat room and whispered that I could come over to his house to play. I didn't want anyone else to hear me and felt unsure of myself.

The following afternoon as school let out Frankie looked across the room at me as if to say, "Well, are you coming or not?" The other kids stared at me as I passed them by. One whispered, "You goin' to that little nigger's house? Better watch out for his Momma. She's big and mean. Be sure to wash your hands when you get home."

I continued over to meet Frankie at the schoolroom door and we walked silently together out of the building along the several blocks to his house, passing the Westmoreland County Grocery where my grandfather worked. That was as far as I had ever gone from my house without my parents being with me. I was surprised when we went inside Frankie's house. What was I expecting? A dump?

The house was smaller than our apartment. Nice, clean, neat, pretty rooms. Living room tidy. Frankie had his own room. I didn't have one. Big garden out behind the house. We could run through the cemetery but must not tramp on any of the graves. We had a really good time playing together.

My father finally arrived to fetch me and Frankie's Mom invited him to sit and have tea. I watched him closely to see what he would do. He readily agreed to the invitation to sit down with this large woman who didn't look mean to me at all. We all had cookies around the polished dining room table. Looking back, it was a rare and unexpected happening.

Dad's departing words as we walked hand in hand out the door were, "We hope that Frankie will come over and play with Rollie at our house real soon."

My folks looked back and forth at each other at the supper table. Grandpap Glenn finally asked me, "Well, did you have a good time?" My one word answer was, "Yes." We all looked at each other; Grandpap said Grace and the eating began. Dad told us stories about a high school friend of his who was black.

I remember being very quiet that evening as I pondered the events of the day. It wasn't easy to fall asleep that night. I looked up and saw my father standing beside me. He sat on the edge of the bed and put his hand on my head. "You feel cool, Rollie, and I think that you will sleep well tonight. I am very proud of you and I love you very much."

We hugged each other. "Shall we say our prayers?" We knelt beside the bed together, as Dad did every night of his entire life, and began to recite *The Child's Prayer*. I always got a bit frightened and confused at the section, "If I should die before I wake, I pray the Lord my soul to take." In the mornings, when I discovered that I was still alive, I would wonder what and where my soul was since the Lord had apparently not seen fit to take it from me during the night.

Frankie and I went on to spend many hours together. He became a member of the gang of kids on my block. My other friends, Helen McColly and Tony Angelino, also learned to like him. We would rotate our playground from Frankie's backyard and the cemetery over to Helen's backyard which was just across the street from our apartment house on South Pennsylvania Avenue. Frankie and I continued to be friends until my family moved to Ligonier, where I entered the fourth grade.

There were only white kids in my classes during the balance of my elementary and high school years. I do remember an ethic that seemed to permeate that region of western Pennsylvania. Blacks were not welcomed. My Mom explained to me that black people were allowed to pass through our town during daylight hours but were never permitted to remain in our village at night. She had no answer for me when I asked her "Why?"

Dad heard this conversation and exploded once again. "Isn't this awful? Will these people never come to realize that Negroes are human beings just like us? You have got to get out of this town. I don't want you growing up here. It is too late for your mother and me, but not for you. We will help you one way or another."

They did help me make my exit from Ligonier by borrowing the $500 that paid my tuition over at Kiski School. After that final year of high school, the Army took over and I was on my way to God knows where. And, my Dad's arms were somewhere back there in the crowd, no longer around me.

A close friend asked me recently, "Do you have any ideas about how your current attitudes toward people of varied racial and cultural backgrounds got formulated?" My Dad is an important part of the answer.

Years later, I still ponder some of these questions as I go through this process of recovering my soul following severe illnesses. Memory is the diary that we all carry around with us. It is the recall of these experiences with my Dad that give me a new perspective on our relationship as father and son. I adored this quiet, gentle fellow and feel very close to him even now. I more fully realize what a profound lesson he taught me when influencing my earliest attitudes about people whose racial and cultural backgrounds were so different from my own. This has made it possible for me to have relationships which I might otherwise have avoided.

My family and I have been through life threatening situations in the past. War. Disease. Community disturbances during the Civil Rights upheavals. Our lives have been saved by individuals whose skin color and family backgrounds were different from our own. We have reached out, on more than one occasion, to these human beings for help. My debt to some of these people can never be fully repaid nor my love for them fully expressed.

The Tweeter Sisters

THERE WASN'T MUCH SLEEP the night I left home with the vision of my family and friends standing there waving good-bye as my mind flooded with memories. The dusty two-car train, pulled by a steam engine, would carry us from the Ligonier railroad station over to the main line station in Latrobe, Pennsylvania. It rattled on past the ice skating pond and slowed as we entered Idlewild Park, the scene of many family picnics. A longer train ahead of us awaited the reloading of hundreds of people who'd enjoyed a day's outing at this famous and scenic amusement park. Band music blared from loud speakers along the tracks.

This reminded me of past times I spent there learning how to make my first real money. Perhaps more than the money, I gained independence and took a few steps up "the ladder of success" that my mother always urged me to climb, by securing my first real job as cashier at the Roller Coaster with a weekly salary of 12 bucks. I saved most of it and counted it frequently, gave some to Mom and Dad for groceries, and opened my first bank account. The Great Depression did bad things to my Dad. Not goin' to happen to me! No it won't! Not to me, I thought.

Then I got a break by being promoted to become the park's Public Address Announcer, a real big deal. This important job gave me the opportunity to play records all day long from my booth over the souvenir stand beside the railroad tracks where special picnic trains deposited and picked up crowds morning and evening. The steam engines came chugging into the park with their whistles blowing while I put on a rousing Sousa march.

Just before day's end, a free performance would be staged in the central meadow of the park where large crowds assembled. One week it would be the circus. Next, would come the Hopi Indians who performed their native dances and sold their beautiful jewelry. Every week or so a new act would arrive.

Of all these different performers, the Tweeter Sisters were my favorites. I enjoyed announcing their act. Picture this. Me dressed in a tux that was a bit too tight, wearing a black top hat, a size too large, and on my feet a pair of dirty sneakers. I would dramatically step out onto the open air stage and into a spotlight holding a mike in one hand and a drum in the other. The crowds applauded as I bowed and began my spiel . . . **"Ladies and Gentlemen! Cast your eyes to the very top of these two hundred-foot, parallel ladders. The Tweeter Sisters will defy danger and slide down these two slender strands of steel holding on only by their teeth.**

And, now! Ladiezzz and Gentlemen! I ask that you remain absolutely quiet so as not to distract their attention during this death-defying feat. You will see this only one time in your life.

Are you ready, Julie and Emily? God bless you both! May your dangerous trip over our heads prove to be a safe one."

At this point each sister would raise one arm in a salute to me as I looked up from the stage beginning to beat on the drum to raise the tension higher. Bright spotlights would focus on the sisters and on the long wires that crossed the entire meadow slanting down from the tops of the ladders. Then the drum beat would suddenly end. The sisters would insert plugs into their mouths that were attached to pulleys. Their arms would spread out at their sides revealing yards of flowing silk and down they would come like two exotic butterflies. Two men slowed their descent with drag lines at the bottom. The girls would mount two white horses and be carried through the cheering crowds looking like two Christmas tree angels descended from Heaven.

These two parallel ladders began to intrigue me more and more as we went through this act twice a day. "Don't you get dizzy going up?" I asked. "Just keep your eyes on the sky and the tops of the ladders and nothing will happen," they said.

Early one morning, before the park opened, I took my camera and started the climb, keeping my eyes on the top that appeared to be a mile in the sky. Sideways glances revealed that I had climbed well above the tree line and could see the lake in the distance. My camera was bumping against my hip and I stopped to adjust it feeling as if I were about to become a trapeze artist. Higher and higher I climbed until I neared the top. And then, I looked down. Vertigo hit me instantly. I froze in place with my eyes tightly shut hoping that I could manage to get myself out of this mess, but not knowing what to do. One of the ground's keepers saw me trapped at the top and raced for the sisters. They climbed both ladders until one positioned herself just below me and the other one opposite me on the second ladder and calmly talked me down, a very long trip as I took each rung ever so slowly. Julie held a hand on my one foot while Emily talked to me as if nothing was wrong. When we finally arrived at the bottom, where a small crowd assembled, everyone but me broke out laughing and applauded while I trembled. The girls hurried me off to their trailer for some hot tea and a round of stories about how they got started and some of the funny things that happened to them. No one squealed to the park management or I would have probably lost my job.

The Tweeter Sisters were teamed up with a circus that featured a horse act holding greater promise for me. They had four really magnificent white Arabians. The Ring Master, dressed in a more dashing costume than the one I wore, made me look like a clown. At one point in the act, he would jump onto the rump of one of the horses and ride around the ring balancing gracefully with a slight up and down movement.

I prevailed upon the Ring Master to use me in the act. Still dressed in my clown's outfit, he would put a harness around me and pulling on a rope would lift me onto the back of one of the horses. I learned to balance fairly quickly and got better and better at it. Just when it appeared that I had mastered the trick, he'd pull on the rope and lift me up into the air while the horses continued their run below me in the ring. A great laugh would go up as I flapped my arms and waved my top hat until he lowered me again to the back of one of the horses. The crowd roared with laughter and I discovered my skills as a performer and got better with each show.

One day the Circus Manager approached me and asked if I would like to join the troupe at the end of their two-week engagement. Surprised and excited by this offer, I rushed home and announced to Mom and Dad, "I'm going to join the circus." Mom glanced over at Dad and then, looking me straight in the eye, asked, "How soon will you be leaving home?""Two weeks!" I said. "Oh, that will give me just enough time to get your clothes ready," Mom answered.

They were going to let me go without making a big fuss. I fully expected a big "NO." As each day passed, the question of whether I wanted to spend the rest of my life on the backs of those horses crossed my mind. Learning to climb those ladders? Becoming a Boy Wonder sliding down those slender strands of steel? I bowed out at the eleventh hour using as an excuse the necessity of my finishing high school. I still wonder what might have happened to me if I'd gone off with them. My parents permitted me to make this decision for myself. What marvelous wisdom on their part.

Idlewild Park became especially beautiful at night as the rides turned off their gaudy lights, allowing the stars to take over. I drove my Chevy back and forth to work. Such great fun for a teenager! One night after the fireworks, an accommodating young woman asked if I wanted to take her for a drive. That sounded like a good idea to me. We drove around and around and finally wound up at the Latrobe reservoir. She knew those back roads so well that I got the distinct feeling she'd been there before. Others must have preceded me as her driver, but it mattered little as we explored each other in the back seat.

I became very fond of making frequent trips to the reservoir that summer. Nice memory!

Unfortunately, my parents stayed up late until I'd arrived home. Dad liked to make fried egg sandwiches for Mom and me to top off the evenings. The recreational activity over at the reservoir took time, resulting in my getting home later and later for the egg sandwich ceremony. One night, near midnight, I could think of nothing to say except, "I had a flat." Dad smiled, winked, and the two of them went off to bed with the usual, "We love you."

I revisited Idlewild Park during the summer of 2001 to attend an Egner family reunion where 40 descendants of Granddad and Grandmother Egner came from all over the region between Madison, Wisconsin and Boston, Massachusetts. They no longer lived within 15 minutes of one another's homes in Ligonier. Cousins who'd attended my departure dinner from Ligonier gathered together once again. Many of us hadn't seen one another since we were teenagers visiting together in the old Victorian house up on East Main Street. We spent hours telling stories of our youth, looking at family pictures and then rode the antique carousel whose horses were once carefully painted by our Grandfather Egner, Uncle Ford and Corky. Three generations of our family had cared for this very special amusement ride that we had cherished over the years. I held my granddaughter, Jemma, on one of the horses that I rode as a child.

A number of years ago I took the train each morning from my home in Redding, Connecticut to New York City where I taught at New York University. One morning I glanced at the obituary page of *The New York Times* and noted the death of Julia Tweeter who fell to her death from slender strands of steel during a performance at the Iowa State Fair.

The last picnic train pulled out of the park ahead of the train carrying us off to join the army. I looked at the scene of my past exploits one last time as our dusty coaches rattled along the tracks beside the lake and on toward the main line station in Latrobe where we were to be picked up by a larger troop train.

Part II

Training For War

Basic Training

We found ourselves standing among another group of relatives and friends who had come to see off the Latrobe contingent, while waiting for the arrival of the long troop train. One young girl, sobbing and holding on to a young man, caused everyone to be on edge. Probably her older brother? Her family couldn't get her quieted down. Outbursts of crying bothered everyone who tried to put a good face on the situation. Momentarily, I thought back to my own little sister who appeared to have cried for all the adults bidding me farewell. Did she have any understanding other than my leaving home? Probably not, but I still wonder. A large billboard displayed a poster of Uncle Sam pointing directly at me again. Planes dropping bombs filled the poster's background with huge explosions reminding me that this wasn't the start of a trip to summer camp. Would I have the guts to kill when the time came?

While another band played rousing marches, we finally boarded the train. More emotional good-byes were said as we leaned out the train windows waving to those gathered on the platform. It didn't seem to matter that we didn't know these folks. They were wishing us well as we waved.

The coal-fired train lumbered east through the Allegheny Mountains where Uncle Ford had taken us hunting. We were in for a long night of restless sleep sitting up. Strange that nobody talked. Each man alone with his private thoughts. A few wrote letters. Some played cards. One group at the far end of the coach sang.

We passed through Greensburg, my birth place, where Grandpap Glenn took me to the movies Saturday mornings. Once he fell asleep during the show and *Tom Mix* ran through twice before Dad finally came. He found us in the balcony and got us home in time for supper at the McColly Apartments.

After midnight we passed through Johnstown where other members of the Glenn family slept. I remember going around the famous horseshoe curve in Altoona, one of the great railroad engineering feats in the country. To this day, everyone riding the rails across Pennsylvania wakes up to observe the beauty of the mountains as the train rounds the massive curve and descends the steep mountainside going east or climbs on the westward route. We passed through Harrisburg and proceeded to Philadelphia where our cars transferred to a south-bound train. Early next morning, we arrived at Fort George G. Meade, Maryland, still a massive army post just north of Washington, D.C.

Fort Meade processed the draftees. While still another band played, we staggered off the train, lined up and marched off to the first of a number of stops where we bagged our wrinkled civilian clothing and mailed the package off to our homes after putting on new Army uniforms. Next was the barbershop. Scalped! Then off to a medical building for mass physicals. Fifty of us stood stark naked getting the once over by a team of doctors. One of them noticed that I had a hammer toe on my left foot and sent me off to another room where a team of doctors dealt with special cases. They asked, "Are you going to be able to walk with a foot like that? You're going to be assigned to the infantry." I told them that I had walked all my life without any problems. "Wouldn't another branch of the service be a better place for you? How about driving trucks?"

"I would rather hike." A bad decision that I would regret later on. Next were inoculations against every conceivable disease. Several guys fainted. A shot against yellow fever? Why? Where?

We took many different tests that seemed to me easier than the ones taken back at Kiski School. I felt good about these tests. You can't imagine the number of different forms we filled out. I learned the word *beneficiary* when asked who would get my insurance in the event I didn't make it home. Ten thousand dollars! My family would be rich.

We scrubbed floors, cleaned toilets, and learned to march. My past experience as a member of Ligonier's high school band came in handy. Some guys stumbled over their own feet. A tailor from Brooklyn, with a straight up and down body which had no hips, had caused his rifle belt to slide down over his ass and fall around his knees causing him to trip. This guy's frequent marching accidents would screw up the entire platoon and enrage our Sergeant. "You are making me very angry!"

A parade at sunset saw us, as new recruits, pass in review. Joan Blondell, the movie actress, stood with the commanding general to review the troops. Wearing a white dress and holding a large bouquet of red roses, she presented most of us with our first view of a real live movie star. We practiced marching for hours in the hot sun and it all seemed to be worth it just to see this beautiful woman, who I had assumed noticed me among the hundreds of men in the parade.

Being recruited to play the baritone horn in the post band led me to believe I might continue as a musician at Camp Meade, but it didn't happen. Instead, I became a bugler in an Infantry battalion. My typing skills were noticed on my record and led to an office assignment resulting in a very funny experience. One night after a full day's work, we scrubbed the office floors before heading back to our barracks, exhausted. Just as we climbed into our sacks, the barracks sergeant told everyone to scrub the floors of that building, a job finally finished about midnight. Climbing up into my assigned upper bunk something didn't feel right. The guys next to me weren't the right guys. My God, tired and confused by the similarity of the buildings, I had returned to the wrong barracks and did all of that work for nothing. The Sergeant came into the room and announced that everybody who'd scrubbed the floor could apply for a weekend pass the next morning. Walking out of the building nonchalantly, I rather sheepishly returned to my own barracks located on the next street. In the morning, after collecting the pass, I headed for the train station and crossed Pennsylvania eating and drinking in style and ready to present myself as a smartly dressed soldier.

One bad experience at that Army post occurred when someone took my new wrist watch, a graduation present, off my arm while I slept. Other than that incident, things went well for me during that time of establishing my independence from my family. Good pay allowed me to send $50 home every month for deposit in a savings account and another $50 back to Kiski School to reduce the tuition loan that I owed. I never missed a payment! Army life could be pretty good and I wondered if it might be a career for me.

We continued marching, scrubbing floors and cleaning toilets for over a month. A large group of us were then transferred south to Camp Wheeler, an Infantry basic training center located close to Macon, Georgia. I thrived on the training, became physically stronger, became a good shot with a rifle, and found that I had a natural know-how in moving fast over the land. In fact, I had greater awareness of the terrain than most of the recruits and attribute this to the coaching received from Uncle Ford

Roland Malone Glenn, III, "Rollie," photos taken in 1943 at Camp Wheeler in Macon, Georgia, a United States Army Infantry Training Center. This center trained thousands of replacement troops for both the European and Pacific wars. From this center, I was transferred to The Infantry School, an officer training center, located at Fort Benning, near Columbus, Georgia. (Photo courtesy of Glenn family archives)

Wilt. And my handling of an army M-1 rifle, many times more powerful than the .22 I had coveted during my teenage years, impressed the drill sergeant who awarded me a citation. But we weren't out to shoot squirrels and rabbits any longer and Uncle Ford wasn't near to provide advice and offer protection.

Intensive daily lessons followed a strict training curriculum on the various ways one could kill. We practiced until our bodies were wet with sweat. These lessons went on for hours with ten minute breaks. The following day we'd be out in the field learning how to dig and camouflage a foxhole and how to dig and use a slit trench. Several days would be devoted to using a compass to follow a trail through dense forest or snake-infested swamps. There were lessons on how to use field radios and the laying of telephone lines from the simulated rear echelons to the battle front. These lessons were more enjoyable than those devoted to killing. There were very long hikes when we were loaded down with heavy equipment. Sometimes we remained out on field expeditions for several days. Kinda fun. Special exercises were staged to have us experience different kinds of possible enemy gas attacks. The gas masks we carried were very bulky. It seemed that whenever a lull came along, we'd be drilled in running in place or doing pushups and sit-ups. Each of us became physically stronger during those weeks of basic training. We were also learning the skills of survival by crawling on our bellies under barbed wire while live machine gun bullets were fired a few inches above our heads. Hand grenades were part of our armor and drills were conducted to teach us how to throw them so that they would explode close to enemy bodies, preferably right in their foxholes where the explosions would paste skin and bones right against the dirt walls of the holes. Never were we lectured on the foreign cultures we would experience once we went overseas. All humanity was stripped from the enemy during this intensive course.

Our days began around 5 A.M. when a noncommissioned officer would come into the barracks and yell, "Drop your cocks and grab your socks." On occasion and unannounced, a short arm inspection would be held and all our cocks would be inspected by a medic. What a way to begin a day! It appeared that our short arms and fire arms were equally important to maintain in a very clean condition.

My Camp Wheeler experiences also compared favorably with the script of Neil Simon's play, *Biloxi Blues*. I got drunk more than once, got kicked out of a whorehouse by the madam "whose girls were not there to service kids," and eventually applied and became accepted at Officers Candidate School. But before going to O.C.S., I achieved a certain, shall we say, recognition as a buck-ass Private. After completing three months of rigorous training and discovering my physical strength, agility, field smarts, manual dexterity, winning the highest marksman medals and bellying up to the bar with the best of them, the Army promoted me to Private First Class and assigned me to be clerk/bugler at battalion headquarters. Big deal time!

As a clerk in a battalion headquarters, I maintained the files, not then one of my better skills. One morning the captain who served as the boss of the office staff came up to me. "*Private Glenn, by the time I get back to this office after today's training, I want to see that these files have been cleaned out. They are a mess. If those files aren't cleaned out by 5 P.M. today you won't be with us much longer. Do you understand me?*" "YES SIR, I DO SIR." I jumped to my feet as this pompous ass marched out of the building. OK, my task was to clean out the files. Nothing complicated about that. I methodically emptied all of the contents of every drawer into a box and made repeated trips down to the cellar where I proceeded to burn the files in the furnace. After every bonfire of files, I went back upstairs for another load until every single document had been reduced to cinders. The only thing remaining in the file drawers were the alphabetical index card dividers. I even dusted the insides of the drawers as an extra effort to "clean out those files." The captain would be proud. At 5 P.M. he came marching back from a day in the field. *"Private Glenn, let me see how you have fixed up our files." "Right, sir, the job is done, just as you ordered."*

The Captain opened the first drawer, looked in, got a peculiar look on his face, and then opened the next drawer, and the next, and the next. *"Private Glenn, what have you done with the files?" "I burned them, sir."* "YOU DID WHAT?" *"I burned them, sir. You told me to clean out the files, sir, and that is exactly what I did."* The man's face was a study. I wasn't sure what would happen next. *"You mean to say that you burned up all the Army records which comprised the entire history of this battalion?" "Yes, sir, they were certainly in a mess and you were so right to order me to clear them out. They hadn't been used in God knows how long. Now we can begin all over with a proper filing system. I have it all figured out. Would you like to hear about my system?" "Private Glenn, you are as of this minute relieved of any further filing responsibilities. Furthermore, as of tomorrow, you will be assigned as the Colonel's orderly and will remain in the field as far away from this office as is possible." "Thank you, sir, I need the air. If you ever need another job done, just let me know."* This ungrateful man stormed out of the building. The other clerks broke up and said that I was lucky I didn't get shipped overseas. Anyway, I liked being in the field and, as the Colonel's orderly, I would have a lot of free time.

Red-haired, Colonel Sanford S. Stanton, III could've been W. C. Fields' twin brother. His bulbous nose would've seemed at home on the face of a circus clown. The middle-age girth on this man was surpassed only by that of Oliver Hardy. How he became a battalion commander of an Infantry outfit was known only to the Pentagon. He had trouble walking. As the Colonel's orderly, I had various important responsibilities including polishing his shoes, making up his bed, dusting his desk, disposing of his empty liquor bottles, and waking him from frequent naps when the commanding general paid surprise visits to our bivouac areas. He was pretty good at jumping out of his cot in a hurry but even better at getting back into it when the higher brass departed.

The Colonel had an Executive Officer who was his constant companion. As the Colonel was fat, the Executive Officer was thin, a spit and polish type of man. They both spoke with heavy southern accents. When either wanted me for this or that, I would hear a long, drawn out, Privatttt Glennnnn. "Yes, sir, yes, sir," I would respond, not knowing what it would be this time.

There were special occasions when the two of them would hire whores from Macon for assignations in the underbrush. This usually happened when we were out on field exercises. The Executive Officer's driver would fetch the ladies from the city and deposit them at the secret rendezvous locations made ready in advance. My role in these little parties, as you might have guessed was the morning after clean-up detail. No stone could be left unturned to obliterate from the face of this earth the telltale evidence.

Of course I realized that I had a limited future in the Infantry so long as I remained in this particular job. Ambitious to get ahead, that was me. The question was how do I get out of this crazy situation without causing the old man to become my enemy? Fate intervened. One hot afternoon, after the party of the night before, the Colonel and his Executive Officer were catching a few winks while I puttered around the other end of our long field headquarters tent. The two of them began to pull themselves together and I heard the Colonel mutter something to his shadow. "Here it comes," I thought to myself. "*Privattt Glennnn, the Colonel has to take a shit. Go out and dig him a hole.*" "*Yes sir, yes sir.*" I took the shovel and went out behind the tent and dug a hole in an appropriate spot. When I re-entered the tent, the Exec snapped, "*Did you dig the hole for the Colonel?*" "*Yes sir, yes sir and I certainly hope that it is deep enough sir.*" First of all, the two of them were stunned and then they completely cracked up. They laughed so hard that tears were running down their cheeks. I didn't fully realize that I had made such a joke of the situation. After this incident, they both became friendlier towards me. It is probably because of the skill which I demonstrated in this role that the Colonel recommended me for Officer's training. Or was the Army desperate? As a parting gift, they invited me to join them in one of their all-night parties before I went off to Officer's Candidate School. Not bad! Great scotch! Too many mosquito bites!

During this period, I befriended a kid from West Virginia. Ed didn't like anything about the service. One day he came up with a scheme to get himself declared 4F. "Glenn, what we need to do is to report in sick every morning. They will eventually send us to see a psych doctor and if we act crazy, we'll get out." I couldn't believe that anyone would pull such a trick as this. Here we were learning how to defend our country and something called democracy. An honor. We should be willing to give our lives for such a cause as that. Ed didn't agree.

"Don'tcha see we can get ourselves killed? Don'tcha want ta live?"

"Of course I want to live. I want to survive this thing and I know that we can make it. God will help us through. You can't do such a thing. What will your Mom and Dad think?" "Glenn, they won't give a shit. They didn't even say good-bye when I left the house. They were both drunk."

I thought about how my family gathered to give me a proper send-off, of how my mother spent the entire day cooking that feast, and of my father marching beside me down Main Street to the Ligonier train station where he told me, "I love you."

■ ■ ■

October 27, 1943
Ligonier, Pennsylvania
11 P.M.

Dear Rollie Boy:

I have been very busy all day running around—first took the car over and had the oil changed. I am taking good care of your car for you and saving up the gas coupons so you will have gas when you come home. Then came home and baked an apple pie, did the wash and ironing, and watched your little sister play with your doggie. They are such friends.

Am planning to bake cookies for you, Corky, and Steve Wuchina. I worry about Steve's parents. They are so sick. Steve should not have been taken. He is needed here to care for his family. Please try to stay in touch with him. He has been stationed in Florida, not too far from where you are located. He wrote us a note and said that he would write to you. Steve is scared and Dad and I feel you could help him. You are strong and have always been helpful to others.

God has been so good to us. Yes, dear, I know he does watch over you daily. Honest, you have made both your Dad and me extremely happy. We know you are trusting in the Lord and doing your best. Your basic training sounds so wonderfully interesting. You surely will have plenty to keep your mind busy. Some time ago I read quite a few articles on the different kinds of basic training and realize how important it is to listen and to be able to obey orders. I well remember reading about those days out in the open and how wide awake a fella must be, able to endure and make the grade. But dear boy, somehow I have no fear for you. I know whatever way things go, you are giving your best—and that is all anyone can do.

Doris always remembers her Rollie Boy. She is always so happy when I mention her name when reading aloud your letters. Her face lights up. I was combing her hair and she said that she wished you would come home and brush her hair because you didn't hurt her as much as I do. Ha! Ha!

One thing you are learning is that every move you make is for the better. That should relieve the nervous strain a little when something is in the air. Yes, we want a college education for you as much as you do for yourself. Here's hoping you get it. O.C.S. would be the next step in line. Always do what your heart tells you to do. We are so proud of you. We feel you are trying to do good things in life with courage and a will. You have never been afraid of doing things and putting in long hours for a boy your age and we are proud to say you are our son. I thought that I would have this letter written and mailed much earlier.

Love, Hugs, and Kisses to our own darling boy,

Your loving Mother.

P.S.: Dad wants to add a few lines before I mail this. Also Grandma Egner sends you her love and will be writing as well as Aunt Lucy and Aunt Pearl. We all miss our boys and are so proud of them.

■ ■ ■

Dear Cappy:

Here it is Sunday night again and it is really remarkable how events happen within a week. I think that you were sent to Camp Wheeler for a good reason and out of this move will come your desired goal of further education. You might have a few more difficult weeks to go through, but my guess is that you will be transferred soon. As you know, the Army moves fast. In my days in the Army back in 1918, I saw promotions come very quickly.

I know the reason that I didn't get so far, Cap, outside of my good character record, was that I didn't have your strong initiative, ability, and your determination. I guess that I got through only on my Irish wit.

We want your Army life to be as cheerful as we can possibly make it. The Infantry is tough, Cap, but you get fine training. Just be very careful of yourself.

We guards had our pictures taken down at the plant the other day. The place is now guarded 24 hours a day. You should see your old Dad dressed up in his uniform wearing a pistol at his side. I look swell. The high brass came out from Pittsburg the other day to inspect our unit. The major told us that we were the best drilled, best appearing, and snappiest unit in his entire district. So that isn't so bad for us old boys of 1918. The plant is now making bomb fittings.

The guards at the Robertshaw Company in Youngwood, Pennsylvania protected this plant during the war. My father, Raymond McCrea Glenn, is leading the first row. These men were highly trained and very proud of their role at this facility that had been converted from manufacturing thermostats to producing very sensitive bombsights for aircraft. Many of these guards served in the United States military during the First World War. (Photo courtesy of Glenn family archives)

We are proud of our war work. Women have begun to come in and work right beside the men. Some guys have gone into the service and there were no men to replace them. The gals are doing ok.

I want to take this letter down so it goes out at 7 A.M. so that you get it Wednesday.

But, Cap, I am thrilled over your progress. Any soldier that has some Infantry training makes the very best kind of soldier, the snappiest and very efficient; so kid, I am with you 100%. Take it as it comes. Get the best you can out of it. You are on your way to a very successful Army life. Keep fit. Keep neat. And always be snappy!

God bless you my boy and keep you safe,
Good night Cap. I love you and say prayers every night just as we always did together.

Your Dad

This sketch, done by a member of my staff, is a fairly good rendition of what I looked like as my trip to war began, following my graduation as an officer from The Infantry School at Fort Benning, Georgia. I was 20 years old at the time and celebrated my 21st birthday crouching in a fox hole on Okinawa. (Sketch courtesy of Glenn family archives)

Officers
Candidate School

Several things happened to me in rapid succession after digging that hole for Colonel Sanford S. Stanton, III. Having received notice that my scores were very high on the Army's various tests, I became qualified for college in the Army Reserve Training Corps. Both a degree and a commission as a 2nd Lieutenant would be awarded upon the program's completion. While pondering that good news, the invasion of Europe took place, resulting in a more intensive effort to win the war in the Pacific. My opportunity to attend college suddenly switched to my being immediately considered for officer's training. Thrilled upon being accepted, I soon became one of 200 men in a class at The Infantry School located at Fort Benning, near the city of Columbus, Georgia. Before departing for O.C.S., I went to see my buddy Ed, who persuaded the medics that his mental problems were severe. He'd been committed to the psychiatric ward at the camp hospital. "Are you nuts, Glenn? Don't you see how easy it is to get out of the Army? I'll be home working at a job in another month with a 4F classification while you're setting yourself up to get killed. These dopes really believe that I'm crazy." "I know Ed, but you and I will always know that you aren't." Ed and I never saw one another again but I encountered other men along the way who were very much like him. I never was certain which ones were really in a state of shock or were just acting to escape combat.

We cadets arrived at Fort Benning, from many different Army camps around the country feeling both excited and nervous, knowing the school's reputation of being physically and mentally demanding. Many men flunked out. The fear of failure was intense and remained with us constantly as we progressed through this three-month program to eventually become "90 Day Wonders." How would I handle the humiliation if I flunked out? What would I do? What would I say? These questions were balanced with remembering my successful record in going through an academically demanding program at Kiski School where I discovered, much to my surprise, that my IQ was very high. I hadn't known that before. Furthermore, I'd been very successful during Basic Training and won various awards. I felt cocky, sure of myself and ready for almost anything.

Just after arriving at this new camp with a group of total strangers, we new cadets were lined up and forty of us assigned to one barrack. We shouldered our heavy duffel bags and went inside to select a bunk and deposit our gear. Everyone became aware that a black man was assigned to our group, a new experience for all of us. At that time, black men were segregated into their own Army units and it was very unusual to have one in the same room with white soldiers. This resulted in a certain mingling around to see where he would land. He chose a corner bunk. The bunk beside his was empty until one of the guys plopped down his gear and introduced himself. I wish I'd have done that. John was his name, and he reminded me of Frankie, my black childhood playmate. I went over and introduced myself and a few others followed. The majority kept their distance.

Some of the other guys thought that it weird for us to befriend him. Harry Harper was one of those. Harry grew up in Alabama and hated "niggers." He and I talked for hours in the latrine at night about why he didn't want to associate with John. It didn't take long for John's leadership potential to become obvious, lessening the tension. Harry, John, and I were assigned together on a number of field training exercises and it soon became apparent to both Harry and me that the color of John's skin made little difference when you were trying to stay alive. A bullet from a black man's rifle would be just as lethal to the enemy as one fired by a white man.

The three of us survived well into the third and final month of the program and escaped the failure which haunted us during the onslaught of the many academic, physical, and tactical leadership training sessions that filled nearly every hour of the day and night. We often sat up on the toilets after "lights out" until early morning studying the training manuals or doing pull-ups using the ceiling pipes. After only a few hours of sleep, we began a new day of strenuous field training, preparing to lead men into battle. Every hour of every day presented a new set of simulated battle conditions. We were being taught how to lead men whose primary mission would be to kill the enemy.

Our platoon leader, Lieutenant Arthur Ramponi, believed in every one of us and demanded our best effort. We called him "The Ramp." When we believed that we couldn't make it over the next hill or do one more pull-up and were ready to collapse from exhaustion, he urged us on. If we did a good job, he backed us up. If we screwed up, he yelled and gave us hell. He frequently sat up all night with us asking questions when we were studying hard for a stiff exam the next morning. Tough but caring, demanding but supportive, he was a model officer and we grew to respect him and attempted to model our own behavior after his example. Lt. Ramponi conveyed both knowledge and authority in his teaching. His home was in Salinas, California. "The Ramp" promised to be there to welcome us home at the end of the war. He treated us like the sons that he didn't have.

One day we cadets were all seated in bleachers overlooking a valley. That day's exercise would be devoted to the art of camouflage. The instructor announced that a number of enemy emplacements were hidden in the underbrush at various distances before us. He asked the class to find the tank. My hand went up. "It's right over there under that tree." "Very good Glenn. Now, see who can find the large howitzer." When no one else volunteered, I told him, "It's over by the cliff." He said, "And, I suppose you know just where the enemy rifleman is positioned?" "Of course," I said, "he was the first one I spotted an hour ago. He's over there by the road."

After this exercise, Captain Ramponi asked to see me privately. "Glenn, how could you see all that stuff before everyone else?" I thought that I might know. My peculiar type of color blindness enabled me to see through most types of camouflage. This capability became part of my military record from that day forward much to my regret later on during the battle for Okinawa. Some overly efficient clerk at Fort Benning entered this fact on my Army records and it followed me throughout combat.

I passed all academic tests, became physically very strong, and gained confidence but hadn't yet been put to the critical test. At one point or another during the program every cadet was chosen by Lt. Ramponi to lead a combat exercise. This particular event could wash a man out even if he did well academically. My number came up one afternoon when "The Ramp" turned to me and said: "Glenn, you are going to lead this platoon in an attack on a village." Fuck; this is just the type of situation where cadet after cadet had gotten busted.

Ramponi gave me fifteen minutes to look over the land, crawl on my belly into the forest to check out the location of the enemy in a group of shacks, and plan the attack. The rest of the guys were sitting back there in the field smoking and waiting for me to emerge from the woods and most probably get knocked out of the program. We supported each other but most everyone knew that the chances for coming through this type of situation were no better than fifty-fifty, if that. At this point, we were in the last weeks of the program and our original group of 40 in our platoon had dwindled to about 25 men.

Once again, I remembered Uncle Ford's lessons. Georgia land didn't look a lot different than the Ligonier, Pennsylvania forests where we hunted. The bumps in the terrain were the same as I'd experienced as a kid. And, I also knew that I was a good actor, remembering my performances at Idlewild Park and having watched enough John Wayne movies to know what you needed to do when talking to the U.S. Cavalry before the attack on the injuns. It was a now or never kind of situation. I breathed deeply, pulled myself up to full height, looked the guys straight in the eyes, and began to lay out the plan of attack.

My voice, filled with authority, barked out strong commands to my classmates who were serving as the Infantrymen in the exercise. They all looked a bit surprised as they observed my portrayal of a confident combat Commander. In fact, I was also a bit surprised at how good I sounded and began to feel like an actor on a stage with his audience right in the palm of his hand. Leadership is the art of acting the way a group expects. You can be scared as hell on the inside but must convey confidence to your audience. I believe now that I did just that. The more I talked to "my men" about what we were going to do, the more I believed we could really do it by laying out a very specific plan of action for each squad. This clarity made them feel that they were the best combat soldiers in the whole world. That enemy village was going to be taken. No doubt about it. The Japanese wouldn't know what hit them.

Everything went like a well choreographed ballet under the close observation of Ramponi as I moved the men from spot to spot through the forest feeling success in my bones from the very first moments of the attack. We creamed the enemy. In the final stages of the attack, the guys were yelling and screaming like the killers we'd been trained to become, similar to the end of a football game where the home team just made the winning goal. I'd carried the ball and knew it and liked how it felt. Damn good!

The entire platoon was shouting and applauding. "You did it, Glenn! By God, that's something else!" I stood there before those men who were about to become combat leaders feeling a confidence among males that I'd never experienced before. As a kid, when the macho guys chose team players for baseball, I had always been selected for the furthermost position in the outfield. One afternoon some smartass hit a high fly ball with the bases loaded. The ball came right in my direction. It looked like it would pass over my head. So, I turned my back to the oncoming ball and ran further out where I figured that I might be able to catch it. A direct hit! The ball came down and smacked me in the middle of my head. The next thing, I was coming to, spread eagle on the ground with all the kids standing around me laughing. I must admit that it probably looked like the re-enactment of a Charlie Chaplin routine. But this time, I was the one who hit the home run. No doubt about it.

At the conclusion and evaluation of the exercise, I pointed out what a terrible mistake the men made by screaming and yelling during the final attack on the village. "Don't you guys realize that you would have alerted every other Jap in the forest with all that noise? When you shoot the first squirrel, you keep absolutely quiet and wait for the second one to show. After you've wiped out the entire nest, then it's time to celebrate."

I sat down. I'd done it and knew it. The exercise was over. My buddies were still cheering. The message got through to Ramponi who came over to me and put his arm over my shoulder as we walked together back to the bus that carried us back to camp. In between singing raucous songs, someone at the rear of the bus yelled, "Hey Glenn, you sounded just like a cricket chirping off those orders back there."

So, "Cricket" I became from that day forward and have worn the name with pride ever since, and as my friend, Jay Williams, once said, "with a certain panache."

The O.C.S. 90-day program always ended with a simulated twenty-four hour battle and I was selected to serve as the commander of the entire company for that final exercise. It was quite an honor.

Our graduation from O.C.S., soon after this concluding exercise, occurred just eighteen months after I'd been drafted in August of 1943. Several of my former buddies from Camp Wheeler came over to attend the ceremony. It surprised me to see Colonel Sanford S. Stanton, III and his shadow sitting in the audience. "The Ramp" pinned the gold bars on my collar at the end of the graduation ceremony after which he took many of us out for dinner and then on to the airport to catch our flights home. We each carried orders to report in two weeks to Fort Ord, California where we would be processed for shipment to unknown places in the South Pacific. Jim Harkins and I caught a plane to Pittsburg. We waved and saluted "The Ramp" as we boarded that plane knowing that we would probably never see him again. We never did. This flight was a first for Jim and me.

Here I am, in early 1945, as a newly commissioned Second Lieutenant in the United States Army, back home in Youngwood, Pennsylvania with my baby sister, Doris Adel. I had a two-week leave before beginning my trip to war to the South Pacific. Mom and Dad had saved up precious coupons for the purchase of gas and food so that I would have plenty of home cooking and be able to drive my car around to see my buddies. Doris and I spent as much time together as possible. (Photo courtesy of Glenn family archives)

When the stewardess asked us if we would like to have a drink, we couldn't believe that we'd fallen into the lap of such luxury. Two army generals seated just opposite us got a good laugh from our naive behavior.

We were on our way. The trip to war had begun.

■ ■ ■

January 15, 1945
Florida

Dear Roland:

I received your letter right after chow this morning. Let me tell you the significance of that letter. It is the first one that has reached me in weeks. Nothing from home, day after day. My folks are so sick and this worries me so. Dad can't walk now and Mom is hardly able to care for him. My brother is already over there. I don't know where or how to reach him or even if he is alive.

*   I am so scared. Our Company Commander told us this morning that we are going across in four months. I almost shit myself in the ranks when I heard that. Understand me, Roland, I'll go if I must*

but I don't want to go so soon. I need to figure out how to get help for my parents first. It just isn't fair that we recruits are being sent over when there are guys here who have been in training for over a year. But there is nothing I can do about it. Roland, I am in a much worse fix than you are. I feel sure that you will get into that college program or some specialized school. But me, I'm nowhere. Just in the toughest Infantry regiment down here. Please tell me who to see or where to apply to get into such a program.

I tried to talk to the First Sergeant about my having been a baker back home. He rebuffed me just like that. I couldn't get him to talk man to man. He just told me that if they needed a baker, he would throw me into the kitchen and see what I could do. In the meantime, he said, keep your mouth shut. I tried to see the Chaplain about my parents. The Sergeant wouldn't allow me to go to church to see him. He made it very clear about going to the Chaplain when something went wrong. He said, "I'm running this company and no Chaplain is going to tell me how to do it." I'm going to sneak out and go and see him anyway. Roland, we are not that far apart. Is there any way you could get a few days off and come down and see me? I need your help in a big way. I would give anything if we could be together to talk. I'm sure that you have always wanted to go to Florida. We could go to the beach and might be lucky and find some girls. Trouble is there are ten guys for every woman down here. Plenty of whorehouses though. I stay away from them, Roland. Clap is one thing I don't need right now.

As far as the basic training is concerned, I can take anything they can give me. But, I am so worried about home. Do you think that your Mom and Dad would be willing to go and see my folks and let me know how they are doing? I would really appreciate that.

I get about $20 a month after everything is deducted. My folks are about 40% dependent on me, so they take $22 out of my pay before I get anything. $6.40 a month for my insurance; I never dreamed that I would ever have $10,000 of insurance. $1.50 for laundry and $1.52 for new leggings which someone stole from me. But if you can come down, I'll try to help pay your way somehow. I've got about $15 left until the first of the month. Try and make it. So, Roland, I must pray and have faith in the Lord that everything will turn out ok. I'll pray for you too."

Your buddy, Steve

. . .

Undated Letter from Pastor Rankin
Methodist Church
Youngwood, Pa.

Dear Roland:

Your mother and I have just finished reading your recent letter from Basic Training. We all miss you very much. Although this is not the first time you have been away from us, it is natural that under the circumstances we should be solicitous. I am just now in a position to understand the feeling of my own parents when I followed the flag to France almost a quarter century ago. It is my concern—born of my own experience—that leads me to write you this lengthy letter, with the prayer that it may add a measure of strength to your Christian manhood in the hours of peril that lie ahead of you.

You will soon learn that many of your commanding Officers are Christian gentlemen of the first order. But others of them are disposed to wink at the moral lapses of their men, so long as they are effective as soldiers. You will find that morally you are largely on your own.

You need to lean heavily upon the training that was given to you during your formative years. We have every confidence that you will commit no act while in the Armed Forces that will cast the least shadow of reproach upon the good name of your home. But I know that it is no easy thing for a young man to live at his noblest and best in the atmosphere of war. Indeed, you will find it impossible, if you rely upon your own strength alone.

Let me urge you, therefore, to take time each day for the reading of your Bible and for prayer. It isn't necessary that you parade your devotions before your comrades in arms. But on the other hand there isn't a reason under the sun why you should be ashamed to pray. As you grow older you will find that the praying men and women know God. And you will find fellows in the service who pray.

Get acquainted with your Chaplain. He may not be of your own faith; but if your Chaplain is a God-called minister of Jesus Christ, he will respect your denominational convictions, and you will discover a vast area of spiritual interest in common. When you need counsel about your personal problems, consult him. He has been trained to render that service, and the probability is that he can give you vital help when no one else can. Of course, we are counting on your regular attendance on divine services of worship.

Use your opportunities to speak a good word for Jesus Christ. Your folks and I have every confidence that you are a Christian, and that you love sincerely the Savior who died for our sins. Remember always that your supreme loyalty belongs to him. All about you will be men who have not known what it is to be saved. Do it discreetly, but don't fail to help lost men to find God.

We are counting on you mightily to keep yourself clean. You will be a long way from home before this war is over. Female camp followers are numerous in some places, especially on pay day. The temptation may be strong to let down in your standards, on the grounds that none will be the wiser, and that, "after all, this is war!"

If such temptations come, remember Jesus Christ, and the remembrances of your own mother who, you can be sure, will be praying for you every day. Then, too, you will need to remember the girl you left behind, and who, I imagine, promised to be true. Until you return, you owe it to her to keep yourself clean.

You are finding intoxicating liquor all too plentiful in this war, more's the pity. That was one evil from which our government tried to protect us in the war of 1917. But now, there is little or no stigma attached to social drinking. I hope that you will leave it severely alone. Beverage alcohol never has helped anyone, and it has ruined the lives of countless thousands. Never take the first drink, and you will have no trouble with the second.

Suffer me a word of warning, too, about profanity and gambling. Swearing has always impressed me as a sign of an impoverished intellect. As for gambling, a soldier's pay is none too liberal. You will need what you earn to take care of personal wants. That holds for the other fellow as well. I urge you to leave gambling devices alone.

We have every expectation that you are going to be a very good soldier. We American folk are a peace-loving people and we want to win this war as quickly as possible. Give your enemy the best that you have in your arsenal.

But in it all, be Christian! There is such a thing as a Christian soldier, in the full sense of that term, and your folks and I are counting on you to be just that. May God keep you.

Yours confidently,

Pastor Rankin

Part III

The Trip to War

February, 1945

The Army gave me two weeks leave following my graduation from Officers Candidate School. It was so good to get home for those few days. I enjoyed every minute of it. Mom cooked great meals and treated us to scarce meat purchased with food coupons she'd saved. Dad produced hoarded precious gasoline coupons so that I'd be able to run around in the family Chevy to visit relatives and friends proudly displaying my new 2nd Lieutenant gold bars on my Officer's uniform. I hiked with my dog across fields and played with my little sister, Doris, who constantly hung on to me. Mom and Dad were so proud of me and wanted to show me off to all their new friends in Youngwood, the little factory town in western Pennsylvania where they'd moved while the army trained me on how to kill and lead men in combat. Dad had recently become a guard at the Robertshaw factory. This rather small facility formerly manufactured thermostats for ovens but was converted to a secure manufacturing center for making gun sights in support of the war effort. Dad looked so good and pleased with himself in his own uniform. Mom and many other women in the community were doing volunteer work making bandages at the Red Cross. Everyone seemed to be busily contributing to help win the war and appeared confident and not worried about me, or at least they didn't show it. That leave went by so fast. I felt light as a feather when I arrived home and heavy as lead when the day came for me to leave for the west coast.

Dad came to see me off at the Greensburg railroad station while Mom remained home with Doris. Another painful departure. As we stood there on the platform waiting for the train, he pressed into my hand a copy of the 23rd psalm, cut from the family bible and folded carefully in silver foil. "Read that often, Cappy. It will help you. You're going to be OK. Your old Dad knows." I put it in my wallet. We remained quiet as the train pulled into the station.

"Get one for me, Cappy," were his last words as we said our good-byes.

It was sobering looking back to him standing there on the platform waving and wondering what was going through his head as he watched me leave for war. Where did Dad find the strength to send me off, knowing that this time I would soon move toward combat and might not return? Both he and Mom were strong people and their religious faith always seemed to be a major support to them. That must be part of the explanation.

The plane carrying my best buddy, Jim Harkins, and me from Pittsburgh to Los Angeles stopped several times to refuel. There were no nonstop, transcontinental flights in 1945. The frequent landings and takeoffs were part of the excitement of the trip. We flew through a pass in the Rocky Mountains where the peaks were higher than our plane. As we landed at the Los Angeles International Airport, I noted the rural character of the countryside with the airport surrounded by orange trees. Never had seen oranges growing before. We spotted a B-29 about to take off, the biggest plane I ever saw. Another first. Only one passenger terminal existed and we easily located the small connector flight which flew us north to Fort Ord, California, a vast army camp being used to process soldiers being sent to the Pacific war.

We met up with our Officer Candidate School classmates from Fort Benning a few hours later. Bob married his high school sweetheart during the short holiday and Betty journeyed from Pennsylvania to California to be with him. The rest of us envied him until we saw how much pain the two of them were experiencing as a result of Bob's imminent departure. We did everything we could to make it possible for them to have private times together in the motel room where Betty was staying. One of us would answer, "Here," for Bob at the twice-a-day roll calls feeling thankful that we were single men and not leaving a wife behind.

The only training we received at Fort Ord during those few days consisted of learning a swimming technique to use if we needed to abandon ship and swim under burning oil on the surface of the ocean. We used the breast stroke to swim under the flaming water and then came up for air by splashing away the fire directly above our heads. Easier to do in a pool than it sounds but a sobering prospect to have to do it at sea. Each one of us needed to master this skill before we could move on. Monterey was the only place where we could go for excitement in the evenings and there wasn't much there except for small shops and interesting places to eat. After a few days of further training and fooling around, we marched behind still another band to the station and boarded a train for Seattle, Washington.

We climbed through the great forests and mountain ranges of the northwest and made frequent stops permitting us to get out and smell the pines and play like kids throwing snowballs at one another. Further north, the train stopped again in the heights of the Cascade Mountains of Oregon and I saw at once that these great mountains made my Pennsylvania Allegheny range seem like little hills. You should have seen those snow-covered peaks slowly turning orange-red as the first rays of the morning's sun reflected from their tops.

The short time we spent in Seattle turned out to be very pleasant thanks to Bill Gilbert, another classmate who lived there. His girlfriend lined up dates with students from the University of Washington. We went out on the town with them several nights all decked out in our military dress uniforms. While well supplied with condoms, we only tied them around the tops of our highly polished combat boots as a way of tucking in the bottoms of our pants to make us look more like dashing paratroopers. Elastic bands would've worked just as well but denied us the opportunity to display our individual supply of rubbers. Men going to war needed to be prepared! I always kept mine in my wallet right beside the little clipping of the 23rd Psalm that I hadn't read since Dad gave it to me as I began this trip to war. Bill's parents did everything they could to make us feel at home during those few days in Seattle by taking us out for good meals, planning early morning fishing trips in Puget Sound, and encouraging the use of their telephone to make long-distance calls to our families. Then that part of the journey toward war ended. Not bad, so far!

Crossing the Pacific

We boarded a troop ship for Pearl Harbor as if embarking on a Caribbean holiday cruise. It was a lovely trip that provided plenty of time to lounge around in the sun on deck to work on our tans. Upon docking at Pearl, another band played while a line-up of Hawaiian girls did the hula. The upper riggings of the sunken Navy ships were clearly visible. Disembarking from the ship, I pondered what happened that Sunday morning on December 7, 1941. It seemed so long ago that I'd sat in the Ligonier High School Auditorium and heard President Roosevelt declare war on Japan.

We piled into open railroad cars for the trip across the island of Oahu. It reminded me of one of the amusement rides back home at Idlewild Park, and I suddenly wondered where the Tweeter Sisters might be performing their high wire act and who did their announcements now. What might have happened to me if I'd joined their circus? The train chugged along and passed through fields of sugarcane and pineapple. We were finally deposited at an Army camp located high in the hills of Oahu.

The further training that we received emphasized strenuous exercising to keep us in good physical condition. An easy life! We were so damn good! Our bodies were strong and incredibly well developed. The first batch of mail from home arrived. When we could get to the beach, we tried to learn how to surfboard. I got all banged up from scraping my legs on the coral just under the surface of the water.

■ ■ ■

Undated letter

Dear Cappy:

I thought long and hard about where you are heading after waving to you as the train pulled away from the station. You boys will be seeing plenty of new places. Sometimes I can't believe that you're only nineteen and already an Officer ready to lead men. You are a very strong person, Cap, and will make it through the good and the bad days with God looking over you. Never lose your faith and remember you have been well trained to handle this important responsibility. Your men will rely upon you and need your strength. Mom and I will be with you all the way. When I say my prayers at night, I wonder where you might be as I ask God to watch over you.

You can't imagine what we did last night. Mom baked 35 dozen cookies and they all needed to be boxed carefully to send to you, Corky and Steve. Do you ever hear from them? We are still quite worried about Steve's parents. Since we moved from Ligonier to Youngwood, we haven't been able to see or help them. Try to write to Steve. He must be very worried about them. We so wish that he'd been sent home to care for them.

Your old dad is doing just fine down at the plant. You should see me in my snappy uniform marching with the other guards. We do short-order drill every morning and have pistol-shooting practice once every week. That plant is plenty safe as the bomb fixtures roll off the assembly lines. Women have been hired to fill the jobs of men going into the Army and I'm glad to let you know that they are doing fine work. We all are doing everything back home to support you boys. This war won't last much longer. The Germans are done for and you will soon kill off the Jap devils.

Well, Cappy, that's about it for this time. The mailman hasn't brought us a letter from you for several days now and that leads me to think that you and Jim and your buddies are on your way. Mom and I love you so much and Sunny Girl looks at your picture all the time. She's a great little kid.

Your Dad

P.S. We went to the movies the other night and saw a colored picture. I mean there were colored people in it. Quite something and about time!

Kirkland Ford Wilt, "Corky," taken in 1943 at the Great Lakes Naval Training Center soon after he was drafted into the Navy. (Photo courtesy of Wilt family Archives)

Jim and I enjoyed a few wild nights at the Moana Hotel on Waikiki Beach. Sex was less easily available than we anticipated. There were thousands of men cruising the streets of Honolulu looking for the same thing—to get laid. Most of us settled for fresh pineapple instead of fresh young women. We located a whorehouse on a back street and joined the end of the line of waiting men which stretched around the block and back. Guards from the Military Police were stationed to keep order in the lines and to keep it moving. Sex would be a quickie. We both finally chickened out. My memory of being thrown out of one house in Macon, Georgia because I looked so young was too recent and we'd heard stories about all those wonderful girls just waiting for us on the South Pacific islands. The army bombarded us with sex education films. They didn't seem to have much effect on our bodies raging with hormones.

■ ■ ■

Great Lakes Naval Station

Dear Rollie:

Well, how's life in the Army? You should be in the Navy. It's a snap. One week we work and the next we're off. I had my first sailing experience this past week. Got sea sick. Guess what? I'm going home for a two-week leave in another month. It takes fifteen hours to travel back to Ligonier by bus but I can hardly wait to eat some home cookin'.

Are you getting any women? There are nurses up here but they keep them behind a high fence. We can't even get a hard-on because they put something in our food to keep it soft. Ha! Ha!

Our buddy Takis was here but he got sent home and I don't know why. He got a 4F.

Has Steve sent you any letters? I guess he's been sent to Italy when he should have been sent home.

I don't write so well but just wanted to let you know that we guys in the Navy are having an easy life.

Corky

■ ■ ■

Oahu Island

Dear Family:

Just have time to jot off a few lines before we leave for parts unknown. This is a beautiful place on earth. Jim and I are spending some good times together on the beaches and in town where we are enjoying fine food. The city of Honolulu is jammed with service men from all branches. The people are very friendly but it is so crowded that it is difficult to get into a hotel. Sometimes the waiting line stretches around the block, if you can believe it.

The only training we are getting is physical exercise to keep up our strength. The Officers seem very pleased with our fitness. We have drills and then sack out and wait for mail. Dad's letter arrived telling me about the baking of all those cookies. I wonder when they will arrive and where I'll be.

I'm taking every day as it comes and learning whatever I can from each situation. Oh, by the way, it's kind of funny to have guys salute me. Sometimes I forget I'm an Officer. I wonder what it will be like to have my own men to lead and if I'll be able to do the job as well as I did while in Officer's training back at Ft. Benning? I do feel my own strength and hope and pray it will carry me through. I'll remember all of your teachings as I face this important cause just ahead.

Keep writing. Tell me everything you are doing. Kiss Sunny Girl for me.

Your loving son, Rollie

One morning several of us were asked to report to the office of the Commanding General of the post. This friendly man told us that he'd been observing us during our physical workouts and had never seen a group of men so fit and well prepared. "You're headed to the front lines of the Pacific war, and men, you are ready. I'm very proud of you. The Pacific war has been going very well. Our forces have attacked across the mid-Pacific islands and also through the south Pacific to the Philippines. We're nearly in a position to cut all Jap supply lines and be ready to either invade the Japanese main islands or force them to surrender. You men will no doubt be in on the most exciting phase of the ending of the Pacific war. I can't tell you where you will be going but it will be way up front. I wish you well."

This was very flattering and our egos soared to new heights. There was a strong bond between those of us who had gone through the entire training program together back at Fort Benning. We were proud of our accomplishments, of the Infantry, the flag, and the United States of America.

The next stop on our trip, Hickham Field, received heavy strafing during the December 7 attack. The barracks where we bedded down, located just beside the landing strip, still revealed shell holes in the sides. We tried to sleep but knew that we might be called at any moment. Ambulances met some of the planes to transport the combat wounded to hospitals. These kids looked awful. Some stared ahead without seeing, their faces blank. We tried not to notice.

A feeling of cockiness still sustained us. Captain Ramponi, our training officer back at Fort Benning, would be proud. But all of the waiting around made us restless. It reminded me of that earlier time in Ligonier when we draftees stood lined up behind the high school band listening to the mayor give his speech before the parade to the railroad station could begin. Only this time my dad wasn't there marching beside me.

During the middle of one sleepless night, we were finally called and told to load onto the big plane parked just beyond our barracks. We hoped to be fortunate enough to get one of those big, silver, four-engine liners with the plush seats for our important flight over the Pacific. Alas, this four-engine troop carrier wasn't so fancy. Upon boarding, we found a stripped down interior with a row of metal bucket seats down each side.

This wasn't going to be a first-class flight to war.

Saipan

After the plane was airborne, we learned that our destination was Saipan, one of the islands in the Mariana group. We were lectured while we flew and learned that the major battle for this island was over except for a mopping-up operation to wipe out the Japanese who retreated to the top of the island's mountain. Saipan served as a staging area to supply replacements to the front. The island supported a large airbase used constantly by squadrons of B-29s for their relentless attacks on the Japanese mainland.

I'd never flown over the ocean before. Our first stop on the flight was a remote coral atoll called Johnston Island. We came off the plane and met up with a small group of Navy officers. Everyone introduced themselves. I shook one guy's hand and said, "I'm Cricket Glenn." He replied, "I'm Robert Taylor." And, by God, he was the movie actor, the third Hollywood star that I'd seen. The first was Joan Blondell back at Camp Meade, the second, Bette Davis back at Ft. Benning, and I hadn't got to shake their hands.

Our flight resumed after we ate a meal in the Navy's mess while our plane refueled. Walking wounded ate at the same tables with us while they waited for their own flights to take them to Oahu hospitals and eventually home. We couldn't avoid them this time while they told grim stories of combat as we prepared to move in the opposite direction. Some of these men were totally silent and stared off into space as if they were alone in the world and the looks on their ashen faces became seared forever in my mind. Jim gave me a jab and motioned for us to walk away from them because they made us nervous. Johnston Island didn't come up to our dreams of a South Pacific paradise. The flat, white-hot land, heavily bombed during the earlier battle, was scarred with deep craters left by exploding bombs that pockmarked the landscape. The pleasures of Seattle and Oahu were clearly behind us.

The uneventful flight to Saipan seemed quieter in comparison to the earlier leg of our journey. Thinking of the faces of those wounded soldiers brought on a chill that soaked my back. For the first time, I felt afraid and reached for my wallet, intending to read the passage from the family bible, but hesitated, thinking that my buddies might not understand.

After landing on Saipan, we hauled our heavy gear off the plane and found the inevitable line of trucks waiting to cart us off to the next stopping place; a tent camp located high on the side of the one volcanic mountain, the major geographic feature of the island. An officer met us and gave us the welcoming orientation lecture which he had probably given to hundreds of others before us. *"OK, men, you are fairly safe here. The remaining Japs, who've survived the battle, are holed up on the higher elevations of the mountain up there behind your tents. They come down at night to steal fresh water and food. Sleep with your knives and guns and see if you can catch one. We've been getting one every night."* Real Japs, I pondered . . . on the same island . . . in the mountains . . . behind our tents . . . come down at nights . . . steal food and water . . . one a night . . . sleep with knives and guns . . . Wow!

Jim, Bill, Harry, John, Peter, and I were assigned to the same large tent. We sat down on our cots and quietly began to sharpen our bayonets, although they were already as sharp as they could be made. Very little talk. The thought of ramming this knife through the guts of a Japanese caused me to remember a demonstration we'd given for Bette Davis back at Fort Benning. She'd come to our camp on one of her crusades to sell war bonds. We were primed to be vicious that day to show her how ready we were for combat. This was different. There were no movie stars watching this time. Sleeping on cots in tents seemed a bit risky to me under these circumstances but we tucked in our loaded rifles and held our knives under our pillows as we tried to sleep. Yes, we still had a pillow under our heads. As alert as we were through the night, we didn't hear a sound. But the large, canvas water bottle was missing from behind our tent the next morning. I wrote a letter home the next morning telling of this incident. The P.S. reads: *"Our only light bulb burned out last night and I wished that I could have run down to the hardware store for a new one. P.P.S.: We are moving on to the front soon and I couldn't tell you where even if I knew. Just keep reading the papers and DON'T WORRY."*

There were no enemy incidents during the short period I remained on that beautiful tropical island. The officer who gave us that initial orientation moved on. He obviously tried to scare us. Now we were the officers who were giving that same lecture, with the same swagger, to those who were following us into the camp. There were new arrivals every day. The military machine of processing men to the front was working smoothly.

We took several patrols into the mountainous region above our tent camp and during one of those patrols we saw our first dead enemy lying in a trench. Not a pretty sight. My mind recalled the far different experience of sitting beside my Grandpap Glenn's coffin and looking at his body surrounded with flowers and his grieving family back in the parlor of our old Victorian house in Ligonier. My only experience with death and dying up to that time was limited to those first family losses that provided me with a realization of my own mortality. I remembered that my little dog, Patty, jumped up into the coffin with Grandpap and curled up and went to sleep beside him as she'd done every day of her life. We allowed the two of them to be there together. It seemed right. Finally, my Grandmother Glenn gently lifted her out of the coffin saying, "Our Grandpap is gone now, Patty." I'd reached into the coffin and patted Grandpap's head, feeling surprised by the cold touch of his skin and remembering how I sat in his lap the day before. Grandmother Glenn died just six months later. They were married for sixty-two years and I guessed that she didn't want to live on without him. It must have been time for her to die. I had to shake my head of these thoughts to get back to the reality of that mountain side.

Seeing a dead body, bloated, deformed, and smelling like rotten meat wasn't the same kind of experience. Peter covered the soldier's body with weeds and branches. Harry got angry at Peter. "*What did you do that for? The son-of-a-bitch isn't worth more than a dead rabbit. Let him rot! Let's go hunt for more of them.*" We hated the Japanese. During previous training, we'd been brainwashed to think of them as non-human creatures. We all seemed to need to actually kill with our own hands rather than to just talk about it and hear stories from others. The expression, "I wanna get me a Jap," was heard over and over.

One of our diversions was to go swimming and there were a number of beautiful beaches. A post officer invited me to join him one afternoon. He had a jeep and drove to a remote location. We swam way out to some large boulders emerging from the water hundreds of yards from shore. He suggested that we swim nude which made perfect sense in view of the fact that we were the only ones there. The warm water was crystal clear and filled with thousands of colorful tropical fish. I pretended that I was one of them as I glided around the coral formations moving my body just like a shark. What a grand swim with the salt water so buoyant! We finally climbed up on the boulders and stretched out. I closed my eyes and allowed the sun to warm my body. "Doesn't that feel good," I remarked. "This will feel even better. Just keep your eyes closed and think about making love with a woman," he whispered. Suddenly I felt his hand rubbing down over my chest. Startled, I opened my eyes and realized that he'd been watching me closely that entire afternoon. This was different than my cousin and me jacking off in the barn. Corky taught me how to do it and kept telling me to "just keep practicing!" That was fun. Confused, I jumped up, got into my shorts, and swam steadily back to the shore.

While driving back to the camp we were at first very quiet. Then he said, "I've been a queer all of my life." I asked him, "Why didn't you declare that you were homosexual? You could've been discharged 4F and avoided this whole mess." "It would've killed my father," he replied. "Dad served in the Infantry during World War I and is so proud that I'm following in his footsteps. Cricket, I couldn't do that to him." "Well, I understand how you feel about not letting your father down. My Dad also served during 1918. Right now, we're both headed for the pit of hell and we must try to stay alive. That was a nice swim. Take care."

Easter Sunday, 1945

Peter intended to become a minister after the war. As Easter Sunday approached, he planned a sunrise service on the mountainside overlooking the sea. We climbed to an outcrop of rock that morning and comforted ourselves by singing hymns and praying together. Except for the drone of the B-29s taking off, a momentary feeling of peace came over us as we looked off at the sea and thought that this was one of the most beautiful places we'd ever seen. In the distance, ships filled the Saipan harbor. The white beaches stretched as far as the eye could see. Under those peaceful waters, the sea's bottom was covered with the rusted hulks of many ships and debris from the attack on the island and had already become a reef home for millions of fish.

During the service, a messenger jogged up the hillside to interrupt Peter's sermon by announcing that we were being shipped to the front that day. Peter calmly concluded with a prayer. I thought of him as a gentle person, not the type one would expect to land in the Infantry. For that matter, neither was I.

We walked down the hillside together while thanking him for planning and conducting the service. "Cricket, I know that I'm going to be dead in just a few more days. Would you do me a favor and write to my parents when I'm gone? I've written their address on this slip of paper." I took the paper and added it to the precious possessions contained in my wallet and tried to change the subject by calling his attention to the beautiful view beyond us. "Peter, how do you suppose God created such beauty? Do you really believe what you just said about his looking over us in the days ahead?" "Cricket, I wish that I'd the time to think more about those questions but I don't now. You gotta believe in something. Might as well be God. Take care of yourself, Cricket, and thanks."

By late that afternoon, dressed for battle and carrying a heavy load of gear in our duffel bags, we were transported to the harbor. Landing craft took us out to the convoy. There were many ships, destroyers, minesweepers, sub-chasers, and troop transports. The transport, which was to be our home for the next few days, lowered heavy cargo nets down over the side that we climbed to reach the deck. I remembered how we drilled to do that back in basic training. Sailors directed all officers to a spotless dormitory where we spread out on bunks already made up with clean, white sheets. Not bad! As music played through the loudspeaker on the wall, we began to relax, unload our gear, change into our clean slacks and shirts, and take in our new surroundings.

There wasn't much conversation. Suddenly a woman's voice interrupted the music and I had my first of many experiences listening to Tokyo Rose. She began by sympathizing with all the U.S. families who were losing their sons to Japanese bullets. Suddenly her voice became more serious and she announced that President Roosevelt had just died and that now we didn't even have a leader. "You will soon be reporting to the victorious Japanese." The room fell absolutely silent. Everybody looked shocked. I felt a keen personal loss, just like another member of my family had suddenly been taken. Then another announcement confirmed the President's death and directed all troops to the ship's fantail where a memorial service was to be held. It was sunset when hundreds of us gathered there together surrounded by the many ships that made up this convoy soon to depart for a destination still unknown to us.

Saipan, the stop at Johnston Island, meeting Robert Taylor, a few days of vacation on Oahu, good meals and drives in Pennsylvania country with my family were all behind me. My old Chevy was back in the garage out of gas. Feeling sad and stunned, I asked myself, "How in hell had I managed to get myself into such a mess?" I could've made excuses earlier on getting into a different branch of the service. I thought of the Army doctor who had asked me if I didn't have trouble walking as a result of a hammer toe on my left foot. "Wouldn't something other than the Infantry be a better place for you to serve?" he had asked. I told him that I'd been walking well for years and had no trouble at all. Now, look where it had landed me!

The voice of the ship's captain interrupted my thoughts. He spoke to us about what a wonderful man the President had been and that someone called "Harry Truman" had already taken over. Never heard of him. We prayed and sang *Nearer My God to Thee*. The service ended with a resounding but solemn rendition of *Onward Christian Soldiers*, a hymn that I'd sung many times in church not realizing then that I was to become one. I walked back to the officer's dormitory saying those lines to myself. Was I really nearer my God to thee, nearer to thee?

> Onward Christian soldiers, marching as to war,
> With the cross of Jesus going on before.
> Christ the royal Master, leads against the foe;
> Onward into battle see his banners go!
> Onward Christian soldiers, marching as to war,
> With the cross of Jesus going on before.

■ ■ ■

April 1, 1945
Easter Sunday

Dear Folks:

Everything is passing through my mind right now. Peter delivered a good sermon. The world looked so calm from the mountain side at sunrise this morning but now under the water you wonder who might be looking at you through a periscope. The horizon looks no different but one peers at it more carefully and wonders what is just on the other side. This moment certainly is difficult and something I will never forget. We grieve the loss of the President.

I don't suppose that I will be able to tell you where I am. Perhaps you can guess. It would be cut out of the letter if I did tell you more. This won't make any difference to us. I still feel close to you and know you folks have the same feeling.

This trip has been a long one and it isn't over. We still have a ways to go. Jim and I certainly have enjoyed it. We stayed in some swell places on Oahu where our treatment was fine. Lots of stories to tell but they will need to be put off for a spell.

So many things await me. I wonder what the future has in store for me.

Faith is one grand thing to base one's life on and I do believe God knows best and by his hand I'll go forward. Always remember that his plans are the best and never will we question them. Remember that! Whatever happens! Believe me, my dear ones, I feel that I can do this task and will come home to you.

Your loving son,

Rollie

Convoy

AFTER THE MEMORIAL SERVICE for President Roosevelt, the ship's communications officer made certain that we didn't hear anything further from Tokyo Rose. Instead, we listened to broadcasts from the States. Kate Smith entertained us with all the old favorites. At the end of the program, she sang Irving Berlin's *God Bless America* and it brought tears to our eyes. Tokyo Rose might have been a better choice at that particular time. At least she would have given us a few laughs.

The non-commissioned troops were billeted in huge dormitories below the main deck, the dank spaces equipped with row upon row of bunk beds stacked four high. Before turning in that first night, I went down into the troop's quarters to move around and talk with the men. They were all going to be replacements for soldiers killed or wounded in battle. Unlike us officers, trained together for the past months, these men came from basic training at many different army camps and were strangers to one another. No bonds of friendship, no interpersonal support, alone, scared, covered with sweat.

As I entered their quarters, I became aware of a metallic sound coming from all corners of that large area. Metal grated against metal. Eighteen and nineteen-year-old kids sat on the edge of their bunks staring at the floor, sliding one bayonet blade against the other to hone these knives even sharper. Some cleaned their rifles, a few wrote letters to their families and sweethearts. Several crap games were going on here and there. The room smelled like an unclean locker room, faces and backs damp, undershirts and shorts soaked.

Peter moved from one to another. He prayed with several men kneeling on the metal deck. No embarrassment at showing fear. Easing stress by openly admitting that we were all afraid of what lay just ahead. "Oh, Lord, we ask you to help us get through this. We know that we've been well trained but, God, we're scared."

A small group, gathered over in one corner, was having a rather jovial discussion and I walked over and listened in. "You know the thing I miss the most in this man's Army? It's women, that's what it is. When's the last time ya had one? I bet you wouldn't even know what to do with your cock." One kid started to answer but this braggart went on. "Why I even had two together once. You should try that sometime." Laughter all around.

And, so it went. Sex talk in one corner and praying in another. Finally exhaustion took over and the room grew quiet. I walked between the bunks and talked quietly with each man feeling almost like a father putting his sons to bed. I recalled my own dad reading me a good-night story and then both of us kneeling beside my bed saying, "Now I lay me down to sleep, I pray the Lord my soul to keep. If I should die before I wake, I pray the Lord my soul to take." When I would wake in the morning and realize I was still alive, I wondered where my soul might be. As I walked from one soldier to another, my mind clicked a picture of Dad kneeling beside his bed every night saying his own goodnight prayers before crawling into bed. Every now and then I would pause beside a bunk and just be with the young kid lying there for a few moments and not say anything.

On the way back to our own bunks, Peter and I stopped at the rail and looked out on a calm ocean covered with ships silhouetted against a dark sky. We stood quietly looking off in the distance. Peter put his arm around my shoulder. Tears in his eyes. I pulled him into my arms and hugged him. So strong down there with the men. Sobbing now. Then we turned in. The convoy sailed silently out of the Saipan harbor while we slept between clean sheets in the officer's quarters.

Sometime during the night our convoy converged with another and substantially increased in size. The next morning, the scene from the deck looked like a travel brochure. We were anchored in a lagoon surrounded by many small tropical islands, each little emerald gem of land covered with palm trees, surrounded with white sandy beaches and appearing to float on the turquoise water. Now this was more like it. We felt better. Had a great breakfast. The Navy certainly knew how to eat.

Abandon ship exercises were held frequently during that day until every man aboard knew precisely where to go in an emergency. We were informed that the convoy would sail after dark, our destination to be announced at sea. The main danger for next 48 hours was potential torpedo hits. The waters were infested with enemy submarines.

Our dormitory so clean . . . bunk sheets so fresh . . . difficult to comprehend that much danger. Our second night passed without any difficulty. The next morning we stood again at the ship's rails like a bunch of tourists on a cruise and watched many other ships surrounding and protecting the troop carriers as our convoy steamed toward a target still unknown to us.

Suddenly our ship changed course. General Quarters sounded and all men raced to their abandon ship stations on deck. Sub-chasers began to drop depth charges. The delayed "thud," followed by huge surface upheavals revealed no evidence of a sub hit. Jim shouted "Torpedo!" Three small wakes approached our ship. Another quick change in course. Torpedoes sailed about a hundred yards across our bow just missing us. Cheers! "How do you guys like that maneuver? We'll run the asses off those bastards." More cheers! "We'll win this goddamn war!" And a sense of pride and hope seemed once again to take over. But the mood onboard rapidly changed. Our ship was the sub's target. Planes from a distant carrier zoomed about putting on a fine display. Clearly we weren't watching an Air Force stunt team at a 4th of July celebration back home. This emergency lasted for over two hours. The ship's captain finally declared, "All Clear!" The men were ordered below deck and the officers were called to a briefing where the captain laid out the plan of attack.

"Our destination is the island of Okinawa, located just south of mainland Japan. We're part of the largest flotilla of ships ever assembled for attacking an enemy, many times larger than the one that crossed the English Channel for the Normandy invasion. Thirteen-hundred ships are underway for the initial invasion underway as I speak. Admiral Chester Nimitz is in charge of the whole show. You're the first wave of replacements. The campaign is designated OPERATION ICEBERG, only you're not goin' to freeze your asses off. Okinawa is sub-tropical. The success of winning this campaign can't be over emphasized. Once the island is in our hands, we'll be within spittin' distance of the Japanese homeland. The invasion won't surprise the Japs. Jap air and submarine reconnaissance spotted our convoys. They know what's comin'. You should also tell the men that our underwater demolition teams worked in advance to clear obstacles from targeted landing beaches. Our arrival time is just after dawn. Brief your troops below. Review disembarking procedures. Be straight with them. Going over ship's side is tough in rough seas. We've lost men while climbing down nets to landing craft below. Jap planes are around. I can tell you that the initial invasion on Easter Sunday went much smoother than expected. The entire landing took place with incredible ease. There was little enemy action on the beaches, and the troops landed right on time. They've

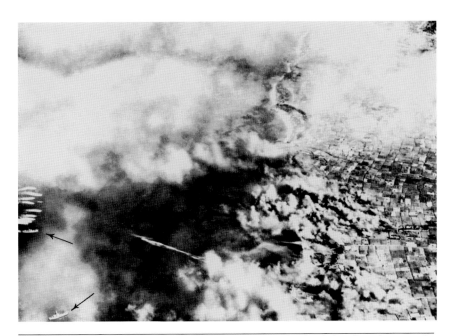

The landings were made in amphibian crafts which were shepherded to shore by control craft (arrows). Heavy support fire which had blanketed the beaches with smoke and dust lifted seconds before the first troops touched down. I wasn't part of the initial landing on Okinawa but came ashore as a replacement officer a day later. (Photo courtesy of Center of Military History, United States Army)

already moved inland. Fortunately for you guys, Okinawa's beach is already secured by the first wave of attacking troops. This means you'll not have to go ashore under machine-gun fire. However, there's some limited enemy artillery action, and beaches and waters you'll cross can still be bombed. Most of the underwater mines have been removed or exploded. Japanese air attacks pounded our lead ships but their shore installations were badly hit by our initial sea and air bombardments. Your landing operation must proceed rapidly when the time comes. We'll get you into shore but it will be tricky. There's a coral reef just off the beaches. We have to hit them at exactly the right tide or the landing craft you'll be in will get stuck off shore. Good luck to each of you. Your country is proud of you."

We went over and over these plans with the men. We were all pumped up . . . alert . . . adrenaline rushing through our veins. No time to pray. Talk of sex long gone. Not much sleep that night, imaginations running wild about whether we'd be alive in 24 hours. The officers remained with the troops. They continued to sit on the edges of their bunks sharpening bayonets. Some stared off into space, an expression of sheer fright frozen in their faces. One kid yelled, "Oh Jesus! Oh Jesus! I can't move, I can't move. Oh please! Oh please!" Peter went to him. Tried to quiet him down. No use. He kept screaming. Finally the ship's medics took him away. A man in shock, the first of many to come. "Can't you keep those God damned knives quiet?" shouted another, but the grinding never stopped.

Peter moved from one to another with a quiet grace, a comfort to many men. Nothing about him suggested that he could injure another human being. I patted my wallet thinking about that little slip of paper containing his parent's address and wondered what there was about this gentle man that led me to believe he'd be more likely to get killed than another soldier. What were my chances of survival?

Sometime before dawn Peter and I were able to leave the men and head back to the officer's stateroom. We paused on the deck and looked out at the moving ships. "Cricket, you won't forget what you promised?" "No, Peter, but . . ." "Let's not talk about it now, Cricket. You'll know what to do." He turned toward me and gave me a hug. "Would you pray with me, Cricket?" We stood silently together thinking our own thoughts and then headed for our bunks for a last few hours of rest between the clean sheets. I took out the little folded paper from my wallet and read the message from the Bible before turning off the bunk light. Dad had said, "You'll be all right."

Before sunrise, dressed in combat fatigues with all gear packed—rifles, ammo, knives checked—we assembled on deck. As the sun rose, several miles to the east, the shore of Okinawa emerged as a distant shadow with sun coming up behind the land. A far away battle, with planes diving at targets, smoke billowing high into the air like from a raging forest fire, reminded me of times I deposited coins in the penny arcade machine at Idlewild Park back home. The toy gun would be aimed at enemy planes moving across the backdrop and you got points when you scored a hit. But these planes weren't toys. Real bombs dropped and exploded with massive clouds of smoke rising in the air. Tracer bullets spewed forth from our planes. The thud of explosions reached us still way out at sea. Jim said, "That's what we're here for, to kill." The closest I had come to killing was chopping off the heads of chickens in the backyard behind the old Victorian house on Main Street.

My buddy, Bill, was standing next to Jim and me. He'd been very quiet. I asked him if he was okay. "I hope we don't have hand-to-hand fighting. I think I'll be able to shoot one of those bastards but I hope that I

We climbed down over the ship's side on a rope ladder into the landing craft that would take us onto the Okinawa beach. It was tricky to do with the ship moving and with all the heavy gear we carried on our backs. Wave after wave of these landing crafts moved together toward the shore. (Photo courtesy of National Archives)

don't have to drive this knife into their guts." Harry overheard him. "Just pretend that you're gutting a rabbit. They're not human."

Somehow or other, we got through those last hours on board where we were still safe. It still seemed like a movie as the convoy sailed closer to the island. The captain ordered us to take our men to previously designated locations on deck and prepare to go over the ship's side. We were each responsible for 60 soldiers. Steel helmets, heavy back packs, rifles, the recently sharpened bayonets, belts with all sorts of gadgets, compass, water bottle, several hand grenades, and extra bullets. It is a wonder we could stand, let alone move, with all that weight on our backs.

We were still about a mile off shore when landing craft began circling the troop carriers—thirty of them, all in groups of ten chugging round and round. Heavy cargo nets strung over the ship's side swayed in and out with the rolling sea as the men crawled down into the craft. As each one was jammed full, it pulled away and the next craft pulled up under the net. My group and I were the last to go over the side. I was the last to leave the deck. A sailor, dressed in his whites, extended his hand. "This is it. Good luck to you, Sir, and your men."

Absence of enemy opposition to the landings made the assault seem like a large-scale maneuver during our previous training as we jumped from our landing craft, waded through the water and quickly consolidated on the beach. (Photo courtesy of Center of Military History, United States Army)

Army units were able to unload massive amounts of equipment soon after the invasion because the Japanese had withdrawn inland and didn't offer opposition to the landings. (Photo courtesy of National Archives)

Our landing craft pulled away and joined others moving toward shore. We were packed in shoulder to shoulder and could not see over the top. There was about two feet of steel reaching above our heads. The helmsman yelled out reports of what was happening. He told us that the beach was loaded with trucks, tanks, piles of ammunition and other stuff necessary to support battle operations.

"When will we hit the beach? How long will this take? Can you see any Japs?"

The helmsman informed us that we were still a considerable distance off shore. Fear was intense in spite of the briefing from our ship's Captain. Not a word spoken. We pressed tightly together as if bodily contact with all those around us would offer more protection.

Finally our craft hit sand, front ramp lowered into waves. We ran screaming out into waist-deep water, waded onto shore without a shot being fired. The battle had already moved inland several miles leaving the beach itself relatively safe. It took only a few minutes for guides to lead us to a receiving station set up for the purpose of processing replacements. We could now look off shore at the convoy of ships that had just brought us into shore. All of this action had taken most of that day.

An air-raid alarm sounded at dusk. Small ships began to circle the convoy and belched out smoke concealing it entirely in fog. Air attacks began

We watched this display of American anti-aircraft fire directed at Japanese planes attacking our ships during our first night on Okinawa. It was like watching a fireworks display. We were still in a reserve holding area awaiting assignment to infantry units on the front lines. (Photo courtesy of National Archives)

and once again it looked like something out of a shooting gallery at an amusement park or a massive 4th of July display.

Enemy planes dived out of the cloudless sky. The fog bank flashed from blasts of exploding shells. Big guns from our own ships fired non-stop. Tracer bullets zoomed skyward. Impossible to tell at first of any scored hits. Then one enemy plane continued diving downward, downward toward the fog bank and crashed. A series of mighty explosions rattled my teeth. Giant red and orange fireballs rose above the fog. The explosions continued, one after the other, just as if a huge ammunition dump had been struck. I wondered about the crew of the ship and the sailor who wished me luck a few hours earlier. Were they safe? Difficult to believe but we were experiencing a high. We were trained for this. Battle sounds could clearly be heard from front lines still several miles away. What would happen next? Sleeping nearly impossible. Each of us took turns standing guard over our buddies dreading the coming of dawn.

■ ■ ■

2 April, 1945

Good Evening All:

I have just a few minutes to bring the situation up to date for you and am not sure when this will get mailed. We're another day closer to the "Target." Today was fairly normal until Jim yelled (...........cut by censor.............) We are now in precarious waters and a zone where anything can be expected. Still, life goes on. I'll pass this on to someone when we land in hopes that you'll eventually get it. You know, there is a real possibility I won't be able to write immediately after getting off this ship. We'll be plenty busy but I'll get word to you just as soon as I can. If you just listen to the news carefully, I bet you'll be able to tell where we are.

It is dusk now and our ship is blacked out. Not one speck of light is permitted to escape. Double hanging curtains seal every door. From the inside here you might imagine your being almost any place taking a cruise. I know the folks at home would feel very much better if they could actually see the safety measures taken on these troop ships. You would marvel at the rapidity with which every man can be removed in case of danger. Our government has spent great sums of money to make our Navy the best in the world. We all know that now even more so than before.

Need to cut this short now and go below with the troops. These kids have come from all over the States, thrown together in a pool of replacements unknown to one another, unlike us officers who trained together and have formed friendships. You were right, Dad, they need lots of support and I'm doin' my best. For that matter, we all need support and that's when Our Father Who Art in Heaven comes into the picture.

Good night with love my darlings. "Sunny Girl" keeps smiling at me from her picture. She's all ours.

Cappy

Part IV

The Okinawa Campaign

Okinawa as seen from the south. (Courtesy of the Keystone Portrait Studio)

Moving Toward
the Front

THERE WERE SIX OF US in the back of the open truck as it pulled away from the receiving station just after dawn the morning after we landed on Okinawa. Sounds of distant explosions overpowered the engine noise of the convoy of trucks carrying us toward the front. Two lines of vehicles, one moving toward the front, and the other returning to the rear nearly clogged the rutted, muddy road. The terrain looked like a great flood had inundated the entire devastated region. Smashed huts, broken down trees, deep craters, overturned tanks, trucks, shell casings everywhere. Stop and go. Stop and go. We talked with drivers of returning vehicles, some filled with troops being relieved and returned to rear positions and field hospitals; ghostly, mud-smeared faces, chalk-white complexions. Silent men in shock.

A sickening, dreadful smell of death from bodies suddenly engulfed us. We paused for a moment beside a truck filled with corpses, one stacked upon the other like a load of logs. The tarp didn't quite hide the load, nothing could totally hide the hideousness of rotting, dead bodies easily observed through cracks between the truck's sideboards. The truck driver and his partner wore cloths around their noses in a vain attempt to protect themselves from the odor. My God, how long were we going to be stuck here?

Finally the truck convoy jerked slowly forward past a panorama of battle scenes. An artillery unit off to the right . . . guns blaring . . . shot after shot . . . puffs of smoke . . . running men . . . trucks carrying more

Mud and flood increased the difficulties of fighting on Okinawa. In this picture, infantry-men trudge toward the front lines past mud-clogged tanks. This scene was repeated time after time as we moved toward Japanese fortifications at the southern end of the island. The northern regions of Okinawa had already been secured during the first days of the battle. (Photo courtesy of Center of Military History, United States Army)

shells. Then a field hospital with ambulances, more trucks, men running in and out of tents, dead bodies lying row upon row outside a hospital tent, each corpse covered with a rain parka, not yet loaded to be sent back to the morgue where the staff couldn't process the bodies fast enough and get them into the ground. More stops and starts, jerks forward, spinning wheels in the mud, very little conversation. Finally our truck pulled out from this endless line and stopped beside a cluster of tents. The driver an-nounced,"You're here, guys. This is your new outfit, the 17th Infantry Reg-imental Headquarters of the 7th Infantry Division, Tenth Army. Someone will be along to get you squared away."

An older man came out of one of the tents and introduced himself as the Regimental Commander. "I'm Colonel Bob Packler and just want you to know that you're badly needed. One of my staff will get you assigned to your new unit. You're feeling scared? Well, I am too. We all are. That's natu-ral. This is a good outfit. Our 7th Division is fighting right beside a division of Marines. The battle is going well. Many of the enemy have been killed. Rapid advances have been made since the invasion on Easter Sunday. Good luck to each of you." We saluted. "Oh, by the way, we don't salute here."

The truck carrying us toward the front lines passed a field hospital. Row upon row of dead Americans stretched outside the tents where emergency doctors and nurses treated the many wounded who were constantly arriving from the front lines. At one point our truck paused beside another northbound truck that held many bodies stacked like cord wood. The stench of death was overpowering. (Photo courtesy of Library of Congress, Prints and Photographs Division)

Directly in front of us stretched the bodies of four U.S. soldiers, one with a rigid, dark brown arm and hand with clenched fist extended into the air like a bizarre salute. We looked but said nothing. We were called over to a tent where we waited for a runner who would take us to the individual companies to which we'd been assigned, each one of us to a different unit. My assignment was Company "I." Someone gave us hot coffee. We sipped while casting an occasional glance over to the dead soldiers.

Captain Bob Odom, Colonel Packler's adjutant, came over and introduced himself. He noticed our side glances toward the bodies. "You might just as well come and take a good look because you are going to see a lot of this." We followed him over and he reached down and lifted the rain slickers, one at a time exposing the bodies, one white and three with dark skins. We stared in silence. One had a gray pallor, one looked sunburned,

Upon arriving at the 17th Infantry Division headquarters, located behind the front lines, we stood beside the tarp-covered bodies of four American infantrymen who had been killed that day. I learned that one of these men had been the luckless platoon leader of the unit to which I was being assigned. He had been killed, while his platoon was resting in reserve, by a stray bullet piercing his bare back while he leaned over to lace up his combat boots. (Photo courtesy of Library of Congress, Prints and Photographs Division)

one stared up at us with an expression of horror on his face, and another looked like he was sleeping peacefully. Then the captain said, "I knew that soldier. He did his best. It's so easy for a man to get killed here." Peter doubled over and vomited. I grabbed him before he fell to the ground.

Odom spoke again, "Glenn, you're replacing that dead officer. He got shot this afternoon. His platoon—your platoon—is now in reserve. You'll have an easy first night. Here comes John Garcia to take you to your unit. He's one of the platoon's scouts. Nice guy but watch him. He's too big for his own foxhole." Things happened so fast that I didn't have time to digest the fact that I was about to replace the dead man lying at my feet.

The man approaching us looked at least seven feet tall. He came lumbering along, scraping his boots in the mud and dragging his rifle at his side. Odom introduced me as Lieutenant Glenn. "What do they call you Glenn? We don't use officer names here, don't want the enemy to know you from anyone else."

"Just call me Cricket."

"Cricket? OK, that sounds like it'll work. Come on then and I'll take you up to meet the guys."

John turned and I followed, waving back at my buddies. Walking beside John made me feel like a midget. He seemed three feet taller, two feet wider, a hundred pounds heavier, skin darker, hair longer, arms dangling at his sides. The army didn't make clothes to fit John Garcia. Pants too short. Ends of sleeves half way up his long arms. A mop of black curly hair hanging down under his steel helmet. Even his rifle looked too short for the length of his body. We headed off down a path with John in the lead. He paused, turned around and asked, "Cricket, do you speak any Spanish?" "Not a word, John."

"Well Cricket, some of your guys are Mexican Americans and they yak at each other a lot in Spanish. Don't let it get to you. They won't hide anything from you. It just comes natural to 'em. I'm originally from Hawaii but many of us live in Southern California around L.A. We've been together through this whole Pacific War and had one officer after another. But we never had a Cricket before. The men will like that. We'll help you. We need you real bad right now. Can you believe it? Just this morning, our last officer got shot in the back by a stray bullet while he was bending over to tie his shoe. And, we were even in reserve at a safe place. That's where I'm takin' you now. Are you ready, Cricket?"

"John, I'm as ready as I'll ever be and scared as hell. I'm going to need your help."

"Cricket, you and I are goin' to see a lot of each other. I'm glad they sent you. Come on, it ain't far. And, don't worry about some of us being Mexicans. We shoot like crazy. Already killed half the Japs on the island. We got them on the run."

"OK, John, let's go."

My Platoon

JOHN GARCIA LED ME ALONG a muddy path beneath some shattered trees. An odor of smoke came from the tops of the trees that smoldered like punk used to ignite firecrackers and reminded me of burning autumn leaves back home. Then a stench of something rotten drifted out of the copse of trees. An acrid burnt smell perfumed the air. My guts grabbed me with intense pain. "John, I gotta take a shit." "OK, Cricket, this is as good a place as any. Go into those trees and I'll guard you from here. You'll be OK. This is a safe place." I went behind some bushes, dug a hole, stripped down my jumpsuit, and released a burst of diarrhea like I hadn't experienced in months. Just then an enemy artillery shell could be heard coming our way from a distance. It sounded like a freight train running at full throttle right over my head. John rushed into the woods and pushed me to the ground with him on top. The bomb passed over us and exploded some distance to the rear. "That's one crap ya won't ever forget, Cricket. Come on, let's get out of here."

"John, if this isn't war, I don't know what is."

"You ain't seen nuttin."

John didn't seem to be upset by this delay and led me out into an open area to a group of men sitting around on a small hillside in the sun. Shirts and shoes off. Some asleep. A few writing letters. Mail had been delivered and some were quietly reading the notes from home. One guy laughed out loud at something his girlfriend had written. "Just wait till I get home, honey. You'll get all that you can stand and then more." Another soldier spit out angry words, "My old lady's getting fucked by a 4F bastard. She's ditching me." One of his buddies put his arms around him. There were glances in our direction as we approached. John took off his helmet and made one introduction. "Hey, you guys, this here man is Cricket. He is going to be 'Our Cricket.' You know what that means? Good luck, that's what."

Hand waves from several of the men, a few words of greeting, several came over and shook hands. One guy laughed and said, "Keep your shoes tied Cricket, and don't turn your back on the enemy." John yelled at him. "Juan, that ain't funny. The poor guy just died this morning right where you're standing. Cricket, that was a stupid accident. He got hit in the back from a stray bullet. Didn't know what hit him. Right through his heart." I'd seen this officer's body just moments earlier at the battalion headquarters lying under a tarp.

John said, "Come on, Cricket, let me get you a proper rifle. That peeshooter you're carrying makes you look like an officer." I was still carrying the carbine rifle that was assigned to officers. Made us look jaunty, or so the Army thought. John fetched me an M-1 standard rifle that I'd learned to fire in basic training. It was heavier than the carbine, a very powerful rifle and I'd earned medals shooting it at targets.

"Where's the enemy?" I asked. "Over that ridge, that's where Company "I" is spread out. Our platoon, your platoon, is in reserve tonight. We join up with the marines over there in the morning. They're fighting bastards. Kill everything in sight." I walked around the area reaching out to talk with the men sprawled out on the ground. There were questions. Where you from? Where'd you train? The fact that I'd grown up in farm country of western Pennsylvania registered. "I'm glad you're not a city slicker." "We got one guy here from L.A. but most of us are farmers. Got across the border and became citizens just in time to get drafted. Hot shit! How do you like that for a present from your new country? But it was worse at home. We starved."

Another day was coming to an end. A messenger arrived to tell me that the Company Commander wanted to see me. Jack, the Commanding Officer of Company "I," was one grizzly looking character, covered with dirt, face blackened, and a man of few words who'd just returned from the front lines over the ridge. "Glenn, your platoon is going into action at six in the morning. I'll come and get you and your men. We have to cross a minefield the Japs put down yesterday. It'll be tricky. Single file until we get through it. Your platoon is good. You're lucky. See you in the morning. Dig a deep hole to sleep in. And, by the way, you won't believe this, but this letter just arrived for you."

I didn't feel good about this exchange with my new company commander. I stuffed the letter in my pocket and headed back to my men. It felt good to get back to them. I already thought of them as "my men" after having just met them. John Garcia was right there beside me when I returned to the hillside. He suggested that I dig my foxhole close to his own. That hole was the deepest one I'd ever dug. John came over and looked down at me while I was digging to China. "We got ourselves a 'Cricket.'"

It was dusk when the air-raid sirens began to sound off toward the sea in the distance. The first night in an actual combat situation had begun and here I was with a group of men who were strangers to me. They looked like a Hollywood cast which was all set to rob the Wells Fargo bank and gallop out of town before the Sheriff's posse caught up with them. What were they thinking about me? I was now their leader. We were about to go into combat in the morning. Would they follow me? I needed to connect again with them before sinking into my hole.

I ate my can of beans, remembering Mom's home-baked pots that she always made for Egner family reunions, and then I began to make the rounds, talking with each man, saying almost anything that helped me to make individual contact. They were friendly. We sat together under the stars on the edges of their fox holes and watched the Japanese planes dropping bombs in the distance. The sky was lighted by flashes of our anti-aircraft fire, and a steady stream of tracer bullets headed skyward. It reminded me of the fireworks at Idlewild Park on a hot July 4th evening.

Just before dark, I met with the squad leaders to review the night's plan for guarding our perimeter. "I'll be out there with you guys because we're a team now and we're going to look after each another."

"Sounds good, Cricket. Did you say that you were a chicken farmer?"

"Yep, raised a thousand chickens with my cousin. Made my first real money. Love chickens." After getting guard detail set, we agreed to meet again at 5 A.M. to go and take a look at the mine field.

The air raids continued all night. I made another round to check on each man and then dropped down into my own fox hole next to big John's. Deep down in my hole, it felt safe. I looked at the earthen sides and ran my fingers up and down to feel the dirt, remembering watching my grandfather's coffin being lowered deep into his grave. He was lying there, dead now for many years. I was here, alive, spread out on my back on some dry grass, looking upwards. The opening above me was partially covered with branches but as I lay there resting beneath a star-filled sky, it seemed as beautiful a sky I'd ever witnessed. Remembering the letter in my pocket, I fumbled to get it open in the dark and then lit up my Ronson lighter. The envelope contained a program of a service, "In Honor of War

Mothers," conducted by women at the First Presbyterian Church in Ligonier. Mrs. Dan Melville, mother of my friend Dan Jr., gave the address of welcome. The program contained, "Our Message to Servicemen." I read the lines slowly.

■ ■ ■

Dear Young Friends:

In your home town on this beautiful day, we have met in a Community Meeting to honor your mothers, who are so bravely enduring the suspense which is part of their service in this time of national and worldwide distress and to pay our due respects to you, the Defenders of our Country.

You belong to us all now; you are our Defenders, not only of Democracy but of Christianity, and of Liberty. The gallantry and patience of you who serve our country is deeply appreciated.

As you are showing courage and high endeavor in the camp or at the front, so will we try to show the same qualities on the Home Front.

We will devote ourselves, heart and soul and mind, to the creation of that better world for which you are serving.

Our hearts go out in tender sympathy for the sick and wounded, with heartfelt thanks to those who tend them.

In your moments of loneliness remember the love of the Heavenly Father and accept His strength and support which are yours for the asking. This letter bears to you who receive it not only the love of the sender, but the high regard of all your friends with the prayer, "The Lord bless thee and keep thee."

Mrs. Daniel Melville

On the back of the program was this note from my mother:

Rollie Boy:

Will you please find the copy of the 23rd Psalm that Dad gave to you just before you boarded the train in Greensburg to go off to war? Learn it by heart, renew your faith in God and repeat or read this Psalm daily. Your Great Uncle Issac had great faith in it and he said many fell all around him in the Civil War but he was never injured.

Your Loving Mother

I opened my wallet and took out the small silver foil envelope which protected the clipping from the family Bible which dad had slipped into my hand as the train pulled out of the station in Greensburg where this journey to war had started. Trying to hold the cigarette lighter steady, I began to read the 23rd Psalm:

> The Lord is my shepherd; I shall not want.
> He maketh me to lie down in green pastures:
> He leadeth me beside still waters.
> He restoreth my soul;
> He leadeth me in the paths of righteousness for his name's sake.
> Yea, though I walk through the valley of the shadow of death,
> I will fear no evil: for thou art with me;
> Thy rod and thy staff they comfort me.
> Thou preparest a table before me.
> In the presence of mine enemies:
> Thou anointest my head with oil;
> My cup runneth over.
> Surely goodness and mercy shall follow me all the days of my life:
> And I will dwell in the house of the Lord forever.

I held a small St. Christopher medal in my hands. My cousin, Cubbie Freidhoff, gave this to me when she said goodbye the last time I visited her in Johnstown. This medal had belonged to her Grandmother Freidhoff. It hung around my neck with my dog tags. There wasn't the slightest doubt in my mind that I had a personal God who was looking over me. I felt scared but did not feel that I would be killed. I knew that, somehow, I would get through this and be able to lead these good men. My God protected me in years past. He wouldn't let me down now when I needed him so badly. Ours was a very religious family. God was always beside us to help us through troubled times. We Glenns were a bunch of survivors. I was on good terms with God.

My enemy and I were about to meet. But first I masturbated, then fell asleep while looking up at the stars.

Follow Me

AT ABOUT 0400 I CLIMBED out of my foxhole realizing that my first day in combat had begun. Clouds scudded across the fading moon casting an eerie blue-white light across the hillside, creating a play of dark shadows that made the light of the setting white moon even whiter. Framed in this dim early morning light, my men were beginning to stir quietly like animals rising from their holes looking around, sniffing the air for predators in utter silence. A wisplike flicker of light rolled across their backs and cheeks, their movements in slow motion like a silent ballet on a dimly lit barren stage. A scene like you might have dreamed. My eyes caught the lights and darks and held them for a moment, and then it was gone. Never quite real, never lasting longer than a moment.

"Son of a bitch, I'm still sleepy," whispered John as we both checked our rifles, ammunition, and grenades while drinking cups of hot java and eating doughnuts, miraculously sent from the rear, then eating C-rations in the cool air while we watched the scene framed in the light and dark of this new day. We did not talk. Our next stop was the latrine trench back in the rubble of the woods. My guts had quieted down leaving a very nervous stomach as a warning. The Army dressed officers in smart looking one-piece coveralls. It was "the look" and clearly identified us. Together with the pea-shooter carbine, this outfit gave us a rather jaunty look. I stripped from the top down exposing my entire body. Had an Officer ever been shot while squatting in this position? "Holy Christ, Cricket! We gotta get you dressed like a regular G.I. You ain't gonna last long lookin like that." John junked the coveralls and produced separate pants and a shirt making me look like any infantryman. Their Cricket had now become one of the anonymous.

The sky lightened. We walked to look over the minefield we would cross. Some mines were easy to spot. No one knew that I had a particular type of color blindness that enabled me to spot hidden objects. The Japanese made some attempts at camouflage. Next, I made the rounds speaking with every man, "I've seen the mines; I know where they are; just follow me and we'll be OK."

Company Commander Jack arrived on the dot of 0600 looking more disheveled than ever after being at the front all night commanding the other platoons of Company "I." He brought two scouts with him who took the lead sweeping the ground before them with metal detectors. Jack came next in the column, followed by me, John, and the rest of the platoon in single file. I spoke up and pointed out the mine locations. That was a mistake.

Jack didn't like it. "How do you know for Goddamned certain just where they are?"

"I can see them, Jack." He didn't believe me. I didn't think it a good idea to go into all the details of my vision. Didn't mind in the least his walking out in front. Every man followed the one just in front of him closely, tramping in his comrade's footsteps knowing that at least that one move would be safe. Once we got through the grass-covered minefield without incident, Jack took the lead down a muddy path bordering a rice paddy. I'd never before seen rice growing in water. There were bomb craters in the middle filled with muddy, stinking water. The stench of death was terrible. A headless Japanese was sitting against a tree, rifle resting across his legs. "Booby-trapped! Don't touch it or you will blow us sky high," mumbled Jack. We carefully stepped across the legs of the headless body to move on. We could see the trip wire connected to his rifle lead off to the hidden bomb. One day of training at that Infantry School at Fort Benning had put us through an exercise on how to detect hidden bombs in situations just like this one. A bridge got blown up because of my not detecting a trip wire. My color blind condition didn't help that time.

After we had walked several hundred yards, Jack looked over his shoulder at me and suddenly stopped. He looked shocked. What next? "For Christ's sake, you 90-day wonder, where are your men?" Looking behind me in stunned amazement I discovered no one was there. Not a single man had followed me. "Get your fuckin' ass back there and bring those guys along. Shit! Didn't they teach you anything at that damned school for boy officers?"

I shook with embarrassment, anger, and fear while running back along the trail, leaping across the legs of the enemy, wondering what had become of his head. Where in the hell had my men gone? Why weren't they right here following me? Damn! What a dumb mistake to have made. Finally I met my stalled platoon. Garcia was standing there, all six feet, seven inches of him. "Damn it, John, where in the hell have ya been?" "Cricket, we just thought that you were walkin' in aways. You never looked back, never gave us a signal. You gotta let me know what you want. Can't read your mind."

"Okay, John, let's begin again. Stay so fuckin' close to me that you can smell the sweat off my back. Do you smell this sweat on my neck? Don't ever get out of my sight again? Understand?"

"Si, Cricket, Si." "OK, FOLLOW ME!"

Off I went down the trail past the dead Japanese once again, looking behind me more than once and giving John hand signals to keep tight with the men strung out behind him. Each guy had to be shown the trip wire. Finally we caught up with Jack. He acted disgusted with me. That was bad. There was a disconnect right from the very first moment, and this incident did nothing to improve our relationship. He turned out to be a master at dispensing chicken shit to anyone he didn't like. The mistake of pointing out the mines when he was leading to show I knew something, followed by not having kept my platoon right behind me, had apparently convinced him that Glenn was a lost cause. He had just lost the officer I'd replaced the day before. Another 90-day wonder.

The front line extended along a set of low hills where soldiers were dug in just below the crest amid broken down trees shredded of their leaves. We walked in a ditch that looked as if it had once been an animal trail, perhaps for oxen. Another platoon was being relieved. Jack led us along the line where my men were assigned to fox holes as other men were sent to the rear area from where we'd just come. They looked terrible, probably been awake all night, needed to get outa there. Big John was like my shadow. He stood so tall and looked like an ostrich when he bent over. "Keep your fuckin head down, John."

"Si, Cricket, Si."

Once my platoon was set in the positions just vacated, Jack led me along the rest of the front line that was the responsibility of the 17th Infantry Regiment. At one point in the line, another officer spoke with Jack. "One of our men is in a forward foxhole just over the top. We haven't heard from him. Someone needs to go out there and check on him."

Jack took over. "We need a volunteer to creep out there and check on your buddy. Who is willin' to go?" There was utter silence from the men. "Okay, I know what you are feelin'. But, what if you were the one out there in trouble? Wouldn't you want someone to come out to help you?" Finally, a young kid volunteered to go. He got down on his belly and began to crawl and slid in the mud over the top. We waited in silence. He returned looking ashen.

"Jack, his body is pasted all around the sides of the hole. There isn't anything left to grab onto." The kid broke down and began to cry. Jack put his arms around him and declared him a hero on the spot. He praised this man's bravery.

But the boy couldn't recover from the shock and was sent immediately back to the field hospital never to be heard from again. Jack decided that it would be too risky to attempt to retrieve the soldier's body until more enemy territory had been taken.

We continued slogging through the mud along the line. A compassionate side of Jack had been revealed to me. This was a war-weary man who had deep feelings. Jack suddenly stopped, turned to me and said "Remember that, Glenn! The kid deserved to be honored before his buddies for what he did."

I met up with Jim Harkins, Harry Harper, and several other classmates who'd been assigned as platoon leaders in other companies. Our energy level was still so high that we ran from one fox hole to the other to say hello and prove to each other that we were courageous and still alive. Christ! We were in combat! The big game had begun! We seemed to need to demonstrate ourselves as being fearless and full of youthful athleticism. The combat veterans, including John, thought we were crazy. We were nuts to be exposing ourselves in that manner. John pulled me aside and jammed me down into a hole with him. "Cricket, I will always stay with you while you're alive but you got to listen to me right now. You never know when a bomb is going to land. You could be killed in an instant just standing out there pretending you are so goddamned brave and clever. That was stupid, Cricket."

"Si, John, Si."

Jack observed what happened as we were showing off. He chewed me out for moving around so much as we headed back down the ditch. There was an explosion just ahead of us. We both dove for the ground. For a few moments, nothing could be seen. Smoke and the odor of hot metal filled the trench. As it began to lift, the body of a soldier could be seen lying just ahead of us. We crawled on our bellies toward him. His face was ashen. "My, God, Jack! It's Peter, my buddy!" There didn't appear to be any wounds in his body. No observable blood. He died instantly from concussion. Didn't know what hit him. I reached in his shirt and pulled out his dog tags to check his name. "I can't believe that we were just walking by here a few moments ago. He believed that he was going to die but Christ,

Jack, he has been in combat for less than an hour. How can this be? Just a few days ago he was standing on a Saipan hillside delivering our Easter Sunday sunrise service. You should've seen him, Jack, on the ship. He talked and prayed with one scared kid after another in the hole as our convoy moved closer to Okinawa."

I reached down and lifted his body into my arms and cradled his head under my chin against my shoulder as my tears fell on his gray cheeks, recalling the love I felt toward him when I hugged him by the rail that last night at sea. I felt Jack's hand on my shoulder as he pulled me up and away from Peter's body. "Glenn, you might have been that man. We don't need you to be super brave and die before nightfall. We need you. Your men need you. Go now and be with them. Take care of them and yourself and perhaps we'll get through this alive. The medics will take care of your friend. I'm sorry, I really am."

Two scared stretcher bearers arrived to carry Peter's body back along the same route that he had traveled just a few hours before. Before we permitted them to carry him off, Jim and I knelt by his body for a few moments but it was dangerous to be there on the exposed ground. My hand reached to my hip pocket to make certain that I still had his parent's address as I recalled the scene of my grandfather lying in his coffin. "There will be no red roses for you, Peter." Then he was gone.

When Peter died, part of the spirit that carried me to war died with him. Only twenty years old. He didn't look anywhere near that. Most of the guys didn't even have a chance to get to know his name. He'd been a replacement for a broken part of the infantry machine. Another one would now be needed and the assembly line that carried us all to this place would quickly produce another officer. The awesome reality that we'd been trained to be cannon fodder in a war that covered the earth's surface and had already ended the lives of millions of people hadn't quite dawned on me. The fact that I might lose my own life violently or that I might be maimed while still a very young man hadn't fully registered until this very moment.

Jack abruptly interrupted my thoughts. "The Japs like to attack our positions at night. Our perimeter has been booby-trapped with tangled wires and packs of dynamite. Cans have been tied to the wires to alert us to any movement of the enemy. Flares will be put up all night to keep the area illuminated. If an attack comes, we'll shoot every damned gun we have, throw as many grenades as we can heave out, and call for artillery support. The general idea is to make them think that there are four times as many men here as we really have. It is the volume of fire, not the accuracy, which counts. Get it, Glenn?"

I thought this was a strange concept after so much emphasis had been placed upon precision firing during our training. Volume of fire power was more important than accuracy. Never did see one of our planes shoot down an enemy aircraft nor an enemy plane get one of ours. Every day tons and tons of ammunition was expended by both sides. Rarely was there a direct hit.

Jack and I crawled forward to another lookout position where we could observe the still enemy-occupied land. A field that sloped away from us looked much like any other field back home. All of a sudden a head popped up and looked straight at us. It looked like the missing head of the booby-trapped Japanese soldier. Only this time the head revealed shoulders and arms pointing a rifle directly at us. He was only 50 yards from us, a stone's throw away. He fired and I felt the bullets pass directly over our heads and smash into the dirt side of the trench behind us. Jack threw a grenade and I threw another, my first. We didn't wait to see if we scored but slid backwards in the mud to a lower and safer location. Other guys in the platoon took up the task with more grenades.

Jack changed directions. "I want to go over tomorrow's attack with you. You and your men will join up with tanks. It isn't going to be easy. Your men are rested. The others have been awake for several nights. We've been in this location for two days and we've got to break out and keep them on the run. The tanks will come down that road over there at 0700. You guys will follow them out across that field. A massive artillery barrage will be put down just ahead of you to bomb the bejesus out of the Japs. We've got to push them back to the next ridge by tomorrow night. This maneuver is going to be hard but we've got to do it. Better explain all this to your squad leaders before dark. And remember, when you fire at the enemy, don't even think of them as men but as targets.

After Jack left, I got my squad leaders together and talked them through the plan to attack with tanks and artillery support. On paper it looked wonderful—tanks, infantry troops following closely behind, under cover of massive artillery barrages. But no one was very excited about the idea. "I don't like it, Cricket. This is the toughest kind of maneuver. We have never done it before during this campaign." The only experience I could remember was going through a few short simulated tank/infantry attacks back at Benning. Could we get through this successfully without encountering serious casualties?

Everyone predicted an enemy attack that night. We spent the next hours making certain that everyone had sufficient ammunition and grenades. Several newly invented rifles issued to us permitted us to see in the dark via ultraviolet rays. When you looked through the gun sights, it looked like you were observing a scene in almost daylight. I saw a Japanese poke his head up over a mound and realized how close we were to the enemy.

Right after dusk, they began bombarding our positions. Shells flew overhead. You could hear them coming from some distance away. The roar of the shells grew louder as they neared us and zoomed over our heads exploding someplace to the rear of our positions. I wondered where they were going to hit. We all got low in our holes until the explosion and then peeked up to keep a watch on the field where we believed they would attack. We didn't have to dig new fox holes because we were occupying positions already dug by the enemy. However, each of us made certain that our own particular hole was plenty deep enough to stand up in and peer over the top and be ready to fire or throw our grenades. Very little sleep that night but, at one point, I must have dozed off having slumped deep down in the hole using my steel helmet as a pillow. Suddenly I realized that a rat occupied the hole with me when it ran under my neck. I jerked up into a sitting position, yelled something and the beast scampered up the side of the hole and out. The guard on duty came running over. "What's the matter, Cricket, you having a dream?"

"Nope, just a rat in here with me." "Oh, hell, you'll get used to that. It ain't fun for them either. They need to hide too." I took out that little slip of paper again from my wallet, lit a cigarette, read the lines by the dim burning light, and then tried to relax. No sexual urges this time. Perhaps the rumor was true that the Army was secretly putting saltpeter in our food to quiet our peckers. How did they do it? Were there a couple of KP's back there somewhere secretly mixing up a witch's brew?

The Japanese didn't attack that night as we'd expected. It was almost too quiet. What were they doing?

The Tank Attack

THE ENEMY DIDN'T ATTACK AS expected. A very restless night gave me some time to think about how I would lead the men in such a dangerous maneuver, remembering the exercises at Fort Benning where foot soldiers followed tanks in simulated battles. Tanks would take the lead with their guns blasting, always reaching and overwhelming the objective. Infantry would spread out behind tanks and fire at an enemy line of cardboard dummies. This wasn't Benning. With only a few hours 'til dawn, we'd move out beyond front lines to fight the enemy on their turf. Could I do the job without getting killed? I had to present myself as confident. I knew what I should say to my platoon before attacking. I rehearsed it in my mind several times during the night while feeling apprehensive and very uncomfortable with my superior, Jack. No trust.

Early in the morning, John Garcia, our two scouts, squad leaders, and I were taken to the point where my platoon and the tanks were to join together. We had fifteen minutes to look over the land, determine location of enemy, go back and brief the men, and then confidently lead them in battle. I only hoped that this attack would go as smoothly as the training exercise back at Benning.

My platoon was stretched out in the early morning mist along the steaming, muddy roadside as the roar and grinding of tank engines could be heard coming from the rear, rumbling closer and closer. When you're on the outside, it is difficult to get personal with a tank, especially when you need to do all your communicating via radio. I didn't even know the tank commander. The lead tank paused when it reached us, the hatch popped open and a young kid climbed out looking very jaunty in his clean

My platoon was assigned the job of attacking a Japanese position my second day in combat. We met up with the tanks after dawn and followed them out into a valley. Half-way to the objective, the Japanese opened fire, disabling one tank and causing the deaths of several of my men who I never got to know. (Photo courtesy of Center of Military History, United States Army)

uniform. "Glenn, I'm Bart. We need to get your radio in synch with the one inside the tank. It's goin' to be tough communicating with all the shooting but we gotta stay coordinated. Artillery are scheduled to begin firing at the exact minute my tanks and your platoon move out together. It's a perfect plan. We take off in fifteen minutes, right after initial bombardment is lifted. We'll cream the bastards." At least he was confident. I chose not to give my platoon a John Wayne rah rah type of speech before the attack but instead walked along the line saying a few words quietly to each man about the plan. The valley to be crossed led to a steep hillside several thousand yards in the distance. The enemy awaited us in their holes and caves. Organizing for the attack in a copse of splintered trees, the road would lead us into this field of battle as if we were entering a vast coliseum during Roman times but without the cheering crowds and the fanfare of trumpets.

The time for the attack came. The six tanks began to move forward, spreading out with my squads deployed behind them. Each tank opened up their guns, spewing out continuous fire as they lumbered slowly forward. "OK, men, begin firing as we move forward. Stay in close to the tanks. Those artillery guys just blew the top off the ridge. Can't even see it now under the clouds of smoke from the explosions that have blocked our view. That's where we expect the enemy to be hiding. It looks like the Japanese withdrew or have been killed by the combination of fire from artillery, tanks, and you men. Move slowly now. We're getting three-fourths of the way toward our objective." Our progress made me feel like we'd just about wrapped up the whole job.

The bastards tricked us into believing they'd retreated from their dug-in positions. When we were totally exposed, they opened up and hit all of us with a barrage of fire. The enemy bullets ricocheted off the metal tank sides. Several men were hit and propelled backwards with arms flailing and rifles flying into the air by the force of the barrage. They dropped dead during the first moments. I immediately radioed our company commander, Jack, requesting more artillery support. We could hear the shells coming. They fell short of the enemy positions and landed in the area of our lead tanks. One tank was struck, blown off its tracks, completely immobilized. The tank commander radioed. "Additional tanks hit! Two can't move! Crews need to escape! Cover us while we get out!"

I began to look for a fallback position. The guys from the destroyed tanks were confused from the concussions and didn't know which way to turn. We were stopped, totally surprised, unprepared to move forward in the attack, and trapped in a very exposed position. "Christ, Cricket, let's get out of here," shouted John. My men and the tank crews all began to move in full retreat toward a slight rise in the rear that I'd spotted. A small ridge in the land, and I mean very small, lay off to the right rear. Using hand signals, I moved the men toward that cover. The three tanks which were still functioning continued to fire at the enemy positions while we maneuvered to get the hell out of there. It wasn't pretty or well organized. It was every man for himself as we ran for cover. The Japanese fire continued to be very heavy as we leapt to the ground and hunkered down into the mud. At the spot where I landed, there was only about six inches of ground above my head. I could feel the impact of the bullets hitting the land just inches from my cheek and the spray of dirt splashing into my face. A flash of memory came to me of Uncle Ford, Corky, and I squeezing down behind a small ridge of land while hunting squirrels in the mountains. Pressing my body deeper into the earth, I remembered what Uncle

The Japanese defenses were in rocky crags at the end of the valley. The position was eventually taken with the support of flame-thrower tanks shortly before capture. The ground was covered with Japanese dead smoldering in the flames. (Photo courtesy of Center of Military History, United States Army)

Ford taught me that early morning about hugging the land and hiding from the animals.

A soldier lying just beside me raised his head just a few inches and was instantly killed. His head, snapped back by the force of the bullet entering through his steel helmet and into his skull and out the back of his head, dangled like a rag puppet against my side with his warm blood gushing onto my neck and shoulder. So much blood that I thought for a moment that I'd also been hit. I didn't even know at first that this was Ben, a popular man within the platoon, an old guy, almost thirty, called "Pop." I felt terrible and guilty that I'd not somehow saved him. We needed to get out of there quickly before we were all killed. Saving the rest of the men came first. Guilt came later. Fortunately our radioman, Rick Wanacott, communicated our situation and the support that we received from the rear saved us.

The artillery bombarded the enemy positions again. This time the shells hit the target. A smoke screen dropped over the tanks and the area where we were stranded. Within an hour, we and the tank crews extricated ourselves and began to move forward again. The disabled tanks were abandoned. The bodies of our men were left behind as we groped forward through the manmade fog. We reached the lower side of the ridge, spread out, and inched our bodies forward on our bellies with the tanks just ahead of us. A squad of flame throwers moved with us through the tank formation or what was left of it, and opened up as we reached the crest of the hill. They blasted every inch of the ground with searing flame. Screams came from the Jap locations. Nothing was alive when the flame throwers withdrew to allow us to move forward again over the smoldering ground. Steaming, bloated bodies were lying everywhere, seared black beyond recognition. Eyes stared out of roasted swollen heads without hair, resembling hogs at a barbecue roast. Some bodies were jammed together in fiery death as they attempted to escape blocking the openings of caves. The air merged the odor of cooked meat with the smell of expended bombs and scorched earth. A total holocaust unfolded before us.

We were still very exposed to the enemy and quickly fell into their foxholes, sometimes pushing their bodies aside and even using their bloated forms as protection in order to provide a deeper cavity for ourselves. Our objective had eventually been reached but at great cost. The sudden loss of Ben lying dead there beside me with his bloody head on my shoulder and the mowing down of the three other men who I'd never really come to know became seared in my memory at that very moment. No time to mourn as I tried to fathom what had happened in such a short time. Their bodies would be picked up by the medics and returned along the same paths which they'd so recently trodden with fear. My men were stunned and I couldn't allow my own deep and sudden shock to divert me from them. John Garcia brought me back to reality when he said, "Cricket, we'll order us four replacements."

"Sounds like we're going to requisition a new mess kit or parts for a broken machine."

"That's just about it, Cricket. When we lose one, we order a new one from supplies. Some of them don't even last more than a day. The three back there lying in the field arrived the day before yesterday, just before you got to us. I don't remember their names. They all look the same. We'll have to check what they're carrying in their pockets and their dog tags for identification. Don't worry too much. Army has a good supply. Cricket, it coulda' been much worse." "Don't see how. Really true though; they all do look the same, except for you, John. You're so damn big. Can't distinguish the rest of the guys one from the other and that's good out here. There's nothing about the look of these guys to encourage anyone toward recognizing them."

While all of this had been going on, Jack moved other platoons of Company "I" up behind us to help secure the new line of positions that we'd just occupied. Much work had to be done before nightfall. New booby traps were to be set to protect us from counterattack. Needing to do all of this work before dark diverted us from feeling the loss of our men, of being afraid, of exhaustion from what we'd just experienced. The fact that so many of us had somehow survived was a miracle. In checking my men's positions, there wasn't much chatter between us and I wondered what they were thinking about my leadership skills. Were they blaming Ben's death on me? He'd been with the platoon for a long time and was very popular.

That bright night made it difficult for the enemy to move on us without being seen. But moonlight also produces all sorts of shadows and presented us with a situation where every blade of grass seemed to conceal an enemy. In spite of all the natural light from the moon, we called for artillery flares all night to better illuminate the land beyond our positions. These flares burst into flame high in the sky and floated slowly to land carried by little parachutes. That night was one of being constantly on the alert. No sleep, shooting at every shadow. The Japanese didn't attack.

A feeling of confidence returned with the morning light, the retreat of the day before now forgotten. Our enemies were on the run. The men believed that we could finish off the battle within a few days if only the Army would let them. I needed the overconfidence now being shown by the guys but became aware that they were taking unnecessary chances by running around and crowing about yesterday's great battle with the tanks. "Cricket, just let us at them. We can get this thing over within twenty-four hours."

How could they think that way? Had they forgotten about the loss of Ben and the other men? Feeling leery of their bravado caused me to take extra precautions. The fact was that it might have been any one of us who had been shot and killed. We didn't dare think of that possibility. John kept bopping around and I kept yelling at him to keep his ass closer to the ground. I was now in the habit of cautioning him as he'd previously done in looking after me. The battle stagnated and we remained in those positions for over a week with the dead bodies stacked by my men in piles like cordwood over to the side of the hill. The stench of death increased until we all were sick and didn't feel we could take it much longer. Jack appeared and told me that he was pulling us back for a day's rest that afternoon. "Be ready to get your asses outa here when I yell." That sounded good to me. We'd been on the front lines for about ten days. It seemed like at least a month. We were very thankful to be getting out of that scene of death and destruction. My mind played tricks on me. The appearance of dead men . . . the headless body with the booby trapped rifle . . . Peter once very alive and then dead in my arms . . . Ben being killed right beside me . . . the enemy bodies . . . black and blistered . . . eyes staring out of their heads . . . their burned hair . . . Grandpap's dead body surrounded with red roses in the parlor of the old Victorian house back in Ligonier.

The replacement units arrived. I looked up from a foxhole and recognized the officer who'd taken me swimming on Saipan. "How you doin', Cricket? Haven't had much of a chance to swim and lay around in the sun out here I bet?"

"I'm alive. That's enough for now. Good luck to you and your men." Then we moved out and he and his men took our positions. As it turned out, the entire company was being pulled back, not just my platoon. We were going back far enough to actually sleep on cots above the ground in tents, eat hot meals, bathe in a water hole, take showers, and walk around in our undershorts without our rifles dangling over our shoulders. It was time to make contact with our buddies from other units, swap war stories, and crow a bit about our successes in battle. We didn't dwell much on our losses.

■ ■ ■

June 5, 1945

Dear Mom, Dad, and Sunny Girl:

Can't believe that this is my 20th birthday being celebrated here in a foxhole on this remote island that no one has ever heard about. Mom, what one of your yummy chocolate cakes would do for me now. Except that I would rather be eating it at home with the three of you. Hope that you did something together with my Sunny Girl to remind her that I still love her. A letter will be on the way soon just to her. Oh, how I miss you all, think of you every day, and am so thankful for all the love and support you have sent my way. No letters from home for over a week because of where we are. Hope they arrive soon. God has been good to us and we certainly need his blessings right now because I am about to take my new platoon into combat.

Dad, you would be proud of your kid. I am now a platoon leader. Wish you could see these guys. I have a number of Mexicans from Southern California. John Garcia is a big, tall guy who has been very helpful to me. He has had much more experience in combat than have I. The two of us stick very close together. We sat on the edge of our foxholes last night and watched a dog fight going on out over the ocean far enough in the distance not to put us in any danger. Sometimes, Dad, this feels like I am living a dream. Up to this point, it hasn't been too bad but there are some tough days just ahead. Down deep inside I feel scared that I will be killed but then those feelings go away and are replaced with feelings of confidence. I read the 23rd Psalm every night. After all, I have been well trained for what I have to do. I can admit these feelings to you because you have also been a soldier in World War I. I don't want you to worry but to realize that I will count on you to take care of Mom and my Sunny Girl no matter what happens. You have been straight with me about what it is like to be an infantryman. Your past words to me have been a wonderful support. You know how much I love you. You are a great Dad and one day we will be able to take a walk together and talk this all over. May God give us that time to be together once again. I need to catch a few hours of sleep now. Tomorrow is going to be tough but I am as ready as I will ever be. Look over our girls for both of us. Pray to God every night for the guidance that I need to get through this. Keep your own spirits high. Enjoy your job helping to guard the plant. You and the others at Robertshaw are making a real contribution to this war by making those bomb sights. I send each of you love and kisses.

Your Rollie Boy Lt. Cricket

Respite and Loss

JIM HARKINS AND I SHARED a tent with Bill Fortuna in the respite camp and we wanted to connect with our other buddies. I got on the phone and called Harry Harper who'd been assigned to another company. The voice at the other end asked for identification. "I'm Lieutenant Cricket Glenn, a friend of Harry's. Just want to get together. Can you get him on the line for me?" "I'm sorry to tell you that Harper was killed yesterday. He tried to save a kid by running out to him at an exposed position. Both of them were shot. Harry covered the boy with his body. The kid was saved but Harry died instantly. Didn't know what hit him. I'm sorry to tell you this. Harry's body was sent north to the field morgue. When this is over, you can go up there and find his grave. Really sorry, Sir."

Jim was watching me as I slowly put down the phone. He sensed the bad news without my saying a word. The guy who I had sat up with all night in the barrack's latrine arguing about race was dead. And Peter too. We rounded up the guys who trained with us, now a group of men suddenly appearing older, sober, and shocked from this latest loss of a good friend and the terrible experiences of the past weeks. We sat around thinking of our past times together, holding each other as we'd not done before, walking together, eating together, not allowing anyone to get out of sight of the others.

We took a walk up along a hillside just to have something to do together. The sun felt good on our bare backs as we plodded along with our heads hung low. Suddenly I spotted an egg lying on the ground in front of me. "Hey, you guys! Look! I found an egg!" But the egg was cracked. As we gathered around to look at it, it moved. A chick was in the process of hatching. Just one egg. No mother hen in sight. Four young soldiers in their skivvies watching the little bird emerge from the shell. "What are we goin' to do

Cricket? We can't just let it sit here. It'll be eaten by a rat." I picked up the moist chick and slipped it into my pocket. It remained very still, not even a chirp, as we walked back to our tents. All the guys were amused by our find. I stretched out on my cot and put the little chick beside me in the bed. I'd grown up with chickens and this little creature was perfectly content to accept me as its mother, never having seen a hen in its life. A bit of chicken shit on my chest wasn't as bad as crawling through all that mud and blood these past weeks. I felt living warmth from its body against my cheek.

It flourished during the days we were resting there, began to scratch around, ate our oatmeal and continued to sleep in bed with me nestling up under my chin on my chest. It followed me around everywhere I went and that brought gales of laughter from all over the camp. When we went to eat, that chick would jump up on the bench beside me and gobble up the handouts. I'd become a chicken mother in the middle of a war zone and felt like I was back home tending my flock out by the barn. Caring for this little creature seemed to ease the pain from the loss of Harry, Peter, Ben, and the other men. The substitution of a baby chick for the life of a man wasn't a fair exchange but, strange as it may seem, it helped.

The men of Company "I" relaxed during those days. They captured several wild goats, butchered them and cooked up several meals of goat stew using root vegetables that tasted like potatoes. We ate together and bathed in craters filled with muddy water that we splashed on each other and then ran naked to the showers. The mosquito bites didn't seem to bother us at the time. There was time to get to know one another, share pictures of our families and friends and crow a bit about how great we were in the recent battle. We began to relax.

I was sitting outside our tent writing letters to the parents of the soldiers who had been killed when an explosive shot was fired inside the tent. Rushing inside, I found that Bill Fortuna had fired a round from his rifle through his leg. I couldn't believe what I was seeing. He was bent over screaming with pain. "Cricket, it was an accident. Honest, it was. I was just cleaning my rifle when the damn thing went off. Get the medics, quick." Jim came running in and we got Bill off the ground and onto his cot. We called the medics who were just down the hill. They were there in minutes. Jim motioned for me to come outside the tent. "What happened? I was just in there with him and he wasn't cleaning his rifle. It was under his cot. He was sitting there writing a letter to his wife."

The medics carried Bill off in shock. He couldn't speak. Jim and I looked at each other still disbelieving what'd happened so quickly. The two of us went to the field hospital that night and sat with Bill while he waited to be operated on. He was under heavy sedation but still conscious. His knee had been shattered by the bullet. We just sat there silently with him holding his hands and wiping his sweaty brow. The orderlies arrived to wheel him into the operating room. He looked over at us. "Sorry, guys." Then he was gone out of our lives forever. His wife, Joan, got her husband back, maimed, but alive.

Before returning to the front lines, I finished the letter to Peter's parents telling them what a fine job he'd done supporting other soldiers during the entire trip to war. "*Peter was a very brave man as he entered combat. He was always close to God. We were good friends. He died instantly and did not suffer. I held him in my arms. I will call you when I get home.*" I did make that call eventually but now had to write letters to the parents of the three young soldiers who'd been killed in the tank attack. I had never gotten to know them. Those letters were very difficult for me to write. Every expression of condolence that I tried seemed trite. What could I say to them? Should I tell them that their sons died in an enemy ambush while their unit was in full retreat? I threw away one draft after another. Finally I tried my best to explain what bravery their sons displayed in battle. I avoided telling them that I didn't even have the time with them to get to know their names.

After finishing this difficult task, I put those letters aside, wrote a letter home, and took another look at the batch of recently arrived letters from home. Reading the words of support from my parents and looking at the scribbled drawings of my little sister were so important to me. They gave me a renewed strength to go on. I could tell from their words how hard it was for them and how much they believed in me. We couldn't let each other down. Somehow, we all would make it through to the end.

We returned to the front the following morning to fight the battle of the escarpment which pushed the Japs to the southern most tip of Okinawa and finally into the sea.

■ ■ ■

From: Lt. Roland M. Glenn

Somewhere on Okinawa Island
14 June 45

To: Mr. and Mrs. Raymond
M. Glenn, & Doris
10 North Third Street
Youngwood, Pennsylvania

My Darlings:

Another beautiful day here at Okinawa. I went swimming this afternoon in a bomb crater & really felt refreshed afterwards. An old letter

*from Cubbie came today. It was the only letter. I certainly can't com-
plain as nearly 10 letters have been coming in daily.*

*By the way, Saipan answered my letter & told me that my lost
footlocker was there & that it would be sent to me immediately. Boy
that was good news. I'm going to send it home right away. It contains
presents for you all.*

*Censorship did not permit me to mention Peter until now. He was
killed at the very first. The shock was great. We all are feeling very
deeply the death of our Lt. Harry Harper from Tenn. His death was
so hard to believe. We also lost Lt. George Goetz. He was the one
from Ohio. I slept right beside George during training. He was a
pilot and was going to fly me home. And, Lt. Fortuna shot himself
through the knee while cleaning his rifle. Lt. Ellis was seriously
wounded a few days ago when a hand grenade rolled back on him in
his foxhole. These things are so hard on those of us who knew them
so well.*

*I have only a few more days of rest left this time so everybody is
doing a lot of sleeping. Our Executive Officer went to the hospital for
an eye treatment. Since I am the senior 2nd Lt. in the Co. the job
falls on my shoulders. I still have my platoon to run also.*

*Guess what? I found a little chick in the process of hatching up on
a hillside. It has been with me during this rest and sleeps in bed with
me. My chicken and I are getting plenty of laughs. How are the hens
doing out in the barn? Are you getting any fresh eggs? Believe it or
not, we are having eggs for breakfast every morning here in this rest
camp. That won't last long. Don't know what I am going to do with
my little feathered friend. It sleeps under my chin.*

I love you all, Rollie

■ ■ ■

Dear Cap:

*We surely do have a nice comfortable place here and I think you will
like it also when you get home. I certainly get a wonderful thrill out
of coming home from the factory each night. Just think, I am home
in five minutes after leaving work. We are still turning out those
bomb sights and I hope that one of them will be used to get your
Nips. We are guarding the Robertshaw plant 24-hours a day now.
Espionage is our main concern but I can't believe this little old town*

in western Pennsylvania would ever become an enemy target. The town does have blackouts once a week. Mom and I have blinds now on all the windows but we turn out the lights when the siren sounds. Our Little Sunny Girl thinks this is fun.

I got two service stripes on Friday from our Captain for my coat sleeve. One for each six months of service. I'll soon be eligible for my third stripe in about two more months. Gee but time does surely go around.

I know that you are doing well. You had that experience of being away at Kiski School for a year before going into the Army. You learned how to rely on your own initiative and to draw your own conclusions. Now these are quite necessary factors in the life of an Army man and help to build him up from a physical standpoint and eliminate that fear in a man which deteriorates his health and prohibits him from gaining weight and thus hinders his mentality and development. Now, Cap, this is not a sermon but are plain facts my boy, as I experienced them in 1918 and 1919 during World War I.

Mamma will finish so I can mail. Good night Cap from your old Poppy.

P.S.: Well Possum and Company took in a show tonight again. It was a good one for it was a colored picture that I had mentioned earlier. Very interesting and about time. It was titled Stormy Weather. *Doris was a pretty good girl and allowed us to remain until the end of the picture. Heh Heh. It seems that every night we go to the movies, it rains.*

Your Old Poppy

■ ■ ■

Hello Darling Boy:

Well we went to Ligonier today and your grandmother was greatly surprised. We had real good eats again and a good time. Edgar drove us home. We really had a carload with Lucy S. & baby Mae, Edgar, wife & baby, your Dad, Doris and I. We had lots of fun.

Now my dear I wonder how you spent this day. Doris and I attended Sunday School this morning—came near missing—as we or I overslept. Our church plays chimes with the church bells and boy did Doris fuss when they rang out and we were still in bed. So up we jumped, dressed and away we went without any breakfast, but we made up for it when we arrived home an hour later. Ha Ha.

We said special prayers for you at church and we also say special prayers for our boy at every meal and at bedtime. I know that God is looking over you.

You won't believe what I did yesterday. I baked 35 dozen cookies. Doris was a big help laying them out on the dining room table as they came out of the oven. When Dad got home, they were cooled enough so we made up three packages. One for you, one for Corky, and one for Steve. We put a few more in your box. It was 2:30 A.M. when we finished. Dad mailed them in the morning.

Now dear I'll write more tomorrow and try and make up for the short note. Love and kisses and remember to take the best of care of yourself, my darling boy.

Your ever devoted and loving Mother

The Escarpment

ONE WEEK IN THE RESERVE camp went by very rapidly, just like any other vacation. Gone were the days of lounging around in shorts, sunbathing, and swimming in bomb craters. While we did have time to write and read letters, be together again as buddies and catch up on our sleeping and eating, regular meetings filled us in on battle progress, the next campaign objectives, and the role of the Seventeenth Infantry Regiment as we returned to the front lines. Intelligence officers briefed us on the strategic importance of winning the battle of Okinawa. We listened intently and came to understand that if won, the island would become a staging area for the direct invasion of the Japanese home islands. B-29s would have an easy time of bombing Japan from the airports on Okinawa and might even cause the enemy to accept defeat without an invasion and the estimated colossal loss of life on both sides. We could almost smell victory and realized that our lives might be saved if we fought well during the days immediately ahead. It was great to know that all of this was masterminded by Admiral Chester Nimitz but he wasn't right there beside us on that day when we were to return to the front lines. Everything happened so fast that we didn't even comprehend that the ship that brought us from Saipan to Okinawa was part of the Nimitz armada, a fleet substantially larger than the one that raced across the English Channel to attack the Normandy beaches on June 6, 1944. Our own troop carrier was one of 1,600 seagoing ships carrying 545,000 American G.I.'s and Marines. The orientation lecture made us more fully aware that the beautiful Saipan beaches where we had recently played cost the U.S. 17,000 dead and wounded while eliminating 32,000 dug-in Japanese.

When the lecture ended, we got back in full battle dress, loaded down with grenades, water bottles, knives, rifles, bullets, and shovels. My steel helmet suddenly felt heavier on my head. I also carried horrible memories of recent carnage and grief of lost buddies. Peter and the others were in their graves up north. No longer as cocky. Less sure of my lifeline but still of the belief that I had a God who would look over me and that I could lead men into battle. The time had come to stop playing around in bomb craters and get ready to fight.

New replacements needed reassurance that we were a strong outfit and would take care of one another. As their commander, combat leader, and father figure, I needed to stress to these new, young boys that they should act like virile, capable, strong men. "Take control! Aim your rifle! Shoot! Take control! Throw those grenades and then another and another! Bomb! Take control! We will take no prisoners. Stab! Kill! That's why you're here. You're a man! Now, act like one."

As we lined up for the march, the little chicken ran around my legs fully prepared to follow me. It had doubled in size and had begun to grow little red feathers. One of the men who helped run the camp ran out and picked it up as we lined up for the long march back to the front lines of the battle. I gave it one last pat and turned toward the men.

Jack was not amused by the chicken incident. I doubt he ever had a pet. It was a long, hot march through ragged country and along roads ankle deep with mud. My neck and back were soon soaked. John Garcia was right behind me walking in my footsteps. "Cricket, I can smell the sweat on your neck." "Si, John. I know."

Considerable advances had been made against enemy positions during the week we'd been in reserve. However, the Japanese had established a formidable fortress along what was called the Naha Shuri line. A major road stretched from the west coast town of Naha to the east where the ancient Shuri castle had been converted into the Japanese Commanding General's Headquarters. We faced an escarpment resembling the palisades along the New Jersey side of the Hudson River. The enemy established strong defensive positions along this line. Vast rice paddies stretched out toward the base of these stark, rock cliffs. It was a natural stronghold for them and presented a formidable obstacle. We looked out at this scene from deep inside a cave, previously an enemy position. The route we would need to follow in mounting an attack would be through this open territory of water and rice.

The enemy felt we would be annihilated here and they would emerge the victors. We weren't fully aware that an entire Japanese army waited for us in the many caves that stretched along the top of this immensely high

Okinawan customs include the burial tomb and the veneration of ancestors. These tombs were honeycombed with passageways and chambers where artifacts honoring the dead were placed. Most of these relics were confiscated by the Japanese and American soldiers during the battle. By going into one of these tombs and peering through the openings, we were able to observe the distant Japanese positions and carefully plan our attack on the escarpment. (Photo courtesy of Center of Military History, United States Army)

cliff structure. Our briefings identified the Japanese army as commanded by Lieutenant General Mitsuru Ushijima. His Chief of Staff was Lieutenant General Isamu Cho. At least we now knew who we were fighting. These "animals" had names.

Our new positions were located about a mile from the base of these cliffs in a cluster of previously enemy-occupied burial mounds honeycombed with tunnels leading to little chambers that once held the remains of Okinawans. Artifacts that had been buried there had been pilfered. Small openings at the ends of the tunnels enabled us to observe the terrain leading up to the base of the cliffs. The mounds provided excellent protection from enemy fire. We settled into this area late one afternoon after our very long and tiring march from the rear. Jack arrived and announced that my platoon was to immediately commence an attack on the enemy stronghold. I couldn't believe that he planned to attack at the end of such a grueling day. "No, we're not, Jack. I'm not taking my men out there until they're rested." I spit out these words. The first time I directly questioned his authority. I was determined not to take any unnecessary risks following the disastrous tank attack resulting in the deaths of Ben and the others. Jack and

Taking the Tanabaru escarpment in late June of 1945 was one of the final battles of the Okinawan campaign. Following the capture of the escarpment, I was asked to ride in a tank behind enemy lines to use my color blindness to attempt to detect the location of Japanese positions. (Photo courtesy of the National Archives)

I tolerated one another. Trust did not exist between us. The week in reserve had done nothing to improve our relationship. It would have been insane to begin such a difficult assault so late in the day with tired troops and insufficient planning for the attack. Plenty of support would be required from artillery and perhaps even the Air Corps if we were to have any chance of surviving. We would literally be sitting ducks for the enemy who would be some 200 feet higher shooting down upon us as we advanced across the flooded plain of rice paddies. Attack would have to be done my way to succeed with minimal causalities. I would not tolerate being badgered.

The men watched in silence as Jack and I fought this out. It was clear to all that we didn't like or trust one another. My points about needing extra time to plan the attack were also strong and clear. Jack called the regimental commander and reported that I refused to attack. Colonel Packler arrived and listened to my proposal to attack very early the next morning before sunrise when we would have the cover of darkness, mist off the water, and be rested. I won the argument, hands down. Colonel Packler decided in favor of my assessment. Jack lost face. I gained respect.

Now I fell back on the lessons learned in the mountains of Pennsylvania, using the remaining daylight hours to study the lay of the land. There was a matrix of rice paddies that presented one possible route. Like snakes crawling through grass, we could slowly and quietly advance to the base of the cliffs without being seen. Once there, tightly hugging the base, we would be protected from the enemy's observation and fire. We could almost reach the objective before daylight.

A smoke screen would be needed to cover us while we rushed across the final distance from the edges of the last rice paddies to the cliff bottom. Artillery could focus fire on the escarpment top. Planes, if available, could bomb the cliff's top. The trick would be getting across those damn paddies alive, scaling cliffs so fast that the enemy would think it impossible for us to accomplish the feat, then shocking them with our sudden presence right in the midst of their fortress. Suddenly being face-to-face with them would throw them off guard and into a state of disorganization. Essential to our success—surprise.

My squad leaders and I talked this over for hours, plenty scared but satisfied with our plan. A meeting with Jack and Colonel Packler explained how I wanted to do it. They agreed to everything recommended, and also realized how difficult this would be. In the meantime, the squad leaders briefed their men. We planned to shove off well before daylight and get half-way across this open plain before our enemy could possibly see us, then have artillery open up, bombs dropped, and smoke laid down. Much depended upon how the men were deployed. At first glance, there appeared to be no natural protection. I knew better. Six inches of land could save a life. I needed to convey absolute confidence and be a competent leader right now. We began to assemble behind the burial caves at 0400.

The men camouflaged their steel helmets with straw from rice plants, their faces darkened with mud—all loaded with extra ammunition, grenades, ropes for scaling the cliff, small mortars, and knives for killing anything that moved once we got to the top.

"I don't want to hear a sound when we get out there . . . keep your ass down real low . . . squeeze against the sides of paddies as you crawl forward through the water. Fix your bayonets. We don't know what to expect in those paddies. We're going out in the open like a possum in a dead tree but it's still dark. We can make it to the base of the cliff before they know what the fuck is going on. You can do it! Hear me! You're great soldiers! Let's go!"

The first sensation of lowering our bodies down into the slime and mud of rice paddies was a real chiller. Only the sound of rippling water as we moved slowly forward and slithered up over sides of one paddy and down into another like snakes taking a zigzag course toward the cliff base. Very quiet. Rippling water. Crawling forward in mud. Platoon now spread out over a considerable distance, organized to arrive several hundred yards from our objective.

The big artillery guns in the rear opened up at dawn. Jack was on the ball. The cliff top exploded right before our eyes. Smoke screen came down on schedule. I gave the signal. Everyone jumped up and ran like hell for escarpment base. One man fell and complained that he had sprained his ankle. He looked up at me crying. Terrified! Useless! A coward! I couldn't take the time to deal with this miserable man. My concern was for too many others. We let him sit at the base of the cliff as we quickly began our climb using ropes to haul each other and the ammunition up from one rock ledge to the next higher level moving up as quickly as we could manage.

On signal, the smoke and shells stopped just as we neared the top. The land was hot from this bombardment and enemy positions right along the top edge had been vacated. Enemy bodies were strewn everywhere. We pulled them out of their holes, jumped in, and used their cadavers like sandbags to provide us with extra protection. Now was the time to make the enemy believe a thousand men were up there instead of the mere 35 who had made it. We yelled at the tops of our lungs just like we played soldiers and injuns as kids. Fired our rifles continually. Threw as many grenades as our arms could heave while moving quickly from one foxhole to another to confuse them into thinking there were many more of us. We could see their heads popping up and down just a few hundred yards in front of us. There wasn't more than twenty yards of rock ledge behind us. We had to hang onto that bit of land knowing that our lives depended upon it. There was not going to be another forced retreat.

The rest of Company "I" quickly moved up to the cliff base and sent up all sorts of provisions, mostly more ammo so we could sustain firing. The Japanese weren't idle during all this time. They were firing at us and throwing grenades. One landed right in John Garcia's lap in the foxhole next to mine. "Lookie, Cricket, what I got!"

"You dumb bastard, John, throw it back quick." It exploded in the air just after he winged it back at the enemy.

One of the men froze with fear behind a rock in a forward, exposed position. I talked to him, and told him to be ready to run like hell as soon as I got to him. I raced out to the kid and got him back in a flash. He was

The expression on the face of this soldier reminds me of the terror I witnessed on the faces of many men who were so frightened by combat that they went into shock and became totally immobilized. These soldiers were evacuated to the rear and never heard from again. This is the face of Post Traumatic Stress Disorder. (Photo courtesy of National Archives)

crying like a baby and I kept him right beside me holding him and telling him that he was OK. He stared at me blankly, probably not comprehending anything I said. Too engaged to help get him back down the cliff, he barely held together during that first day and night, like a cracked china cup of no further use. At least he'd tried. As he departed for the hospital the next morning, I told him that he'd been brave to remain with his buddies. I doubt that he understood me.

We survived the first night by laying down continuous fire. We didn't care what we were shooting at. We just wanted the enemy to believe that a million troops were about to come and get them. It worked! By dawn the enemy had pulled back and we were able to get more men to the top and really secure the position. Colonel Packler, Bob Odom, and Jack scaled the cliff the next morning to look over the situation. They were excited about our accomplishment, were very complimentary to me and to every soldier in the line. The Colonel conferred a field promotion on me and I suddenly became First Lieutenant Glenn. My father would be proud. "Lieutenant Glenn, I'm instructing Jack to recommend you for a Silver Star for bravery. We are very proud of you and your men."

We felt cocky and certain that we could finish the war in one day if they would just let us go full speed ahead. That short-lived bravado felt good at the time. Exhausted by the previous night's experience, we couldn't let up because air reconnaissance reported that the enemy had some heavy gun emplacements hidden in the jungle caves not far ahead of us. The plane spotters could not determine just where these guns were hidden. My past caught up with me at this point. Colonel Packler asked me to come down to the base of the cliff and I didn't know why.

"Glenn, I understand that your eyes permit you to see through camouflage." I told the Colonel about my color blindness and the experience at Fort Benning. He asked me to ride in a tank behind enemy lines in order to spot gun positions reported from the air. Several tanks would move in formation. I could see them approaching from the rear as he spoke. I never rode inside a tank before and it wasn't one of my high priorities in life. I clearly remembered the disastrous tank attack right after I had entered combat and didn't want that experience again. I felt guilty and angry at Jack for having sent me into that situation only one day after I'd entered combat. I walked over to the road and intercepted the tank column. The commander crawled down out of the first tank. "Are you the chum with the eyes?"

"I'm the one, Commander. Let's go."

"You're about to enter one of the greatest tanks running these roads. Among other amenities, we have the best chocolate this side of Hong Kong. We will make you comfortable, give you the best eye scopes that have been invented, and treat you to one hell of a party. And, by the way, what's your name?"

"I'm Cricket Glenn."

"Well I'll be damned. You guys! We got ourselves a 'Cricket.'"

The different levels and compartments within the tank amazed me, each one designed for a different function—driving the vehicle, firing machine guns through various openings, firing the bigger guns, operating the radio. The commander had a special place where he could observe all levels and functions. It was almost comfortable.

When the tank started it felt like a conveyor belt in a well-run factory moved us along. It was amazing how much I could see through the portholes equipped with sophisticated optics. These have been greatly improved since those days and are now used to assist nearly blind individuals to see in the dark, my son included. The spirit among the tank crew was unbelievable. Proud, cocky men with a wonderful sense of humor, kidding me about my color blindness, joking about whether or not I would be able to spot anything out there. I soon felt a part of their team. This was nothing compared to climbing that cliff.

The tank roared over the crest of the hill and into the territory directly in front of where my men were now perched at the cliff top. There were all sorts of bunkers, trenches, and nets covering abandoned guns. The area had apparently served the retreating Japanese as a major field headquarters and I was able to point out these positions just as easily as I did sitting in the bleachers back at Benning. The radio man reported my observations and then put me directly on the air to talk with Colonel Packler. The tank rolled here and there sticking its nose into every nook and cranny where I thought that I might have seen something. Not an enemy in sight! Company "I" took this opportunity to move forward and take over these positions.

"Cricket, what do you want to do next?"

"I suggest we move toward the enemy positions. Let's find out where they are." They weren't that far in the distance, observing every move we made. Through the porthole, I noticed a huge cylinder coming through the air. Not a typical shell, about four-feet in length, resembling a stovepipe, it looped end over end, landing close to our tank. Big thud! Blew a huge crater in the ground almost under us. No concussions felt but our bodies were tangled together from the shock of the explosion. No one seriously injured. Good chocolate all over our faces. Everybody laughed. Seemed a bit strange to me. But we were alive. Our radio was still intact. The Commander communicated with the other tanks in our formation. They surrounded and protected us. We were finally rescued with all mechanical systems still functioning, and got the hell out of there without further incidents. Something to write home about!

Upon returning to the top of the escarpment, the Colonel moved the entire battalion into the positions we'd taken. I said goodbye to the tank guys below and walked around talking to my men who were about to be relieved from the cliff top by a fresh unit. Dropped my pack and rifle in a pile and strutted like a peacock crowing about our feat in taking this critical enemy position. "We saw you out there in that tank, Cricket. What was it like?"

"I'll tell you later, guys, when we are back in reserve. You did a wonderful job. What a great bunch of men you are. I am very proud of you all. You're the best platoon in the damn Infantry." Felt super confident. That always invites trouble.

The area came under a heavy bombardment. The enemy knew exactly where we were and had us in their gun sights. Smoke from exploding shells hid the reality of what was going on. Dazed, unable to see, groping for my rifle on hands and knees, unable to find it or see anyone. I heard John's voice. Felt someone dragging me away by the legs."Cricket, you're covered with blood. You've been hit. You woulda' been killed if you hadn't moved away from your gear to come along the line and talk with us. That spot got a direct hit from a mortar shell. Let me get you outa here."

John picked me up in his arms, carried me to the edge of the cliff, and assisted in lowering me with ropes under my arms to the bottom where they carried me by stretcher back to the burial mounds from where we had begun the attack. A medic's unit had been set up there. It all happened so fast. Dazed and not fully aware of my surroundings, I felt one of the technicians give me a shot in the arm and another in the mouth. The medics were always well supplied with booze. My wounds were to my face and hands and I was still having difficulty seeing. Felt very fuzzy while they cleaned away blood and applied bandages. "You're on the way to a field hospital, Cricket. I guess this is good-bye. You'll soon be on your way back to Oahu."

"John, you're wrong about that. I'll be back before you know it. You better look out for yourself and the guys and be there when I get back. And, John, stick close enough to me to smell the sweat on my neck."

"Si, Cricket. I'll always be right there." I felt his hand tighten around mine and realized how much I had depended upon him. There was a bond between us. He saved my life. I didn't want to let go.

They strapped me to another stretcher on the back of a jeep and sent me on my way to the hospital unit. My injuries were not critical. I waited and waited while the more seriously wounded were rushed into the operating room. Both my eyes had been bandaged. Could only listen to the wounded on either side of me moaning. Crying men! Hushed voices of doctors and nurses. The sound of female voices was very welcome. Didn't have much pain from my own wounds—had been sprayed with shrapnel, none of it too big to do serious damage. Must have dozed off from the sedative. Finally I looked up into the face of a young doctor sewing up my cheek. Local anesthesia had been sufficient. He told me my wounds were easy to fix and I'd soon be on my way to a larger hospital unit and then returned to Hawaii. I didn't like that idea. I was worried about my men and wanted to remain right there. "Lieutenant, we'll talk later. Go to sleep! You're exhausted and can't think straight, and don't know what you're thinking or saying."

John and several other guys from the platoon showed up the next morning full of news. Everything was going well and the enemy was on the run. The men missed me. The doctor didn't want to let me out of the place for several days but I finally convinced him that my platoon needed me now, not later. There was too strong a bond to leave them. I considered myself a competent combat leader. I'd never be a follower again and had no intention of missing out on the conclusion of the battle. I wanted to lead them to the southern tip of the island. I wanted to see the job finished.

By the time I returned to my unit, Company "I" had taken several miles of territory south of the top of the escarpment where I received my wounds. It felt good to be back. There were several more attacks during the next few days and we worked together like a well-oiled machine. My men had learned to hug the land like reptiles because of the lesson I'd passed on to them from my Uncle Ford. They made jokes about what six inches of land or skin could do for a man.

During one patrol, we rescued an entire family of Okinawans who had saved themselves by hiding in a cave. They feared that we were going to kill them. Little kids screamed and hugged the legs of the adults. My men carried some of these smaller children to the rear area once we had calmed them down. These people were starved. We fed them from our C-rations and turned them over to others who were processing civilians. Later we learned that several Japanese soldiers were in the group dressed as native Okinawans. The enemy had begun to steal away from their units in an attempt to save their own lives. We were not yet in the business of taking live enemy soldiers.

On another patrol we rounded a bend and discovered a complete, untouched tea house. To this day I do not know how it managed to stay intact when all around it was bombed. This little building looked like it was ready for customers. Little cushions were arranged around the low, lacquered tables. Exquisite tea cups were positioned on small black trays. The whole building resembled an inviting oasis, like something you might see in movies.

One man broke away from our group and ran toward it, stepping just inside to retrieve a souvenir. We yelled at him in time to prevent a disaster. He pulled back as the building exploded. The kid's foot had hit a trip wire. He was injured but not killed. We looked among the debris but there was little of value remaining except one very small tea cup that I still have among my war mementos. That was a very close call. It had been an error in judgment on my part to have allowed the platoon to even approach the place. Where was my head? Another lesson had been learned the hard way.

The insight gained at the tea house soon helped us to avoid another trap. We passed through the smoldering ruins of a small village which had recently been occupied by enemy soldiers. They had set fire to all the straw houses except one. The entire open front of the building exposed a floor strewn with all sorts of household objects including several china vases. A small child was tied to a beam at the rear wall. He was screaming for his mother who lay wounded beyond his reach, blood oozing out of her side, her face imprinted with pain. Our instant reaction was to rush to them. It was such a pathetic sight that I still can't erase it from my memory. Some instinct stopped me. The woman waved her arm in a warning gesture, another trap ruthlessly set. Mr. Kim, our interpreter, confirmed that the woman was warning us to keep our distance. I immediately called for specialists in bomb detection and a crew of medics. Within a short time, experts had located the trip wire and defused the bomb hidden under the woman's body. Mother and child were removed and treated for their injuries. Then we torched the building. It rained so hard that night that my foxhole became waist deep with water. I leaned against the earthen side of the hole, couldn't sit or lie down. Another night without sleep. In the middle of that night I realized that it was my twentieth birthday. What a way to celebrate!

The sun was a very welcome sight the next morning. Mail was delivered. Several letters and a package. Everybody assumed that my folks had sent me a box of cookies. The guys stood around while I opened the package. Light bulbs! Not one broken! Useless! Mom and Dad had responded to a letter written months earlier telling them that light bulbs were scarce on Saipan. What a present to receive under those circumstances. Later on, when we were back in tents, one of the guys hooked them up to a generator. We were among the few to have electric illumination.

The view was getting better. The southernmost tip of Okinawa could be seen jutting out into the sea. About fifteen miles to go. Unlike the men who would fight in the Korean and Vietnam wars, the end of our battle was now in sight. The guys were so excited. "Just turn us loose. We can end this war overnight. We've got them licked." We badgered the higher-ups to get on with it. We were feeling feisty, cocky, and sure. Colonel Packler also felt this way. Our skills at staying alive in dangerous situations had been well honed. I had learned how to deploy a platoon of men in an attack just like a choreographer blocked out the movements of dancers in a ballet. I had a feeling for the land and could move swiftly over it. My judgment was respected and trusted, earned as a result of my insistence on how we should attack the escarpment. Watching our platoon attack a hill across a rolling field was like viewing an excellent training film. Sometimes the high brass would come up to the front to watch us in action.

Jack was sent home. My appointment as Commander of "I" Company followed. As he departed by jeep, his last words to me were, "If you want that Silver Star you will have to write up that battle for the escarpment and recommend yourself for the medal." I never did that. It was reward enough to be alive and be rid of Jack. We did not shake hands. He wasn't much missed. Didn't have a friend in the group. In all fairness to Jack, the man was totally exhausted from having been in combat since the beginning of the war in the Pacific. His judgment had been affected by the sieges that he had endured. Jack began his military service as an enlisted man and received his commission as an officer earlier during the campaign for the Aleutian Islands. He had not attended Officer Candidate

School. He didn't like me from the beginning and resented my relationships with my men. I led by instinct supported with excellent training. The guys knew from the beginning that we needed one another if we were to survive. Our bonding was something foreign to him.

Be a good follower? Not me! I liked to take charge and now four platoons, or approximately 200 men were my direct responsibility. My closest friend, Jim Harkins, had also been wounded, shot in the leg. He returned from the hospital and hobbled over to congratulate me on the promotion. We stood there together feeling a strange combination of elation and depression. Harry Harper, Peter, Ben, Goetz, and the others were dead and in their graves somewhere on that island. Why? What did they ever do except be brave and willing to give their lives for the protection of others? That was real courage.

We were still alive but the fighting was not yet over. Could we hang on for a few more days? The end was in sight if we could somehow make it through this last battle. The enemy had retreated to the very end of the island and was waiting for us in caves.

I looked at Jim and saw a young man aged beyond his years. Where had the tall, handsome man gone? The one who I had caroused with back in Georgia, in Seattle where we dated respectable girls, in Oahu where we attempted to ride both the surf and the whores. The youthful energy that we brought to war was gone. There was no time to play as we had in the mountains of Oregon during the trip to war.

We, two boys from the sticks of western Pennsylvania, had become tired men. We stood silently together looking off at the southern tip of Okinawa wondering if we could all make it. "Why did you come back from the hospital, Jim? You could have been home by now."

"I don't know. Why did you?"

■ ■ ■

19 June 45

My Dear Family:

Several days have passed since my last letter informing you of the deaths of Peter, Harry, Ben, and George Goetz. George was a pilot and had promised that he would fly me home. His bunk was next to mine at Benning. We are feeling terrible about their losses. I need to write to Peter's parents, as promised. That will be a hard letter to write.

We have been in and out of action. Never have I been so darned busy. I am still Company Executive Officer. There is much to do with this increased responsibility. I am now in charge of the full company, Dad.

Our battle is still raging as bad as ever just a stone's throw from here. Just don't understand the optimistic view the papers have back home about the war ending soon. However, this campaign's end can now be seen. It should be only a few more days from this writing.

Can you realize the thrill we all had when our platoon reached the highest part of the escarpment? We can now look down and see the ocean around the southern tip of Okinawa. It makes me hope that no more of our men will be lost.

Oh, by the way, you will probably get a telegram telling you that I was wounded. Well, don't worry. Nothing serious happened. The docs were great and patched me up fast. I got back to the guys in a hurry. Yep! I now have the Purple Heart award. Not intending to get another.

I know that you are very anxious about me so let me assure you that each day I become more capable. This job is very hard but I feel very confident in my ability to lead these men. Oh, sometimes we all feel just a bit scared but we help one another over the bad spots. That's what you taught me. I couldn't be doing this were it not for your support.

May God help you to know that I will be safe and back home one of these days.

I think that I might get to see Jim tomorrow. He is still in the hospital up north from his leg wound. It takes about two hours by jeep to drive up there.

We really enjoyed that week of rest. I discovered a baby chick and adopted it. Or, I should say that the chick adopted me. You know me and chickens. Can hardly wait to get back to my own chicken coop.

We just threw five grenades into a small pond here and killed about forty fish, all different colors. They are all cleaned now and we are ready for a fish fry. While we were scooping them up, a dead Japanese came floating to the pond's surface. Not a pretty sight. The pond looked so peaceful before we did that. I would like to have a pond of my own one day.

I'm very well. My wounds have healed nicely. There are many things to be thankful for. Only I am sad to be missing Sunny Girl's childhood. I love her so much. Don't take any chances with her. Dr. Mary is just down the block. Can't believe that my little sister will soon be ready to go to school. It's not fair that I am missing this period of her life.

Everyone out here calls me "Cricket."

I love you all so much,

Rollie, The Cricket

The Last Stretch

JIM AND I STOOD TOGETHER looking toward the southern tip of Okinawa. A craggy outcrop of rocks rose from the sea, a kind of land's end with steep cliffs rising several hundred feet from beaches along this last stretch of island. The Japanese were holed up in caves.

Our 7th Infantry Division, together with a marine division, was closing fast on this last enemy stronghold. The choices were either to force the enemy to give up or to slaughter them. They failed in a badly conceived, disastrous counteroffensive, by attempting to make an amphibious landing behind our lines on both east and west coasts. Hundreds in rubber rafts were blown out of the water before they could reach shore. Bodies floated in on waves like seaweed.

Our new mission, to conduct mop-up operations, looked like a piece of cake. Just like going on vacation! We would knock this one off in jolly short time. Nothing could stop us now as we headed off to this southern tip of Okinawa just like a troop of scouts departing for Camp Mohawk.

The base and face of this escarpment presented tropical rain forest conditions. Looking down over the top edge, we could see nothing but the tops of palm trees, giant ferns and other lush foliage. Well worn paths descended through this dense jungle to the beach below where one might have expected tourists spread out on blankets sunning themselves.

Our enemy utilized these paths at night. The fields surrounding the mountain of rocks were unlike the rice paddies we crawled through in attacking the escarpment. Okinawans farmed this territory growing a root crop similar to potatoes. Enemy soldiers came up at night to dig for this food having run out of basics with all supply routes cut. We also collected this vegetable during daylight and made delicious stews with meat of captured goats.

My company, now dug in across these fields on slightly higher ground, could observe the entire area. Now that the monsoon season had ended, we rested at night in dry foxholes while our sentries patrolled and protected us. The men constructed a grid of trip wires connected to flares crisscrossing acres of these fields. If an enemy attempted to escape or collect food, he would hit one of these wires and flares would illuminate the entire region. Machine guns were manned all night and positioned to spew out massive numbers of bullets knee high. These "monkeys" were instantly killed just like rabbits. No escape possible!

The trip wires were just as lethal during the day as at night. Souvenir hunters appeared almost daily. Many of them were officers from rear units who wanted to take home a Japanese knife, helmet, uniform, flag - anything that would prove they'd seen combat. These soldiers presented almost as much difficulty as the enemy. They came wandering into the area believing it to be safe. One accidentally hit a wire that released a flare that exploded right in his groin. I can still hear his screams of pain as the medics carried him off. Another caught a flare in the eyes. Blinded for life. We called for reinforcements to set up road blocks to prevent this infiltration of soldiers searching for war relics.

The native Okinawan population, confused, frightened, and starving, did not know where to go or whom to trust. They observed our vicious behavior toward the Japanese. Could they accept our caring overtures toward them? Kim, an American Nisei, served as my interpreter throughout the campaign and assisted in organizing these uprooted Okinawans, not an easy task. We fed hordes of people as they found their way to our camp from the caves where they hid from the Japanese who hated them. One of my squads did nothing else but deal with these frightened natives. We tried every way we knew to allay their fears and reassure them that they would be treated fairly and sent to the rear where they would be sheltered, fed, and have their medical problems attended to. Several of these people also stumbled into our trip wires and were seriously wounded.

We questioned these civilians and discovered that the Japanese had brainwashed them to believe that the huge Americans were really sub-human animals intent on killing and raping them. Some Okinawan families had killed their children by tossing them over the cliffs and into the sea before taking their own lives. It wasn't easy to deal with their fear of us as we passed them back toward a camp where their basic needs could be met.

We put up two tents, one for the cook and another for Rick Wanacott to use as a communications center. The light bulbs that Mom and Dad sent were put to good use in these tents. Other than these two above ground set-ups, we still slept in foxholes at night. However, the mood felt more like going on safari than being in deadly combat. The enemy died while we lived it up. Killing the enemy who stumbled into our wires didn't fully achieve our mission. We needed to communicate directly with larger numbers. We now knew the name of their Commanding General. A captured Japanese officer volunteered to take General Ushijima a message offering him one last chance to surrender. How would we handle such an event if he agreed? The surrender never did take place in spite of our efforts. The Japanese commanders and many of their men chose to die rather than be taken alive.

Kim and I sought out a pilot who flew a light reconnaissance plane. He agreed to assist us in our effort to convince the enemy to surrender. In his light plane, we made several flights out over the cliffs and low along the shore nearly touching the escarpment sides just above the waves. Kim used a hand megaphone to broadcast my words encouraging surrender. Every now and then we would see a soldier darting in among the palm trees along the beach. I loved taking these flights in this little open plane. It felt like riding a kite! Like a gull soaring over the waves!

While Kim and I were flying through this wild blue yonder, feeling like members of the Air Corps, patrols from my company moved along the cliff top setting up more booby traps to kill the Japanese soldiers. That these two efforts were diametrically opposite objectives didn't seem to bother us. The traps consisted of trip wires connected to large bundles of TNT. Anyone coming up the paths at night and tripping one of these wires would be instantly killed. This was John's new idea. He knew his stuff when it came to blowing up things. His homemade bombs exploded during the night with a fierce noise giving the impression that a mighty battle raged. With every boom someone in camp would yell out, "Hey, Cricket, there goes another Jap to meet his Emperor." Our cook put a notch in his kitchen tent pole indicating the number of exploded bombs. A search party would leave camp early mornings to make trap rounds. Reminded me of the Pennsylvania mountains when Corky and I headed out every morning at 5 A.M. to tend our trap line, killing the luckless muskrats with Corky's rifle and bringing the animals back home to be skinned. We sold the pelts to earn our spending money. Now, helping to tend another trap line to find out how many enemy we had caught overnight, reminded us that we could also get killed. We weren't home free yet. Sometimes the bombs killed more than one. The explosion's force often removed everything from the victim's bones. Someone would yell, "Soup bones today!"

Japanese prisoners in late June 1945. Some hid their faces in shame. We made efforts to seek their surrender through the use of pamphlets and loud speaker announcements on the ground and from piper cub planes, but didn't take many prisoners. (Photo courtesy of the National Archives)

The lives of Japanese weren't considered to be one bit more significant than those of the muskrats and skunks that we killed as kids. Did we ever pause to consider more deeply what we were doing? Not often. I doubt that we, so-called civilized men, could have carried out our mission in combat if humanity toward the Japanese had entered our heads. We'd been brainwashed to hate these creatures. But somewhere in the back of my head lurked a thought about the capacity of human beings for brutality. How easy it became for us to fight and kill. Or had it?

We were burying those experiences of killing deep in our subconscious minds. It would take years to work it all out. Is it really so strange that wars are fostered by political leaders who are the products of this same type of brainwashing as they pursue their relentless quest for personal power and control? I wondered at the time if many men were trained from boyhood on to fight and kill, to exert control by being violent. My dad and Uncle Ford were not that kind.

What about me?

The 7th Infantry Division, part of the Tenth Army, suffered 1,120 killed and many more wounded and an equal number sent home psychologically dead, totally in shock. Lieutenant General Simon Bolivar Buckner, Jr. commanded the Tenth Army. This "fearless leader" wanted us to get on with this mission so that he might fulfill his heart's desire: the invasion of Japan itself. Several expressions which he loved to pronounce over strong bourbons were, "May you walk one day soon in the ashes of Tokyo! We will take our time and kill every one of the Japanese gradually!"

It might be easier to accept if I could tell you that we tried very hard to capture the Japanese soldiers alive and get them to a prisoner of war camp. Not the case. We'd set out to kill them and that's what we did. One morning we found the body of a dead woman lying between the corpses of two men. All three naked. All clothing blown away by the explosion. Someone shouted, "Hey! The Japs have Red Cross Girls!" A real laugh! We knew they weren't civilized enough to have women working in that capacity. These animals might need to fuck but they wouldn't need females for anything else. Japs certainly wouldn't be capable of love. They were savages. We were civilized.

By breakfast each day, the count of nightly kills would be called into regimental headquarters. The commanders thought our bombs were a brilliant tactic. High-ranking officers came to visit and awarded medals. I promoted John Garcia to sergeant. The bombs were his idea. In a little ceremony, we decorated John for bravery.

Some enemy soldiers did escape through our perimeter of traps at night. They hid in bushes and high grass waiting for a chance to go on. One patrol will always remain in my memory when leading the platoon on a search and destroy mission. We needed to scale the mountain cliff at the end of the island by pulling each other up, hand over hand. Once at the top, we spread out and moved forward ready for anything. A shot fired directly behind me nearly blew the head off my shoulders. Something hit my back before I could recover my senses. One of the escaping Japanese had permitted me to pass closely beside the bush where he was hiding. He suddenly rose up behind me, pointed his pistol at the base of my skull, and fell dead against my back. My ears were still ringing when it became clear that John Garcia had made a well-placed shot that killed the soldier, thus saving my life. He didn't have time to pull the trigger of his own pistol before John killed him. His body slumped against the back of my legs. "Cricket, I was so close to you that time that I could smell the sweat on your back." "Si, John, si." That was one of those times when I believed that my life had been saved by my God with the intervention of John Garcia. I hugged John and kissed the St. Christopher medal that my cousin, Cubbie Freidhoff, had given me before I left home. I didn't forget to read the copy of the 23rd Psalm that night in my foxhole.

We knew from intelligence reports that General Ushijima and General Cho were somewhere in the immediate area where we were patrolling. It would be a great plum if we could kill or capture either of them. Our commanders wanted them, but their Shinto religion and their honor would never permit them to allow that to happen.

There are several accounts of the Okinawa campaign that include descriptions of the last hours in the lives of these officers who commanded the entire Japanese 32nd army we fought. A captured Japanese soldier told us some of the events that took place on the night of June 21 while we

The leader of the Japanese Army on Okinawa was Lieutenant General Mitsuru Ushijima, shown here on the left in May of 1943, as Commandant of the Japanese Military Academy. His Chief of Staff was Colonel Isamu Cho, shown in this picture in 1938, when he was still involved in the Cherry Blossom Society's ultranationalist activities. We attempted to capture both men before they committed suicide. (Photos courtesy of Mainichi Shimbun Press)

were still dropping hand grenades down through the vertical paths and air shafts from the clifftop.

The two generals decided that they would take their own lives in an accepted ceremony of hara-kiri. However, according to Robert Leckie's account in his book *Okinawa, The Last Battle of World War II*, they appointed one Colonel Yahara, their Planning Officer, to be the one to attempt to escape and return to Japan with the full story of what had happened on Okinawa.

The officer we captured reported that the two generals and their ranking officers sat down to a farewell dinner of rice, salmon, canned meats, potatoes, fried fish cakes, bean-curd soup, fresh cabbage, pineapples, tea, and plenty of sake. General Cho brought forth a bottle of Black and White scotch from his large stock of liquors. Many toasts were offered to one another. The ritual suicide of Ushijima and Cho would proceed.

Leckie records a last message written by General Ushijima to Tokyo:

"Our strategy, tactics and techniques were all used to the utmost. We fought valiantly, but it was nothing before the material strength of the enemy."

"22nd day, 6th month, 20th year of the Showa Era. I depart without regret, fear, shame or obligations. Army Chief of Staff Cho; Army Lieutenant General Cho, Isamu, age of departure, 52 years. At this time and place I hereby certify the foregoing."

Our captured Japanese officer reported that about 4 A.M. the last ceremony began. The two generals stepped out from their cave through a fissure in the cliff face to a ledge overlooking the black ocean. They wore their full dress uniforms, complete with medals and saber. A white quilt and a white sheet symbolizing death were laid over the ledge. The scene was illuminated by the moon. One of them carried a fan and stated, *"It is getting warm."*

The generals sat on the quilt and bowed in obeisance to the Emperor. At this time we had been only a hundred feet or so above them hurling our grenades not knowing they were so close. Our prisoner told us that the two generals bared their stomachs for the upward thrust of the ceremonial knives, at the same time bowing their heads for decapitation by their adjutant's drawn saber. The end came quickly, according to Leckie's account.

"A simultaneous shout and a flash, then another repeated shout and flash, and both generals had nobly accomplished their last duty to their Emperor."

We heard those shouts coming from below while we patrolled and watched the moon sink into the sea. That day—June 22, 1945—marked the end of organized Japanese resistance on Okinawa. Later that day while on patrol, we located the site of their buried bodies, marked by beautifully carved wooden plaques inscribed with their names, ranks, and date of death. We were the first Americans to discover the final resting place of our enemy's Commanders. We stood there looking at those freshly filled-in graves thinking that capturing them alive would have been the biggest prize of battle, now denied.

We continued our patrol along the top of the cliff realizing that many of the enemy still remained below in the caves. The generals had launched one final attack before they died. Many of their men were encouraged to race up the paths to either escape or be killed. Not many of them had made it through our traps. Bodies were piled one on top of another as they ran to their deaths tripping over each other and the wires. They'd consumed so much sake that it was like wildly disoriented sheep being led to slaughter.

One Japanese ran across our front. Several guys fired as he disappeared behind some rocks. Our patrol cautiously approached that spot. One of my men yelled, "Cricket, I've found him. Come on. He's dead." We found a young man about 18, stretched out, face up wearing a clean uniform with medals pinned to his chest. He looked like he was sleeping peacefully and didn't respond to our voices. I knelt beside him and felt a faint, irregular pulse. Alive but seriously wounded. Blood gushing from his abdominal wall staining his pants. No medical supplies available. No means of transport to get him down the cliff and to a hospital.

I asked my men to leave me with him, took his hand in my hand, and fired a bullet into his heart and two into his forehead. He was gone, just like that. I removed a badge from his uniform that identified his unit before covering him with ferns. Sent the badge to Dad. This one was his.

"Get one for me, Cappy." Those were his last words to me as I boarded the train at the Greensburg, Pennsylvania railroad station when my trip to war had begun.

We reformed our patrol in silence and returned to camp by scaling down the cliff face. That incident seemed to be over, or so I believed at the time. But I could not get the face of that young Japanese man out of my head. I still can't and probably never will. Could I somehow have saved him? Was it absolutely necessary to "put him down" like a sick or old pet? Was it murder?

These questions haunted me and were the subject of many hours of my psychoanalysis following my return from war. My throat would become paralyzed when I tried to speak of the incident. My therapist held me in his arms as I cried until exhaustion would overcome me. I drew pictures of the boy's face and then could talk about him. My doctor repeatedly impressed upon me that I had no alternative. Those pictures are imbedded in my brain.

I killed a number of the enemy during the various battles leading to this conclusion of my combat experiences thinking of them as animal kills. While holding this boy's hand in mine, I made a very different, deliberate, and personal choice to kill him. The alternative of allowing him to slowly die there alone behind that rock didn't seem right. He didn't seem to be a sub-human animal to me, like the enemy pictured as "monkeys" back home in the press.

I put a human being to death. At that precise moment I fully realized that my government had given me that right.

I became as much a victim as the young man I'd killed. Now I have the responsibility to tell this story as I read and hear the daily news reports of more killings by bullets and lethal injections.

I now know it nets us nothing and diminishes us all.

■ ■ ■

June 22, 1945

Dear Pop:

Two letters arrived from you yesterday. You sure have been busy writing to me and that really is important. Those letters keep me going through these rough days. You don't have to tell me to give them hell at every chance. My boys would fire at the drop of a pin and so far we never give them a chance. Our total would really shock you. Enough of them met the mark of "The Cricket" to round out our entire family and then some. Yep, Pop, I sure wish we could work together. We would make a great team and have a top-notch platoon. My outfit is the best in the regiment.

Our regimental commander, Colonel Packler, watched us work several times. He was there when we crossed the valley to attack the escarpment. Nobody thought we would make it. We fooled the Japanese at each turn. Instead of going up the thing the easy way, I took my men up the sheer cliff. It was so steep we had to pull up the men behind us with our rifles and ropes. Before the enemy knew it, we were all up on the top and made a surprise attack on them. We got a slew of enemy. Bodies strewed everywhere.

Yesterday was unbelievable and I had to make a hard decision. We will need to talk about this when I get home. But, for right or wrong, I put down a Japanese 2nd Lieutenant about my age. I am sending you his rank insignia, a Japanese battle flag, some Japanese money and a picture of his family.

Dad, he looked like me.

Do you remember when we put down my little dog, Patty? I knew the instant she died. It was something like that. I felt life go out of him. I was holding his hand in mine. There was no way I could save his life. He was severely wounded as he crossed running in front of my patrol. I am feeling such a conflict about all of this killing. But we need to win this war.

The big question is what will happen to the 7th Division after this campaign is over. We will probably be sent back somewhere for rest and get ready for the next campaign. I certainly hate to think of going into another battle. It would be the attack on the Japanese mainland. Please pray for all of us that the war will end before that becomes necessary. I don't see how the Japanese can go on much longer. We have just about wiped them out.

Pop, take care of our girls for both of us and continue your good job of guarding the plant. We need all the gun sights you can turn out. And, Pop, how are the women doing as workers at the plant?

I love you so much Pop. Thanks for the copy of the 23rd Psalm.

Cappy

A City Called Hiroshima

COMPANY "I" FINALLY WITHDREW from grisly killing activity and moved to a rear area where we sat around telling war stories to the guys who'd heard our bombs going off down at the southern tip of the island. After the bragging about how many Japanese we got, speculation about our next mission to attack the Japanese mainland began to take over our chatter. The attack on the Japanese mainland meant one more battle to fight and meetings were held to brief us on our mission.

The 7th Division would be the first wave in the attack on the Tokyo plain. The outcome of this mission became very clear to us. A combination of luck and good training had helped us escape death up until now. But would it see us through the next battle? We began writing what each of us felt might be the final letters to our families. What to write when you believed that you would not survive? How to mask fear? How to tell every family member that you loved them over and over again? What words to use? What did Peter say to his parents when he realized he would die in combat? The Army quickly organized a strenuous training program to prepare us for this last mission. Exhausted at the end of each day, we stumbled back to our tents feeling depressed about our future.

I had a small flower garden around the outside of my tent using tropical plants collected in the jungle. Taking time to make things grow gave me temporary freedom from stress. When I planted and weeded, all else escaped my thoughts. The planting of a seed intrigued me. Mom had sent me zinnia and marigold seeds and those young plants looked a bit strange among the orchids.

In the evenings, Jim and I and others sat around drinking Japanese beer that we had found in some caves. One night, during one of these binges, guns began to go off and flares fired into the air. Running out of my tent with our helmets and rifles, we saw the sky becoming bright as day. What was going on? Were the Japanese attacking from the air with a parachute battalion?

An announcement finally came over the camp's loud speakers. A huge bomb had killed most of the population of a large Japanese city, a place called Hiroshima. I had never heard of it. How could one bomb level an entire city?

We wanted to believe it but couldn't comprehend what had happened. Finally more announcements. This time Colonel Packler spoke to us. He confirmed the report. Cheers rose up from every quarter of the camp. An instant celebration began and the drinking and revelry went on until morning. What a great night! Wiping out an entire city! What power!

We lost track of the time as we caroused through the camp celebrating with our comrades. Several G.I.s were wounded that night, struck by stray bullets. The careless firing of rifles got so bad at one point, that we dropped drunk into a foxhole beside the tent for protection, pulling a very smashed 250 pounds of John Garcia with us. He fell in like a bag of wet cement with me on top of him. Uncomfortable but safe.

Sometime during the night of celebration, a patrolling guard heard noises in the underbrush. He surprised two soldiers engaging in man to man sex. They were hustled out of the camp to the Army stockade never to be seen again. Probably sent home with dishonorable discharges. The morning after they were apprehended, everyone attended lectures given by the chaplain and a doctor. They spoke seriously about the "sick and immoral behavior" that led to the disgrace of these two soldiers. One could have concluded from their words that what these men did, in a few moments of abandoned ecstasy, constituted more of a moral sin than all the butchering we participated in during the previous days.

Our mission suddenly changed. We were being shipped to Korea. Discharge orders for John Garcia arrived the day before we departed. My faithful companion would soon leave me. I took the orders to him with conflicting feelings. All 6 foot, 7 inches of John was sprawled out in the sun. "Whatcha want, Cricket? We goin' on patrol again?" "Not this time, John. You're goin' home." "Aw, shit! Who's goin' to walk so close behind you that they will smell the sweat on your neck? What am I supposed to do back in L.A. while you guys are gettin' laid in Korea?"

We staged a big farewell party that night for Big John. The Japanese beer supply ran out early. Someone found a case of scotch that had belonged to the Japanese generals. We retold all of the stories of our times together.

Before departing Okinawa for Korea, Jim Harkins and I visited the Military Cemetery and the graves of Harry, Ben, Peter and others from the 17th Infantry Regiment. Some 12,281 Americans, 110,071 Japanese, and roughly 150,000 Okinawan civilians were killed. A small park has now been created on the island to honor both the American and Japanese who died. (Photo courtesy of Center of Military History, United States Army)

"Remember when you saved my life? "Remember?" . . . "Remember?" . . . "Remember?" We talked until dawn and then we hugged and said good-bye. I walked with John to the jeep that would take him to the ship, remembering the first time we met when he came to lead me to my platoon and to my first experiences in combat. John, who had "followed me."

Three days later the city of Nagasaki took the second atomic bomb. The announcement of the Japanese surrender followed soon. Jim and I took a jeep and drove north to observe a Red Cross plane, painted white, fly south past Okinawa. It carried the Japanese delegation on its way to meet General MacArthur to arrange for the formal surrender ceremony. After watching the plane fly past, we visited the cemetery and located among the thousands of small, white markers the graves of Peter, Harry, and Ben. Jim and I stood beside each grave and silently said our good-byes to each man. Astounded, we gazed over this vast cemetery that resembled a sea of grave markers. Our victory on Okinawa had cost the Americans 7,613 killed or missing, 31,807 wounded, and 26,211 other casualties, most of them victims of combat fatigue.

The Japanese Thirty-second Army was no more, with roughly 100,000 dead, and surprisingly, another 10,000 captured. There was little left of the Japanese airpower after losses of approximately 3,000 planes, 1,900 of them kamikaze, compared to 763 for the Americans. The sinking of the Japanese major battleship, the *Yamato*, and 15 other ships meant the end of Nippon's Navy. Though the United States Navy had been stunned with 36 ships sunk and another 368 damaged, there were still plenty left to mount the invasion of Kyushu from Okinawa.

After this solemn visit, we jumped into our jeep and headed back toward our units. Driving along silently, we spotted a peculiar looking unexploded bomb with wings lying off to the side of the road. Never seen anything like it before! It must have been one of those funny rockets like the Nazis had used on London. Think of that, a flying bomb! What will they think up next? The death of Hitler and the destruction of the Third Reich meant little to us embattled Americans on Okinawa.

The Army didn't give us much time to lounge around and get fat. Our 7th Infantry Division would carry out the occupation of Korea. We were given only a few days to convert ourselves from killers of the Japanese to "Storybook Soldiers." Clean new uniforms replaced combat gear. We polished our boots, buckles, and rifles. Hours were spent relearning how to march in a formal parade.

We were to embark from Okinawa within a day or two. The convoy of ships was already assembling in the harbor. Jim Harkins got the idea that we should take one more drive around the island and see if we could locate the nurses' headquarters. It would be nice to at least feast our eyes on a woman, if not our hands.

The territories we recently fought over were already transformed into busy centers for supply build-up in preparation for the attack on Tokyo, that never took place. We realized that not only our own lives were saved but thousands of Japanese lives as well.

But all of that slipped from our minds when we finally found where the nurses were housed in tents along a hillside. A few other guys got to the spot before us but none of us could get close enough to even say hello. We just sat on that hillside and looked at these women through our field glasses. Speculation about how soon it would be before we could get some real sex was the conversation that afternoon. We craved sex remembering earlier flirtations with the girls back home. Our rich fantasy life focused on all those Oriental women who awaited our hot, young bodies. My groin was filled with all sorts of interesting sensations. The real thing awaited us soon we hoped!

Everyone in the camp could hardly contain themselves once the formal surrender took place. No time to be lost. The Occupation of Korea must begin. We were scheduled for another few days of sleeping between clean sheets and dining at the Navy mess aboard ship. Fresh eggs, hot pancakes, warm baths, showers and toilets. No more taking a crap in a hole.

A sudden decision to load the ships and get them out to sea before a typhoon hit required that we board at night. The rough water and high winds were getting worse by the minute. One man was lost as he attempted to jump from the landing craft to the deck of the troop transport. He sank like a stone, slipped into the sea and was lost. Climbing down the rope ladders to the deck of the transport became extremely difficult under these conditions, far different than the more quiet and serious beginning of the convoy in the Saipan harbor that coincided with the sudden death of President Roosevelt.

This time the men, my men, who were billeted in the ship's lower deck, were shining their boots rather than sharpening their knives. I didn't need to go from one to the other to allay their fears. Six new replacements, assigned just before we boarded ship, were more nervous than the others. They were untrained recruits rushed over to enable soldiers with months of combat to return home. I paused to talk with one of them. This kid remarked, "I want to get me a Jap whenever we get where we are going." "Soldier, the war is over," I told him. "It can't be, I just got here. What do you think I came all this distance for? No, I've got to get me a Jap."

As I spent time with my company in that ship dormitory, I visualized Peter kneeling with frightened young soldiers during the previous voyage to war. He'd done his job. The men didn't miss him now, but I did. Such a gentle man! I noticed a poker game over in one corner. I went over and listened in. One guy was holding forth. "You know what I want more than anything? Women! I bet some of you guys never even had one. Well, let me tell you about the time that I . . ."

Before turning in for the night, I stood for awhile by the ship's rail and watched the convoy sailing full speed ahead in the rain. No danger now from enemy submarines like when we sailed in the darkness of another night toward Okinawa. Peter and I shared that experience. I could almost feel the hug we exchanged. Suddenly I felt very alone and longed to hold someone, anyone, in my arms. There were no more battles to be fought. In the morning, we would be briefed concerning our next assignment as Storybook Soldiers. Before turning in, I reached inside my shirt to hold the Saint Christopher medal as I thanked God for my survival. The medal was missing.

The war over! Tokyo Rose a thing of the past. I took out the little slip of paper and reread the 23rd Psalm before going to sleep, thinking of my dad's strong support through all of this.

■ ■ ■

30 August 1945

Dearest Folks:

My reason for not writing more often during the past few weeks is, this time, a good one. We have been very busy tearing down every last one of our swell buildings put up since the end of hostilities.

Our 7th Infantry Division is being put into the Army of Occupation. Yes, my dears, I am going to Korea. We were just notified this evening that we could let you all know. Everybody is wiring their folks about this exciting news. It certainly is better than preparing to attack Tokyo. We are going to Korea as liberators and feel sure no trouble will come up. Everyone is very anxious to get on the move. We have the urge to see the world and excitement is in the air. I'm not permitted to mention exactly where I will be but know that I will be much better off. We are going as show troops and will make an attempt this time to be "storybook soldiers" rather than killers. We're getting our uniforms fixed up and our helmets polished. It ought to be something. Yet, we also hate to leave Okinawa now that the fighting is over. This is really now a paradise island. The climate is wonderful.

My garden has grown so well thanks to all those seed packets you sent and I planted every one in the very rich soil on this island. It's kinda funny though to see zinnias and marigolds blooming in the tropics right besides orchids.

My plans for a college education are now at a stand-still. I will get back to thinking about future schools when the time comes. Right now, I have a big job to do. I am still Company Commander of "I" Company and will proudly be taking my company into this next important operation.

Now, dear ones, you will now know why there will be a lapse in time between letters. There is no need to worry. I am out of danger. The situation is well in hand.

With all the love in the world from your boy,

Rollie, The "Cricket"

P.S.: I still can't believe that the war is over.

Part V

The Occupation of Korea

Storybook Soldiers

IT TOOK LESS THAN A month, following the Japanese surrender, for the Army to convert us from mud-covered combat infantrymen into their Storybook Soldiers, a term the Army used to impress upon us the different role required of occupation troops. Our new image required spit and polish, good manners, and the ability to march in straight lines.

A typhoon blew in from the South Pacific as our convoy departed Okinawa. It was a terrifying experience. We felt like chaff caught in a whirlpool. The tidal swells, huge waves, and winds of over one-hundred miles-per-hour almost smashed our ship against the steep cliffs of the harbor.

We became instantly seasick. The ship's Captain announced that there had been much worse storms. Hard to believe while we heaved up our guts. The storm blew throughout that night with the convoy attempting to outrun it with some success. The weather was calmer the following morning when an orientation meeting took place.

Our new mission was to repatriate a large portion of the Japanese army to their homeland. They had occupied Korea for many years including the war period. The briefing touched on the historical conflict between the Koreans and Japanese. One uppermost objective during the months ahead would be to lessen the conflict between these two peoples who would look very similar to us. Their cultures and particularly their religions, were quite different. The Koreans were Buddhists and the Japanese followed Shintoism.

How would we be able to face the Japanese across a conference table? Could we possibly cooperate with them in planning movements of thousands of men, tons of supplies, and in assuming control of the many buildings they occupied? We learned later that some of these buildings would become essential to running the new Korean government.

The Japanese had taken over school buildings and had kicked the kids and teachers out into the streets. Court houses were also occupied by Japanese troops. Judges were sent home. There was no civil government in place during the Japanese occupation.

How could we manage our hatred for a former enemy who just shortly before had killed Peter, Ben, Harry, and so many others? Just as important were the thousands of Japanese slaughtered by our forces a few weeks previously. Would each side attempt to stab the other in the back?

I felt deep reservations about our ability to conduct ourselves appropriately in this new situation where collaboration between former enemies would be essential. Also of concern to me were the men who had so recently joined our outfit after the hostilities ended on Okinawa. Would they be mature enough to conduct themselves responsibly in their contacts with the Koreans? We knew nothing about Korea, the people, or their culture. This reality weighs heavily on my mind today as I see our youth in the military being sent to foreign lands on so-called peace keeping missions with little preparation or knowledge of the people they are supposed to protect.

We considered the Yellow Sea to be just another body of ocean water until we noticed that the color of the water wasn't blue like the Pacific. It actually looked greenish-yellow. Deep layers of mud apparently affected its color. Another theory was that it wasn't as salty as the ocean. One sailor remarked, "Sea water is always less salty than the ocean and refracts light differently. That's why sea water is greener than ocean water." To this day, I am still uncertain about this.

As our ships pulled into the Inchon harbor, specks of white appeared on the hillside overlooking our landing site. It looked like the largest rookery ever seen but did not turn out to be a flock of birds at all. Thousands upon thousands of Koreans came to watch and welcome us to their homeland. An incredible sight beyond our wildest imaginings. We weren't prepared for anything like this.

Our approach, even from a mile away, stirred up another overwhelming vision. Thousands of sea birds flew out to look over the ships, no doubt expecting a handout. I can still hear their squawks and cries over the snarling sound of the landing crafts circling below ready to carry us to shore, a maddening combination of noise.

The calm water made it easy for the crafts to get us to shore. There were no shells dropping beside us. I recalled the approach to the Okinawa beach and the loss of some men riding in another landing craft. This time we were taking a trip to peace, not a trip to war.

As we approached the shore, we began to identify specific buildings along the harbor that were pointed out to us during the orientation. A brewery designated for us to occupy turned out to be a folly. Who thought that one up? How ridiculous to assign the guarding of a brewery to a bunch of thirsty guys so ready to party.

To better observe our arrival, citizens crammed themselves into every spot on the hillsides and along the lower streets. Everyone in town, including hundreds of children, were there to greet us.

Our manners were impeccable as we unloaded from the landing barges. We tried to act like the handsome, uniformed men in Gilbert and Sullivan musicals. We had polished up our boots, shined our rifles and belt buckles so carefully, that anyone of us might have become a Colonel in the Queen's Navy.

Wouldn't you know it? An Army band was unloaded first. We formed in ranks and were ready to step off as the color guard raised Old Glory and our unit flags. Company "I" came right after the band at the head of the parade. I felt great pride at that moment for all the men who had followed me into combat. As the band struck the first note, we pulled ourselves up to our full heights and stepped off smartly to the cheers of that mighty crowd.

Hey! Look us over ladies! Here we are!

The parade from Inchon to Seoul, the capital city of Korea, was everything you might expect. John Philip Sousa would have been proud. Koreans, dressed in formal clothing, lined the streets for miles, sometimes ten deep, waving little American flags. Where had they gotten them in such a short time? Were they "Made In Japan?" These people looked so happy. The women were more beautiful than any we had seen since Oahu. They welcomed us as heroes. We felt good. Our spirits were high. They got even higher later that night with the assistance of various beverages from the brewery that some of our men carefully stashed in their backpacks.

We spent the first night in Korea on the floor of a Seoul schoolhouse. Massive celebrations were taking place outside the building. Delegations were arriving at the schoolhouse door to present us with baskets of food that we weren't permitted to eat because of probable bacteria. We politely accepted these gifts, learning quickly how to bow deeply to show our appreciation. Several young women presented themselves at the door. Kim translated. They were prepared to service the entire company, a gift diffi-

One of the first sights we saw upon our arrival in Seoul was this ancient gate to the city. It still stands but is now surrounded by skyscrapers. The buildings in 1945 were only a few stories tall. (Photo courtesy of Glenn family archives)

cult to turn down when feeling sex-starved. The men thought that I was mad to reject their offer. You should have seen the looks on their faces.

"Calm down, you guys. You'll get all you want later. I'm not about to turn this public school into a whorehouse the very first night we're visitors in their country. Come on. Think!"

Firecrackers of every description were going off outside. The men wanted to get out and roam the city and to find the nearest whorehouse to get laid and drunk. Colonel Packler had given strict orders to sit tight and not leave the building. We posted guards at the doors to keep our men in. The roar of the celebration continued.

Sometime during the night, a delegation of older Korean men came to the door with more cases of beer. No further attempts were made to sleep. We drank until dawn. During the night, one of the new recruits from the States slipped out past the guards, went into the city, got drunk and shot a Korean man in the back, killing him instantly. Fortunately, he was not a member of Company "I." The MPs picked him up and brought him in.

"Now, I've got me a Jap," the kid yelled as he collapsed in a drunken stupor. The victim was the father of a Korean household; leaving a wife, three children, and an aged mother. The boy, just 18 and in the army for under six months, went to prison for many years after being tried for murder. The untrained soldiers had been hurriedly sent over to replace combat-weary veterans. This factor caused me more difficulties than the future negotiations with defeated Japanese soldiers.

Early the next morning, Company "I" was moved to a small hotel on a hill overlooking Seoul. The main feature of this place consisted of a large bathing pool in the basement filled with steaming hot water from an underground spring. A waterfall at one end cascaded down over rocks and presented a perfect spot to stand with that blissful water pouring over our shoulders.

We were to enjoy oriental hot baths many times during the following months as we traveled around the country. This particular hot bath, the first of its kind in our lifetimes, became a favorite place for us to relax, but the exotic bathing didn't last long.

The women of the streets soon arrived at the hotel's entrance to offer their services. A strict quarantine, imposed by our regimental Commander, separated us from those inviting-looking girls. Some of the guys thought this restriction was ridiculous because we were lounging about in all those private hotel rooms where sexual activity might have been private. A half-dozen women were, however, not a sufficient number to service 200 men.

The following morning, trucks carried us to occupy Kimpo Airport, located some distance outside of Seoul, now one of the world's largest international airports. That morning, the airport could not receive any planes because the Japanese had bombed all the landing strips which were now pockmarked with deep craters. The huge holes were eventually filled by a construction battalion of black soldiers. Cargo planes could then arrive with the supplies needed for the occupation. Upon our arrival, a celebratory mood still prevailed.

Japanese motorcycles were located in one of the hangers. Jim Harkins, Sam Darby, myself and many others rode them at high speed in and out among the craters. It is a wonder that we didn't have serious accidents. I had never even driven a motorcycle before.

This picture shows me just after our arrival at the Kimpo airport on our second day in Korea. The Japanese had bombed all the runways to prevent our planes from landing. We found many motorcycles in the hangers and rode them around the craters. We also found and wore Japanese leather jackets that made us appear like pilots. This site is now a major international airport serving the capitol city of Seoul. A small dog adopted us and was named Kimpo. She traveled with us throughout the country and delivered a litter of puppies. (Photo courtesy of Glenn Family archives)

Several of the guys found a supply of Japanese leather flight jackets, white silk scarves, and goggles that we all donned. We were young, saved from certain death by the dropping of the atom bombs, and the wind blew through our hair. We were dashing, well-dressed adolescents gone wild. The worst horrors of the recent past were momentarily out of our thoughts.

All this tomfoolery ended with notification that a ceremony in Seoul would be staged to transfer power from the Japanese to the American Army. Our battalion would represent all the American units at the ceremony. We managed to get ourselves all spruced up and were trucked back into the city.

Once again, thousands of Koreans lined the main boulevards leading to the Capitol where we spread out on the grass behind the impressive white marble building and tried to catch up on some lost sleep from the successive all-night binges.

I wrote home to my family in Pennsylvania.

■ ■ ■

September 5, 1945

Dear Mom, Dad, and Sunny Girl:

At last, I have the time and am able to write at length about some very good things that have happened.

Today was very special for those of us who have survived the war. It was the day when Company "I" represented the American forces at the formal lowering of the Japanese flag and the raising of the Stars and Stripes over the Capitol building in Seoul.

Colonel Packler informed me that Company "I" would lead the American contingent in the parade, quite an honor for us.

We hit the deck early this morning at Kimpo Airport in order to be trucked into the city in time for the ceremony. The trucks that carried us from the airport to Seoul were driven by Japanese soldiers. It felt very strange to have men working for us who so recently were our mortal enemies. We were dressed in our best uniforms.

Seoul was quite a surprise for us. It is a large city. You might believe that you are in Washington or Philadelphia. As we passed the impressive railroad station, I thought of the one in Pittsburgh. Streetcars were screeching along filled with people, some riding on top of the trolleys. We could see nice-looking cars everywhere.

My men went wild yelling at the girls. The attractive girls yelled back. It has been so long since we have seen such lovely women. It appeared that the supply of these girls stretched as far as the eye could see.

Little kids ran along the streets beside our trucks. They handed up little American flags that we waved at the crowds. The excitement was so great that it reminded me of those earlier times when I was a little kid in Greensburg standing on the curb watching a parade go by. Do you remember how we all joined in at the rear of the circus parades and marched with the clowns and pretty ladies to the circus grounds for the afternoon performance?

I also remembered you, Dad, riding in the open convertibles with other WW I veterans in Ligonier's Memorial Day parades. Sunny Girl, Mom and I stood on the curb waving the little American flags and calling out to you and feeling so proud of you. You were such a fine soldier, Dad, and looked so handsome in your uniform. I now know how you must have felt looking out from that car at us and the cheering crowds there to honor your service. You taught me how to be proud of our Country, Dad. Now I know.

It is hard for us to believe that this city is so modern. You wouldn't believe this, but several of the buildings are at least ten stories high!

Kim is still our interpreter and alerted me when we were about to turn into the broad avenue leading to the government buildings. In the distance, I finally saw the towering, white dome of the Capitol building of Korea. The cheers of the crowds grew louder as we approached this building. I felt so proud of my men and our country. The dome of the building recalled to my mind the first time I saw the dome of our own Capitol building in Washington, D.C. during my trip to war.

The Korean capitol in Seoul is surrounded by a high, white fence. Once our trucks had driven inside the compound, I took the men behind the building where we could wait in the shade for the ceremonies to begin. The flag ceremony would be at 1500 hours just after the signing of a peace treaty that would transfer authority from the Japanese to the American command.

The crowd outside the walls reached to the many thousands. Their cheers were deafening. We formed up and were in place when the high brass arrived. Our commander, General Hodges, arrived first in a long limousine. He was followed by the Japanese Commanding General riding in a splendid Buick limousine.

Both generals went inside the Capitol to sign the formal papers. It is an impressive building with marble everywhere. Fountains and miniature gardens made the place appear more like a museum than a government building.

Following the signing ceremony, the Japanese general departed before the lowering of their flag. I guess this respected his rank. We would, however, have given anything to see him standing right there as the Rising Sun was lowered and Old Glory was raised.

At precisely 1510 hours our band struck up a march and the parade began with me in the lead. As we rounded the flagpole, a large number of movie-camera people began to shoot the scene. We passed in front of the generals. They looked so very pleased. All of the scared feelings of the past seemed to have slipped from us.

The band stopped playing when we were finally in position. The cameras were whirring as a command was given to lower the Japanese flag. I have never heard anything quite like the shouting of the Koreans as they saw that flag descending and being presented to General Arnold, our Division Commander.

A bugle sounded a moment later and the band struck up the Star Spangled Banner. I had thought the earlier shouts and cheers were the loudest. Not so. The crowd broke into a frenzy. Perhaps they realized that they were once again a free people after years of tyranny under the domination of the Japanese. Whatever it was, we all felt it and realized that this minute was one of the greatest of our lives.

The band played "Stars and Stripes Forever" as we paraded again before our Generals at the conclusion of the ceremony. I must say that we felt that we represented the best country on earth.

Company "I" led the column of troops as the parade passed around the Capitol, through the gates, and onto the main boulevard. We were surrounded by cheering people as we marched toward the cathedral where a service was conducted to commemorate the beginning of a new period in Korea's history. I have never been in such a large church. It is so long that, sitting towards the rear of the sanctuary, one could hardly see or hear what was going on at the alter. It didn't seem to matter much that we missed hearing what was being said. All of us just sat there silently and said our own prayers. It was enough to be alive and back in church after what we had so recently been through.

Trucks were waiting for us as we came out of the cathedral. Seoul was really celebrating as we were driven back to Kimpo airport. We wanted so badly to remain in the city and join the party. Not permitted. When we did get back to the airport, we continued with our own private celebration drinking more of the Japanese beer. Really tasted good!

What a day this has been! What a way to end this period of my life. How very thankful I am to be alive. I don't know how long I will be here in Korea but I am going to enjoy this country and these people and learn as much as I can.

I think of each of you every day and send you my love and prayers. I couldn't have made it through this war without having your love and support. God has been looking over us. Stay well and write soon. I love you very much.

Rollie

P.S.: I have just been informed that I am being appointed as the American Liaison Officer to the Japanese Army located in Taejon, a city located in south central Korea. We will be going there soon. Watch the papers for pictures of the ceremony in Seoul. You might see me marching at the head of Company "I" down the main street!

As we traveled around the country, we saw many Koreans dressed like this man. Some waved a welcome and some just stared. Their country had been occupied by the Japanese for many years. Now, the Americans were taking over. (Photo courtesy of Glenn family archives)

The partying went on all night following the Seoul parade. We were well stocked with beer and hard liquor from the Japanese supplies. It didn't take long that night for our thoughts to turn to sex. Several of us commandeered a Japanese sedan and, with Kim as our guide, headed back into town in search of the whorehouses that we knew were there and waiting. We located a whole block of them in one of the back neighborhoods. The lines of men waiting extended for many blocks, just like back in Honolulu. Little kids ran around soliciting.

"G.I., you wana fuckie ma sister?"

The M.P.'s were everywhere turning away the hordes of soldiers. There were so many intoxicated men in that neighborhood pushing and shoving to get near those houses that a riot might easily have broken out. More M.P.'s arrived by the truckload. Bullhorns were now being used to threaten our troops with arrest if they didn't leave at once. That was the end of that excursion. We headed back to Kimpo Airport to our own party.

The following morning, suffering from a hangover, I learned that a local politician was waiting to see me. The older man, dressed in his formal white flowing floor-length clothes, spoke fluent English. His garment looked like a long kimono. He wore a black, stovepipe hat. I listened as he addressed me after bowing low.

"Lieutenant Glenn, the people of Kimpo village wish to receive you this afternoon. Our village is but a short distance from this airport. Will you please bring some of your men to the public square where we may show the American forces our deep gratitude for your recovery of our country?"

I accepted the man's invitation. Jim Harkins and I took off that afternoon for the village of Kimpo with a truckload of our men. Kim was right there with us as we drove down a dirt road, along the rice paddies, and under triumphal arches constructed of the straw from rice plants that were being harvested and hurriedly erected over the dirt road in our honor.

One of the most beautiful experiences of my life awaited me in the village of Kimpo.

Kimpo

Long ago and far away amid lush mountains
A little hamlet lay.

It was spring in a strange land.
Blossoms came, crops grew,
and the white man came to replace the yellow enemy.

A winding dirt road
passed the patterns of rice paddies.
The oxen helped carry the farmer's load
of seedlings along the edge of the fields.

Planters stooped over the shallow waters
and placed each seedling carefully
as the sun gleamed from
the steel helmets on their backs
as they planted.

A band played
and children danced
along the road to Kimpo.

Cymbals, Drums, Flutes,
Cherry blossoms
Steel helmets and
Straw hats.

White and yellow men.

Photos on pages 160–163 taken by author

As we approached the village of Kimpo, a crowd began to gather. The people were marching along side of us and waving. My men were waving back from the trucks following my jeep. The eyes of these Koreans seemed to be asking, "White men, what are you really like?" The village square was jammed when we reached the municipal building sprawled under a thatched roof.

An elder, dressed in a long white robe, pointed the way to a ceremonial hall. We sat around a huge polished table that was only inches from the floor, permitting space for our legs stretched toward the center where a sunken charcoal fire warmed our feet—both white and yellow.

A young woman served tea in beautiful china cups. One of the elders spoke in fluent English and introduced each man seated around the table. They were all district leaders and heads of provinces from near and far who had come to pay their respects to the victors, the white men, the United States of American, her representative, me.

All eyes were focused on me. "Tell us, Lieutenant Glenn, tell us about democracy." For a moment I looked out a window at the waiting crowds. Then I began, as best as I could, to tell them of my life in a small village in America and how I became a chicken farmer and almost joined a circus before I was 15. I told them of my family, my dog, raising rabbits, planting, harvesting—my life story in thirty minutes. They listened, laughed and then it was over.

The lovely young girl, who had served the tea, entered again carrying a package carefully wrapped and tied with a ribbon. She held the tea cups and saucers that I had admired.

I was escorted from the room and the crowd looked at me. After a moment, a space was cleared and the native band struck up "The Star Spangled Banner." I felt tears come to my eyes. The flag was brought forward and everyone grew silent. All eyes were upon the flag. I felt absolutely sure inside. Proud! Certain! Sure of my beliefs.

After the ceremony, the elders asked if we would mind driving along the road for several miles.
Children wanted to see the biggest men ever. They looked from the arms of their mothers and looked from behind trees and looked up from the swimming hole just like kids back home.

Later on, we entered the hall again. A formal victory banquet was held. Many were to follow in other hamlets as we moved through the country.

The same girl, Sungja, who presented the tea set, tended me throughout the meal. We stayed with each other through the night, and many to follow. The warm white wine, her body close to mine unexpected but welcome. An aura, a dream. These were the colors, smells, touches and tastes of what I had imagined while in combat. They intoxicated me. Now it seems stranger and further off than a dream.

We paraded from the Capitol building down the main boulevard by the cheering crowds to the cathedral.

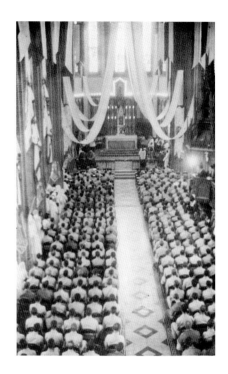

We assembled to give thanks for being alive in Korea rather than having to fight the Japanese in their homeland. We asked for help with our mission to bring peace to Korea.

After months of killing the Japanese on Okinawa, we had survived.

The Inn at Chongju

THE JOYFUL EXPERIENCES WITH the villagers of Kimpo got us off to a very good beginning with the occupation of Korea. I carried away wonderful visions of that little village and warm memories of the friendly Korean people.

Our truck convoy left the Kimpo Airport early one morning on the first leg of our long journey south to the city of Taejon. People waved excitedly at us as our trucks rumbled down the dirt roads. Colonel Packler, our Regimental Commander from Okinawa days, impressed upon me the importance of our conduct with the Koreans. He stressed that my appointment as Liaison Officer to the Japanese Army billeted in Taejon would be a very big and challenging job. I needed to be very sensitive to the Japanese who were keenly feeling the results of having been defeated in the war. Our new mission was to coordinate the repatriation back to Japan of the remaining Japanese soldiers in the Taejon region of Korea.

What exactly did "repatriation" mean?

As these thoughts drifted through my head, I settled down for a long and dusty trip south. We were headed to a country inn half-way to Taejon for the first night's stop. The closest I had ever come to an inn was back in Ligonier at the Hotel Breneiser, when my job as dishwasher and luggage boy earned me enough to fill the gas tank of my old Chevy.

Before our departure, we had picked up a small black and white spotted dog at the airport. I named her "Kimpo" and she sat on my lap as we passed through Seoul and out into the countryside. She escaped being eaten by the locals who loved dog meat and raised them for food.

The views included barren hillsides, very few trees, endless patterns of rice patties, oxen pulling "honey carts" full of human waste for fertilizing crops, people sleeping and defecating beside the road and children waving excitedly. There was no productive soil left on the hillsides from the massive deforestation. I said to the guys, "Look at those barren hills. Thank God we didn't have to fight here. There's no place to hide."

The day passed slowly as our convoy moved ahead in a massive cloud of dust. We would be ready, very ready indeed, for the inn when we reached it, but nothing had prepared me for what we found upon our arrival. It was located just outside the small city of Chongju in South Central Korea. Low buildings were clustered among a grove of gnarled pines. The trees surrounding the grounds of the Inn were preserved, creating the impression of an oasis in a barren desert.

We entered the compound through a series of gates connected to bamboo fences surrounding the perimeter of the property. The fences had created a very private space by separating the interior from the outside world. The buildings and beautiful gardens were all linked together inside the enclosure. A path to the front door led around a pond with a surface of dark, quiet water resembling the background of a painting, brightly highlighted with a multitude of large, spotted goldfish that swam toward us as we approached. They were funny-looking, brightly-colored creatures with whiskers, unlike any fish we had seen before except for the ugly catfish back home in the Loyalhanna creek that ran through the Ligonier valley. One of the guys threw in a handful of bread and the fish nearly jumped out of the pond toward us. The path led us around the edge of the water over large, flat, irregularly shaped stones placed in a meandering pattern. Moss grew between the stones and over the gnarled old roots of the trees whose weeping branches reflected in the pond. The garden plants gave a cool, restrained, and quiet feeling to the enclosure.

We crossed a small, arched, stone bridge at the other end of the pond and quietly wound our way toward a stone water basin placed just outside the front door. Crystal clear water trickled out of a bamboo stake into the basin, seeping over the sides and down into a little pebble stream leading into the pond. A wooden ladle, placed across the top of the rock water basin, invited visitors to pause and take a cool drink. We were ready for those sips and passed the ladle from man to man. Kimpo helped herself by drinking out of the pond. We became quiet as one would in a museum standing before a magnificent painting.

The innkeeper met us at the door bowing deeply. His rotund body, thick arms and coal black hair reminded us of a heavyweight wrestler. It didn't take us long to get used to bowing as a gesture of greeting or farewell. He didn't speak English but his smile conveyed a warm welcome. Kim interpreted his request that we remove our shoes before entering the building. There were wood racks for shoes that were not quite large enough to hold our dusty combat boots.

The floors in the entrance and along the hallways were highly polished and revealed not so much as a scratch. The darkly stained floors contrasted sharply with the off-white paper walls. You could see your reflection by looking down.

In the center of the building was a large rectangular, open-roofed sand garden with only a few giant boulders for accent. The hallways encircled the garden. This unusual garden took my breath away. I had never seen anything like it before.

One of my sergeants had arrived the day before with an advance party to arrange for our overnight stop at this special place. Bill had met us at the door with the innkeeper. Both men were wearing long kimonos with funny looking slippers on their feet.

"Wadaya think, Cricket? Isn't this a bit better than a foxhole in Okinawa?"

I readily agreed. "You picked a good place, Bill. Where are you going to stick me? I'm tired and dirty."

"Well, Sir, this Inn is a spa and we have a wonderful treat for you after we get you settled in. Now, it's your turn to follow me!"

Bill led the way down one of the halls. He paused, and with a funny bow slid open what looked like a screen made of white paper and waved me into a room that I'll never forget. Straw mats covered the floor. More sliding screens hid compartments within the walls. A charming, miniature garden, surrounded by bamboo fence, was located just outside one of the glass walls of the room. The branches of a giant pine tree hung low over the garden wall. The tree appeared to have been shaped in the form of a giant bonsai over the many years of its life.

An ancient stone lantern stood just below the tree's branches resting on a bed of small black pebbles. This contrasted with various shades of green in the ferns, moss and slender bamboo plants in this garden. The transition from the interior of the room to the outside garden took the eye from very refined materials to rough hewn natural ones, just a foot apart. I hoped that I could keep it in my mind forever.

A tall vase containing one flower and a twisted branch, stood in a small alcove at the base of one wall panel. A fabric scroll hung on the wall above the flower. Several large silk cushions were positioned on either side of a low, black, lacquer table holding a tea service beside the garden window. No other furniture accented the simplicity of this room—no bed, chairs, dressers, or tables—nothing to remind me of my room back home in the old Victorian house.

"What do I do now, Bill?"

"Cricket, just get out of your dusty clothes and into this kimono. I have something to show you on the lower level of the Inn." And then he left me alone in this beautiful, simple and uncluttered space. I wasted no time in packing away my uniform in one of the cubbies I found. Bill led me further down the hall and then down a flight of stairs into a steaming pool where the men had already slipped into the warm water. Small wooden buckets, at the edge of the pool, were used to wash down our bodies before submerging ourselves in the steaming water. It was a blissful feeling to just float in that water. An unforgettable experience.

An invitation had arrived from the Mayor of Chongju for the officers of Company "I" to come to his home for dinner that evening. We dressed in clean uniforms and Kim drove us to the Mayor's secluded home, which looked more Western and less Oriental. The Mayor met us at the door. There were deep bows all around and then we retired to what appeared to be the living room of the house. I was surprised to find couches and chairs furnishing this room. We engaged in friendly conversation about our mission in Taejon. The Mayor offered us the use of the inn whenever we could come back.

The aroma of food soon took over our attention. Sliding doors were opened revealing an adjacent dining area. It was simply furnished with a large, low, round table surrounded with cushions. We were invited to sit down and were served hot saki by several women dressed in beautiful kimonos. Just as soon as we emptied our glasses, they were quickly refilled with this delicious, warm rice wine. Then there was a major presentation of the raw fish that was an Korean special course. It took me awhile to learn to love this unusual treat. The delicate pieces of fish were served on a long wooden platter. One course after another introduced us further to the cuisine of the country. One of the women brought in a brass cooker and placed it in the center of the table. It was in the shape of a large bowl that had a chimney coming up through the middle. Charcoal was burning in the base of the cooker. There was a bubbling broth with noodles and pieces of chicken in the bowl. The head woman served each of us a bowl of the delicious soup. I thought that I must have such a pot one day and prepare this meal for my future family. We were then served a chicken dish and finally, sweet cakes. At this point the Mayor stretched out on the floor and invited us to do the same. It was traditional that after such a fine meal with lots of wine, dinner guests took a short nap. What a wonderful idea! From that meal, I developed a lifelong passion for dining in Asian restaurants.

We thanked our gracious host for the pleasant evening of conversation, food, and drink and made our way back to our rooms. Unbelievable! Sungja was there waiting. She had followed me from Kimpo. What a sight she presented standing there wearing a long, flowing kimono with her black hair reaching down to her waist. After those nights we spent together in Kimpo, I believed we would never meet again.

I gradually recovered from my stunned reaction at her appearance and began to excitedly ask her how she managed to get there. Sungja held her hand to my lips as a gesture that I should keep quiet. Then she took my hand and led me from this room down the flight of stairs, and on into the room steaming from the hot underground spring waters bubbling out of the wall of rocks and flowing down over a mossy bank of ferns into the natural pool in the floor.

As I stood there taking in this beautiful, natural bath, Sungja unbuttoned my shirt and slipped it off my back. Placing her hands on my shoulders, she eased me down onto a low wooden bench, loosened my belt, and pulled off my pants. It didn't take us very long to finish the undressing. Sungja allowed her own kimono to slip from her shoulders. What a picture she made! The top of her head came almost up to my collar bone.

Sungja picked up a small wooden bucket and filled it with warm water from the pool. She splashed the water down over my back, creating an incredible sensation. I returned the favor and allowed my hands to rub down her back as the water washed over her. We lowered ourselves into the steaming water. Every muscle in my body tingled as I thought that this must be heaven. Our bodies floated without effort. We swam and rolled around in those warm waters trying to catch one another just like two fish during the spring mating season. I had never felt such warmth with a woman before.

Sungja looked over at me and remarked, "You're my Baby Lew-Ten-Nut."

"No, Sungja! It's Lieutenant! Call me Lieutenant Cricket."

"No! No! No! You're Baby Lew-Ten-Nut." And, that is what I became for my duration with this doll of a woman.

We returned to our beautiful room and stood naked together over by the glass wall and looked out at the little garden. Moonlight fell upon our bodies and made them glow. I picked her up in my arms, kissed for a long time, and then lowered her onto the silk comforters. I became dizzy from her attentions and thought that it all must be a dream. The images and sensations of those moments when lying quietly in Sungja's arms remain with me to this day.

My experiences with sex were not extensive at that time. The usual adolescent stuff in darkened rooms, back seats of cars and haylofts of neighbor's barns. Being a prime candidate, dedicated student and prepared to learn all that Sungja could teach me, I approached my twenty-second birthday with gusto. Not a moment to lose!

We played with one another most of that night, falling asleep toward dawn. Sungja awakened first and it felt like she was doing something to my penis. I rolled over on my back, looked and saw that she tied a ribbon around it, reminding me of the flag pole out in front of the capitol building in Seoul with Old Glory rising to the top. It was a patriotic moment.

We missed breakfast. What a night! There were many more to follow. Sungja told me that she would be staying with an old woman in Taejon and would be waiting. I watched as she made her exit across the little bridge and out through the gates of the Inn at Chongju. At that moment, I clicked a picture of that scene in my brain. My men and I had survived the horrors of combat and had been brought into this paradise. I would never forget how fortunate I was to experience such a beautiful place and wondered if I might one day have one of my own.

Now, we needed to move on to Taejon and begin the repatriation of the Japanese.

Taejon

WE ARRIVED IN THE city of Taejon after another long drive south from the Inn at Chongju. Taejon, although not nearly as large as Seoul, was an urban environment of approximately 50,000 Koreans and another 20,000 Japanese. A major boulevard stretched from municipal buildings at one end to the railroad station at the other.

The advance party spotted a building where we spent the next several weeks. The building looked like a large schoolhouse but had previously served the city as the courthouse. The Japanese Army had replaced the entire judicial system during their occupation of Korea and the judges were in hiding. We came along and replaced the system of justice created by the Japanese. Most of us were in our early twenties and knew little about Korean culture or history. The older, more experienced officers were in positions of higher authority at Regiment, Division or Army Headquarters many miles north of Taejon, but I doubt that many of them knew much more about Korea than we young company commanders. Experienced officers and combat troops were being sent home and replacements for all levels arrived daily, many with very little training before being sent over.

It took us the better part of that first day to get ourselves settled. Platoons of men occupied the various courtrooms stripped of desks and benches. Our Company "I" office adjoined a room that Jim and I shared across the hall from a real bathroom with running water for bathing but not for drinking. The toilets were slit trenches that could be flushed and were a considerable improvement over taking a shit in a dirt hole in Okinawa combat with bombs flying overhead. We were comfortable with this set-up but it didn't quite meet the standards of our country inn.

Captain Isobe presented himself soon after our arrival. I looked up from behind my desk at a man small in stature, twice my age, who spoke fluent English and proceeded to explain his role as my liaison with the Japanese Army that had occupied this south central area of Korea.

The Japanese Commanding General and his staff were prepared to meet with me and my staff to begin working out the details of transferring supplies and buildings to U.S. forces. These planning arrangements were to include repatriation of all troops back to Japan. There were several thousand soldiers in Taejon and many more stationed outside the city at distant locations. A major airport, located near Taejon, had served as headquarters for the Kamikaze pilots.

In addition, there were planes, trucks, and passenger vehicles of every description, including the General's Mercedes limo. There were warehouses containing tons of equipment; clothing and crates of food, fifty horses, including a Palomino stallion, a large kennel of German Shepherd scout dogs, a pen full of carrier pigeons, two white geese, a pond full of goldfish and a pair of cats with six kittens. All were part of the extensive inventory for which we were about to become responsible.

We were to have our first scheduled meeting with General Minoru Itoki and his staff the next day. A discussion of our feelings toward the Japanese lasted long into the night. There were still many questions concerning our ability to collaborate with soldiers who we still considered to be our enemy. How should we act? Should we be friendly, hostile, cautious? Many of us remembered all too well the recent experiences of battle. And yet, the realization that we were no longer in combat became stronger. The atom bombs had saved us from certain death at the hands of the Japanese. We would do our job in a formal, military manner, not become friendly, speak when necessary and present ourselves neatly dressed with all medals proudly displayed on our uniforms. If General MacArthur could manage the surrender ceremony on the deck of a battleship, certainly we should be able to handle this business in Taejon.

The first meeting took place at General Itoki's headquarters. Captain Isobe and I met several times before to arrange details of what would take place. A storm blew in from the sea that morning with pelting rain falling as we drove up a long road to what appeared to be a small mountain covered with trees. It looked like a little forest planted in the middle of the city. The driveway passed by a tall off-white stucco wall with a slanted tile roof covering bamboo plants. Captain Isobe accompanied me in my jeep and pointed out the general's house. He explained that a Shinto shrine surrounded the property. The house actually belonged to the Shinto priests now assigned to live in a back room to make room for the General. Captain Isobe escorted us through the compound and to the Japanese style house that resembled the country inn where our bacchanal took place only a few days earlier.

Once again, we removed our boots at the entrance before entering the exquisite building containing a large ceremonial hall in the center. At one end of the hall was a raised platform that appeared to be an altar where the priests had presided. One large flower rested on the floor at the rear of the platform. Glassed-in hallways surrounded the central room where one could look out at the sand and rock garden. Smaller rooms, floored with tatami mats and enclosed with sliding screens, were located around the perimeter of the house.

At the rear of the building, a kitchen with a charcoal-fired stove was readied for meal preparation. A bathing area with sunken pool could be reached by passing through a bamboo gate. In addition to the sunken pool, a rather tall wooden tub, large enough for two people, overflowed with hot water. The tub rested upon an earthen fireplace where charcoal was burned to heat the water. I began to have visions of what it would feel like to sit in that tub with Sungja.

General Itoki occupied a series of rooms close to the bathing area. We were met and escorted to his suite by several members of his staff. The expressions on the faces of these men were sullen. They remained in an outer room while Jim, Captain Isobe and I were ushered into a sitting room. The casually dressed General knelt on a pile of silk cushions behind a large, black-lacquered table. He gave every appearance of being a retired grandfather rather than the former commander of an army. On his lap rested a small German Shepherd puppy, who wagged his tail as we entered the room. The General placed the pup on the floor. He came running over to me and began to lick at my feet. He didn't seem to feel the tension between us.

The spell was broken. Everyone began to laugh. By clever intent or accident, the General found a way to get to me without so much as uttering a single word. He gestured to us to be seated on the opposite side of the table. The pup jumped into my lap after he broke the spell with his liveliness. Captain Isobe made the introductions and proceeded to serve as interpreter during the meeting. I wondered if the Japanese officers sitting directly behind me were mentally in the room with us or were still on the battlefield. The General nodded his head as I explained the objectives of our mission in Taejon. General Itoki seemed as old as my Grandfather Egner back home in Ligonier. He came across as a simple family man who wanted to express friendship towards us.

We were faced with a big job to do together of sorting out, finding out, and working out all those details. He must have been at least 50 years old and seemed more interested in asking questions about my life than dealing with the various issues of repatriation of his forces. I felt so much pride sitting there as the young leader, bright and smart, with a girl back there in Chongju. But now we were sharing a love for puppies, a love for architecture, and it began to feel to me that there sat a nice person.

"How old are you? Are you married? Do you have children back home? Where did you grow up? Are your parents alive? Would you like to have a woman live with you while you are here in Korea?"

While attempting to respond to these questions, I tried to get on with the planning that needed to be done. Finally we arrived at a decision to have Company "I" begin to take over the airport facilities. The General's staff agreed to arrange a meeting the following day.

It appeared that the meeting with General Itoki was over and we attempted to make our exit. Suddenly he began to speak to me in fluent English. He invited us to remain and have tea with him. We accepted. He wanted to talk more. There were more questions.

"Do you like to climb mountains? Have you ever heard of our great Mount Fuji? Would you like to come and visit Japan when this is over? Do you have your own dog back home?"

The General rose and Jim and I hurriedly got to our feet. He picked up the puppy and very formally presented it to me. "I would like you to have this puppy as a gesture of the friendship that I hope will develop between our two peoples in the future. Both of our countries have been through a terrible time. My wife and daughter escaped the bombs that your planes dropped on Tokyo. I want to join them as soon as possible. You and your men will have my fullest cooperation, Lieutenant Glenn. What name will you give your new puppy?"

"I think that I will call him Taejon."

As we departed, General Itoki bowed deeply. We returned the gesture and made our exit quietly wondering about this thing called war, made for young men to survive and old men to grieve. I remembered looking into the faces of the young Japanese soldiers who I had so recently killed, thinking of them as nothing more significant than rabbits. Now they took on a more human form.

We walked around the grounds of the compound after making our departure from the General's house. A long path led to a temple located some distance from the house. Several massive, white stone arches rose above the path. Captain Isobe explained that the small temple at the far end of the path contained sacred objects.

"What will happen to this property after you and all of your men depart?" I asked

"It will all be yours."

I stopped right there and looked around at the beauty of this place and contemplated what it would be like to live in that house. Jim and I looked at one another silently. The pup ran around our feet.

"Come on Taejon, let's go."

The Taejon Airport

A FORMAL MEETING TOOK place the following day at Taejon Airport. The airport Commander and his staff strode aggressively into the conference room, saluted and seated themselves at the table opposite Jim and me. These men were combat veterans and had been leaders of a training program that specialized in preparing Kamikaze pilots. We were there to sign documents transferring responsibility for all equipment stored in various hangers and warehouses. Behind the seated delegation was a group of younger Japanese who we assumed to be pilots. We were outnumbered ten to one and it felt strange to be facing such a group who we sensed hated our guts. Their faces were serious, their manner brusque.

Captain Isobe, seated at the end of the table, served as interpreter. Long inventories of items to be transferred were presented. These lists, written in Japanese, rendered us unable to distinguish one thing from another. I insisted we be given a tour of the airport before signing anything. The Commander showed a brief flash of anger and barked out a command to one of the men standing behind him.

This handsome officer, assigned to take us around, turned out to be Lieutenant Ioto Masayuki, the tallest Japanese we had seen while in Korea. He looked like he had lifted weights all his life. He had coal-black close cropped hair, a fine mustache, broad shoulders, muscled arms, and narrow waist. His height of about six-foot four topped Jim's, and his finely-chiseled features could easily have qualified him for a role in a Hollywood film.

Unlike his Commander, this young man became friendly and eager to please. He took us from one building to another explaining the contents of many unopened crates. There were tons of equipment including one building that contained nothing but short-wave radios. We immediately spotted the leather flight jackets and were each given one to wear. Several buildings were stacked high with bags of rice and shelves of canned food. The Japanese lieutenant explained that one of their major problems consisted of protecting this inventory from the Koreans who infiltrated the post every night to steal food and other equipment.

As we toured this airport facility, the Japanese guards were replaced with men from our own company. The Japanese soldiers laughed and talked as they met their G.I. replacements. At first my guys seemed uncertain about how to act. This didn't last for long. Our plan to act in a very formal manner seemed to be an idea whose time quickly came and went. Within an hour, everyone wore a Japanese flight jacket of the softest leather fringed with rabbit hair. It became increasingly difficult to distinguish a Japanese soldier from an American G.I. We returned to the conference room after the inspection and signed off on the papers, still not knowing for certain what we were getting and what problems we would encounter. Captain Isobe translated the lists for us.

Lieutenant Masayuki, asked us to come with him and we followed him out of the room, down a hall, and into what seemed to be a dining room. Once again, the central piece of furniture consisted of a large, low, round table under which a charcoal brazier warmed our feet. The heat from the coals felt good. Warm sake started a meal that would further our appreciation for this style of dining which became more and more familiar, gracious, and inviting during the following months of that first, frigid winter in Korea. In later years, I still ate many of my meals seated at a low, round table in front of a fireplace. My sake cup remained full.

At the end of the meal, Lieutenant Masayuki mentioned that game birds were plentiful in the rice fields surrounding the airport. "Would you like to go pheasant hunting with me?"

"I certainly would. When can we go?"

Jim took off with Captain Isobe to continue assigning our men as guards. Lieutenant Masayuki and I proceeded across the fields with our rifles at the ready. At one point I felt an uncomfortable awareness that the Japanese man walking directly behind me carried a loaded rifle. A metallic click intuitively caused me to swing around ready to kill him on the spot. In an instant I recalled the moment on Okinawa when John Garcia shot the enemy soldier who rose from a bush behind me and aimed his rifle at the back of my skull. Masayuki dropped to the ground. I quickly put down my rifle and went over to him feeling suddenly embarrassed and foolish.

"I guess I am still in shock from being in battle so recently. That click scared me. What were you going to shoot? Let me help you up. Let's begin over and I beg your pardon."

"Lieutenant Glenn, that's the closest I've ever come to getting killed. Let's go for the birds."

I spotted a cock pheasant some distance ahead across a rice paddy, raised my carbine rifle and fired. The bird dropped in its tracks.

"Banzai," shouted Ioto. We ran along the edge of the paddy and when we reached the bird we both looked, incredulous. The bullet pierced the bird's eye killing it instantly. Not a feather disturbed! Iota drew in several deep breaths.

"I have never seen such a shot as this. No wonder the Americans won the war!"

My mind took me back to hunting with my Uncle Ford Wilt and cousin, Corky, who would have been proud of that shot.

Lieutenant Masayuki and I broke up laughing while we walked over to a rise in the land and sat down. It felt like we'd known one another for much longer than just a few hours. I didn't understand my own behavior toward this man. Why did I feel so friendly toward this member of the enemy forces who I came so close to shooting moments earlier? Within the past 24-hours I'd accepted a puppy from his General and gone hunting with a man who carried a loaded rifle behind my back. Appropriate or not, I couldn't deny feeling friendly toward this Japanese soldier. We were both enjoying ourselves sitting together wearing identical Japanese leather flight jackets.

Ioto became very curious about my little rifle that brought down the bird. He didn't know U.S. carbines were the most inaccurate weapon in the U.S. arsenal. It was a lucky shot if there was one. I pushed the carbine towards him. He jumped and almost fell over backwards until he understood my attempt at presenting him with a gift.

"Forgive me. It's sometimes so hard to trust anyone. We have been taught to suspect everyone."

After he calmed down, he seemed very pleased and, in turn, presented me with his pistol. We sat there by the rice paddy, talking. Lieutenant Masayuki reached into one of his pockets and took out a wallet extracting several pictures.

"This is my family. Here is my mother and father. They are very old now. This picture is of my little sister. She probably won't remember me when I get home. I never thought that I'd live to see them again. I am a

Kamikaze and the schedule called for me to make my sacrificial flight just before the Japanese surrender. I was scared even though my death would have honored our Emperor. I wish that we were the winners instead of you, but I am very glad the war is over. Now I can go home and get married. Here is a picture of the woman I will marry. And here is one of my grandparents. My grandfather died some years ago. I hope my grandmother is still alive in Nagasaki, but I don't know if she survived the atom bomb. Why did your side drop that terrible bomb?"

The key question, posed in a rice paddy field by a Japanese soldier about my own age, reminded me that Colonel Packler had alerted me to expect this possibility.

"I might not be here either if it hadn't been dropped," I responded. "Perhaps your family would have died also. We were being trained for the attack on Tokyo and feared that all of us would die in that battle. Like you, I became very scared of being killed after having survived combat during the Okinawa battle. We were told that many thousands of people on both sides would be killed were it not for the dropping of those bombs. But if you really want to know what I think, it is this. We dropped the bomb because our side developed it first. Once we made the decision to develop the atom bomb, it became a foregone conclusion that it would be used. Our new President is Harry Truman. He made the decision. I believe he felt that it would save many lives on both sides. Your military leaders would probably have done the same thing."

We sat there together silently, two young lieutenants raised in different cultures, sent to war, trained to kill, and miraculously escaping death; both admitting that we were scared of dying. What a way of maintaining face before the enemy!

The dead pheasant rested on the ground at our feet. I looked over at Ioto and thought about how my government had brainwashed me to think of Japanese as sub-human creatures. Only a month earlier, before our departure from Okinawa, I had shot and killed young men just like him, and possibly the General's son with almost the same abandon as shooting this beautiful bird through the eye.

Here I sat talking to another human being my own age, looking at his family pictures while wondering if the bomb had killed his grandmother in Nagasaki. I thought of my own Grandmother Egner working in her garden with a bonnet on her head. Lieutenant Masayuki's family looked like my own. His parents were the same age as Mom and Dad Glenn. His little sister reminded me of my own little Sunny Girl who probably wouldn't remember what I looked like either. I looked over at him wondering how it could be that we had hated his comrades so intensely who now lay buried somewhere in the Okinawa soil. How did I bring myself to do it? Would I be able to put to rest that part of my life's experience? Neither of us knew what to say next. He looked through his pictures one more time before returning them to his wallet. I felt that I wanted to talk with him longer and try to sort out the feelings that were suddenly coming to the surface. I almost reached over to touch him, but this wasn't yet the time for a handshake. We walked silently back to the buildings of the Taejon airport.

As we parted, he remarked, "I would like to talk with you again before I go home. There is a special place where we could go together some night. I would also like you to meet an old Japanese woman who fears for her life from the Koreans. She is the one who taught me English. A young woman is living with her now." I nodded.

Captain Isobe was waiting for our return. My new puppy ran around as we walked toward another building. "I want to show you something else before we leave here," he said.

The new building reeked with a smell that reminded me of home. Manure! By God, there were animals nearby in this barn. I heard a horse whinny. Inside the barn were many stalls, each containing a horse: forty geldings and one beautiful, chestnut mare. Captain Isobe motioned for me to follow him to the far end of the barn where in a much larger stall stood a handsome Palomino stallion. My eyes popped when I first looked at the large, regal and spirited horse. He tossed his head from side to side, his white mane flying through the air as we got closer. Then cautiously, he came over to the rail to get a better look at us. I reached out to him causing him to quickly pull back. He stomped his feet and pranced about the large stall.

"General Itoki asked me to bring you here to see this animal. His name is Takashi. He is the general's horse and he is worried about what will happen to this great animal when he goes back to Japan. The Koreans have already tried to steal these horses. They will kill them all for food or work them to death if your men don't guard this airport carefully. Our soldiers know that their job here is finished. They will all get drunk tonight, head for the whorehouses and will be of no use. Your men will need to take great care or this place will be wiped out. All the dogs will be killed, too. They raise dogs for food. Little Taejon here will wind up in a pot if you aren't careful. Will you promise, Lieutenant Glenn, to take care of these animals but particularly this stallion? General Itoki would like to present him to you as a very special gesture of friendship."

"Captain Isobe, I would be honored to have him. Tell General Itoki that I raised farm animals and learned to ride horses as a young kid. I will be honored to take great care of his horse and enjoy him as my own. Please thank him for me until I see him again."

What a day! The night ahead promised a possible reunion with Sungja. Within several hours we might be sitting in a hot tub rubbing each other's backs. We jumped into my jeep and headed back into town in a cloud of dust with the young pup sitting right there beside me.

Could this life in Korea turn out to be a feast?

Repatriation

THE MONTHS FOLLOWING OUR arrival in Taejon were initially focused on the task of taking over warehouses, supplies, animals, and vehicles from the Japanese who were focused only on their primary objective of getting home alive. The Koreans became their enemy. The airport facility did not offer sufficient security for the protection of either men or materials. The Kamikaze Battalion needed to be relocated to town where they would be safer and where the U.S. forces could offer them better protection. All of the materials were trucked from the airport to a more easily defended camp just outside of the city. While the relocation of supplies proceeded, we were also involved in initial preparations for moving the Japanese troops out of Taejon and to the ports of debarkation where troop ships were being organized to carry the Japanese men home.

Our Company "I" headquarters remained in part of the courthouse while most of our men moved out to our new camp made up of horse barns, warehouses, and fields, all fenced and supposedly easy to defend. Not so. The Koreans infiltrated the camp every night attempting to get at the reserves of food. Sometimes they succeeded. They picked off the two white geese the first night. The pigeons were taken a few nights later. I had fed and enjoyed those birds. They reminded me of my chickens back home. Their loss taught us a lesson: to guard the dogs and horses more carefully. The kennel held a dozen German Shepherds besides little Taejon. Those forty horses included the General's stallion. My men experienced in animal management took over the kennel and horse barn. Several others who worked in grocery stores back home were assigned supervision of the food warehouses. Most of the guys guarded the perimeter of the camp. This task bored them during the days and threatened them with hostile Koreans at night. Company "I" was in the awkward position of firing at the Koreans while guarding materials that we didn't really want or need. It didn't do much for our emerging relationships with Koreans who we were sent to protect from their evil enemy. Instead, we found ourselves protecting the Japanese. Quite a switch in our mission.

The Mayor of Taejon emerged from the shadows and invited a few of us to dinner at his splendid home. He was a tall, regal, elderly man with snow-white thinning hair and a long, gray beard. Several of his staff sat with us on cushions in a living room while the women of the household prepared a meal. A healthy number of sake cups were emptied before the shoji screens were parted revealing another large, circular dining table. Another unusual cooking device in the center of the table, fired with charcoal, boiled the stew. The beautifully dressed women served us bowls of the steaming broth filled with vegetables. At the end of the meal, we all stretched out backwards for the ceremonial nap. Why haven't we adopted this custom in our country?

I don't recall the Mayor's name but I remember him as a wise man. We discussed the problems that were being encountered at the camp where attempts at stealing supplies continued. He helped us to see that many Koreans were starving since their rice crops were immediately turned over to the Japanese army. He ventured the suggestion that all the food and supplies that were not needed by my company be given to the locals. We made a good decision together that evening. Within a few days, the distribution of bags of rice and canned goods to the inhabitants of the city began. Hundreds of people lined up at the camp gates to gratefully accept the distribution of food.

The nightly attempts to infiltrate our camp came to an end. This led to further collaboration in restarting schools and getting the courts back in operation. Jim Harkins, an engineering graduate from the University of Pittsburgh in 1939, took the lead in locating former teachers to get them back into classrooms. Korean children were excited about returning to their schools. The Japanese were quite content to remain in their camps, having been relieved of all responsibility. They couldn't care less what we did in this city, still so strange to us. The decision about distribution of the food to locals and getting schools back in operation were good ones.

There were incidents during those early days that I will always remember. During a tour of Taejon's hospital, the guide took us right into an operating room where surgeons immediately stopped working on a patient to bow and greet us. I quickly told Captain Isobe and Kim to tell them to get back to their task and we made our exit quickly.

Captain Isobe asked if I would agree to meet again with Lieutenant Masayuki who wished to introduce me to an elderly Japanese woman. I looked forward to seeing Ioto again and wanted to talk with him more about his experience as a pilot trained to give up his life and about his Shinto religion. He and Captain Isobe took me to a small house in the center of the city where a petite, elegantly dressed woman greeted us warmly. After removing our combat boots, she led us into a sitting room where, surprisingly, there was a Victorian table and chairs. We were not seated on the floor this time. The real surprise came when Sungja entered the room and served tea. Ioto and Captain Isobe knew about my girl. They arranged this meeting purposely so that we could meet again. I didn't know what to do with myself or how to express my very confused feelings about Sungja. The old woman seemed to realize my embarrassment and intervened with questions about my life.

Curiosity about democracy in the United States kept surfacing. While attempting to explain how our system of government worked, I didn't realize that simultaneously General MacArthur's efforts at drawing up a new Japanese Constitution were well underway. Ioto would return home to a Japan with a new system of government where average citizens would be given the right to vote and where his Emperor would be divested of his former imperial powers and begin to circulate and talk with his people on the streets. Some of the films taken at that time indicate that the Emperor wasn't entirely comfortable in this new role.

The elderly woman presented me with several gifts after learning that my grandmother and mother still lived back in Ligonier. She gave me a beautiful gray kimono, lined in white silk, for my mother and a more colorful one for my future wife. I still have these beautiful garments. The obis that go with the kimonos hang in my den as a constant reminder of that old lady and the Oriental culture that I came to love.

She presented another gift that needed to remain in Korea. She and her brother owned and operated an inn outside of Taejon utilized by the Japanese Commanding General and his staff. They would no longer need that special place. It would be available to me and Sungja and the others of Company "I" as I wished. She instructed Ioto to take me out there to see the place.

We found a very quiet and beautiful home. The old woman's brother greeted us, escorted us to the bathing area, and told us a meal would be served later. Another young woman awaited the arrival of Ioto. She knew Sungja. They both worked at a local brothel. The four of us relaxed in the baths together. Ioto and I performed our jobs during the day and met secretly at this house with our girls in the evenings. We enjoyed nights for several weeks until it came time for the Japanese soldiers to depart. I turned the management of this inn over to my Sergeant Bill who had organized the party at the Inn in Chongju. The men of Company "I" relaxed with their women secured at the local brothels. This golden opportunity for enjoying women rather than killing Japanese made life more pleasant for us all.

Captain Isobe continued to be our liaison with the Commanding General during preparation for the actual day of departure of the Japanese soldiers. Troop trains were scheduled to arrive one evening to transport the men south to a port where ships awaited to take them to Tokyo. Certain formalities were planned. General Itoki would arrive at the train station and remain in his limo until all his troops were loaded on the trains. He would be the last to board after bidding me farewell. Captain Isobe would accompany the General.

The Japanese troops began their march down the main boulevard in a double column between thousands of Koreans who lined the sides of the road to watch this silent procession. The soldiers approached slowly carrying their gear on their backs. They looked straight ahead. Many Koreans hissed at them. My own men were stationed along the street to protect the Japanese from possible attacks from the Koreans. All weapons of the Japanese had been previously collected except for the General's ceremonial sword.

I noticed that many of the Japanese soldiers carried small boxes covered in white material suspended around their necks with cloth slings. There were so many of these boxes that my curiosity led me to ask Captain Isobe for an explanation. "They are taking the ashes of their dead comrade's home to the families of those soldiers for placement in family shrines."

The magnitude of their loss struck me. As hundreds of men boarded the train, their faces seemed to reveal a mixture of relief and sadness. No cheering. No laughter. No spoken words. Just silence. I cannot remember a situation where so many hundreds of moving men were so quiet. Lieutenant Ioto finally came along. I asked him to walk with me along the platform away from the crowd so that we might talk privately for a few minutes.

"Ioto, I wish you a good life. It's been nice getting to know you and I'm glad you didn't need to make that last flight. Let's hope that your family will be there to meet you."

"Lieutenant Glenn, you are a great shot. I'll never forget you. Come to Japan. I'll show you around. What are you going to do about Sungja?"

"I don't know. I just don't know. Take care of yourself. Marry that woman in the picture you showed me and raise a good family."

Finally, General Itoki stepped out of his car. One of his staff rode his palomino stallion to the station. The General made a formal gesture of presenting the horse to me just before boarding the train after we saluted one another. He told me that his house awaited my arrival. "I hope that you get to see Mount Fuji before you return home." He stepped back from the door of the train, shook my hand and whispered. "Take good care of the horse."

Captain Isobe, Lieutenant Ioto and I exchanged salutes as the train slowly pulled out of the station. Captain Isobe and I had spent many days together. Our efforts at collaboration had turned into a friendship. Ioto and I also became friends as much as was possible. It felt strange to think about life in Korea without them. What a rare experience we were presented. There appeared to be something going on inside of us that recognized what horrible things the war had inflicted upon both of our countries. We seemed to be trying to make up for a terrible set of circumstances and to set the stage for a new relationship between the peoples of our two countries. It didn't seem to be a conscious effort. It was more of a gut reaction that led us to reach to one another across cultural boundaries. I often wonder what became of them and where they are today. Could I find any of them if I went to Japan? I feel a pull inside me to try to do that, to get back over there, attempt to locate them and visit shrines to the Japanese war dead. I did get to see Mount Fuji rising above the clouds far off in the distance from the deck of a ship transporting us home.

I rode the horse, Takashi, from the station, down the main street and back to the house while the crowds cheered. The mood of the Koreans changed dramatically, with the hated enemy gone. The celebrations began and the party lasted until dawn. Takashi carried me through the crowds from the station, up the inclined drive and through the gate to the Japanese house. All mine. I noticed that two Shinto priests stood watching a group of soldiers hauling religious relics from the temple and tossing them onto a pile. An officer I didn't recognize approached and told me that his orders were to destroy anything remotely symbolizing the Japanese, particularly artifacts connected with their religion. Another officer introduced himself as a representative of the Smithsonian Institution in Washington, D.C. He said that supervision of this unbelievable task would be his. I didn't believe either of them and insisted that they stop until I could verify this mission with Colonel Packler. My phone call to our regimental headquarters confirmed that these two officers were acting on orders from Army headquarters in Seoul. Gasoline was thrown on the pile and ignited with a mighty roar. The two priests stood together and openly cried. Moments later a demolition crew blew up the graceful stone arches over the path that led to the temple. A peaceful place for prayer had become a smoking ruin before our eyes. I didn't understand then and I still don't comprehend the necessity for destroying these works of religious art to pander to the Korean's hatred of the Japanese. I later learned that this command policy of symbolic destruction of Shinto artifacts took place in many other locations occupied by U.S. Army forces.

The officer from the Smithsonian later proved himself to be an unscrupulous character. He had secreted away some of those artifacts knowing better than most their value on the black market. Many of us became his customers. We helped him become rich while carrying home items that probably should have remained in Korean or Japanese museums.

I enjoyed living in that beautiful house for the next several months. It really hurt me, however, to see the rubble of the temple constantly there before us. If I ever return to Korea, I would want to go there in hope that it has all been restored to the beauty that we found on our first visit to meet with the General. That is probably unlikely. In all probability, a return visit would result in expressions of anger toward those of us who came to rescue the country from the Japanese.

I also wonder if I would discover Sungja still alive.

Information and Education

COLONEL PACKLER CALLED ME several weeks after the last of the Japanese forces departed from Taejon. He promoted me to his Seventeenth Infantry Regimental Headquarters' staff in the city of Chongju where I served for over a year as the regiment's Information and Education Officer. In this position, the regiment's training program became my responsibility. This required that I travel considerable distances from one unit to another to determine how to keep the men occupied. The day and night guarding of supplies at the various installations didn't do much to relieve boredom. The only diversions were training, movies, women at the many brothels, and alcohol. The army brought in boxcar loads of booze and sold it to the G.I.s for practically nothing. Drunkenness rapidly became a major issue and very little education addressed this problem. My intuition and discussions with Jim led us both to the conclusion that some sort of classes should be set up to occupy the soldiers' time and to help them plan for their eventual return home. Very few of the infantrymen had received a formal education beyond high school. Because of this issue, we organized a school with traveling teachers that included my buddy Jim. There were others among our regiment with specialties of one kind or another, for instance, a master carpenter, a landscape specialist, a painter, a garage mechanic, and men who spoke Spanish. We sent out a questionnaire to all units, and identified a cadre of men who became our traveling faculty. They would teach a class in Taejon one day and move on to Chongju the next. While many of the classes would not have been accredited at home, they did provide a very useful tool for helping some of the soldiers keep their minds alert and diverted some of them from becoming alcoholics. My lifelong career in education began at that time without my fully realizing it.

Red Cross girls arrived in Korea about this time. Four of them were assigned to our regiment. The regimental staff officers were billeted in brick houses on a rise overlooking the city of Chongju. Elaine, Jean, Betty, and Helen occupied the main house where we ate our meals, drank, and watched movies at night. Jim and I and several other staff officers lived in an adjoining house. To have white women in our midst created excitement and competition for their attention. The women worked at a canteen in town set up for the pleasure of the G.I.s. Everyone wanted to date them. But they wouldn't go the whole way with us as the young Korean prostitutes did so eagerly and expertly. This caused plenty of sexual frustration for all of us who lived so closely together, both men and women. The women always found out about the times when we would import Korean prostitutes to our house for an evening of sex. The next day we would get the cold shoulder from them. They remained above and beyond the carnal reaches of those of us who were rapidly learning how to fuck and needed as much practice as we could get.

Sungja taught me a lot during that period. I spent leisurely times examining her body and learning that a vagina is beautiful to see, touch, smell and taste and that a woman can experience orgasms just like a man. Didn't know that before! Wonderful discovery! Kept sex going all night. How dumb and inexperienced could a guy be? The Baby Lew-Ten-Nut practiced, learned and kept practicing and learning some more.

The fact that we were partying with Korean women didn't mean we weren't enjoying the company of the Red Cross girls. Some wonderful times were shared with them. Elaine finally agreed to go hunting with me. My reputation as a good shot grew considerably with Ioto having spread the news of my shooting a pheasant through the eye.

While shaving and getting ready for the date with Elaine, Jim, sitting in the tub beside the sink, asked me if I realized that Elaine was forty years old. I almost cut my throat in surprise. My God! She was old enough to be my mother. I couldn't believe it. "You're shitting me, Jim."

The date couldn't have been better. We each shot several birds and took them back to the cook who always allowed them to hang on the porch for several days before preparing them for an evening meal. That aging of fowl before cooking them was a new one for me. Back home we shot, cleaned, cooked and ate the birds the same day.

I also hit it off with Jean, younger than Elaine. She and I became friends. We often talked about planning for my departure for home. Jean gave me womanly advice such as as how I should manage my return so that my girlfriends would be most impressed. We often discussed whether I should arrange to have them meet me at the airport where I could descend from the plane in my full dress uniform with all the medals hanging from my chest or have them meet the train in Greensburg, Pennsylvania from where I had departed. Sungja was back south in Taejon and I was beginning to have other female friendships.

Before I left Korea for home, some great times took place with the Red Cross girls. We went on a tiger hunt and I'm glad to report that the beast got away. Villagers had asked us to kill it since it threatened their livestock. I got chased by a wild boar while hunting for birds one afternoon. Looked like a giant pig to me until I noticed the horn. It gave a wild squeal and started at me across the field. I outran the beast and finally leaped over a ditch to safety. Tigers and wild boars were prevalent in Korea at that time. Riding the great horse along mountain ridges also thrilled me. He and I vied for who was going to be top horse and I finally won. I can still see him rearing up on his hind legs and flailing the air with his front hoofs trying to impress me that he, not I, would make the decisions. He lost that battle but we both won in the long run and enjoyed many hours exploring the mountains. On one such ride, we came upon a Korean family funeral procession up the side of the mountain. We stopped to show our respect and then went on our way down the mountain very carefully because of the steep slope. At one point, I got off his back and carefully led him over some treacherous terrain. We formed a bond.

Taejon grew rapidly into a handsome adult German Shepherd during that year and a half that I remained in Korea. He went everywhere with me riding proudly in the back seat of my jeep. I began to call the horse Taka and he and the dog became friends. During the hours I spent in the office, Taejon would remain under my desk where I could give him a pat. He went to church with me every Sunday and would sleep at the foot of the pulpit. At the end of the service, he would jump back in the jeep for the short ride to our house. We were never separated.

One Sunday, sickness kept me from going to church. Jim decided to go and to drive my jeep. Taejon went with him and never returned. According to Jim, he went through his usual routine of sleeping by the pulpit but got separated at the end of the service, probably confused by my absence. Jim drove the jeep back to the house without him and delivered the upsetting news. We concluded that local Koreans might have caught him and killed him for food. I began a campaign to locate him by sending out notices to all units in south central Korea on the chance that another soldier might have found him. I traveled miles in every direction in an effort to locate that dog. I intended to sedate him and sneak him onboard the ship in a duffel bag. My family knew that I would be bringing a dog back with me. That never happened. All my efforts to find Taejon continued over many weeks to no avail.

I finally gave up hope of ever locating the dog and turned my attentions to Taka. In the meantime, little Kimpo had delivered a litter of puppies. One of my favorite long horseback rides took me up a mountain where a temple rose above the trees in a remote valley. The approach took us along a twisting road following a serpentine path as it ascended through plateaus of rice paddies. As we would reach successively higher elevations, the tremendous views down the hillside were breathtaking. A ravine with a rushing stream, located about halfway to the top, was a good stopping place where I could swim like a rainbow trout in a deep pool and Taka could rest and drink the cool water. Then we would continue up the mountain to what I thought of as "the secret temple in the valley." This spot remained one of the very few places in Korea where there were still trees. I could see a very tall idol standing high above the treetops as we rode over the final rise in the mountain. It must have reached well over a hundred feet in the air. A cave at its base had prehistoric drawings, many of tigers carved into the stone walls. Apparently the importance of the sacred shrine accounted for the fact that the trees hadn't been cut.

In the main building rested a huge bronze Buddha. Natives walked many miles to make food offerings at the base of this religious statue. The Canadian priests who looked over the temple spoke English and invited me to their house for tea. They appreciated the presents of food which my men later delivered to them by truck. I visited them a number of times before departing for home. This place drew me to it like a magnet. My hunch is that it still remains, but I wonder.

Many years later, on an evening at Boston's Symphony Hall, we attended a pre-concert dinner. I sat beside a Korean who played in the orchestra. I spoke with him eagerly about my memories of his country. The stories began to pour out of me at the table. He remarked, "All of those roads have become super highways lined with apartment houses. You hardly ever see a rice paddy." I remained very quiet for the balance of the meal. We did not bow to one another.

The weeks in Korea had turned into months. We were all preparing ourselves for the trip from war with a mixture of joy and sadness. The thought of leaving our buddies and this exotic style of living behind us caused some concern. Our futures were uncertain. What would we do when we returned home? I imagined that life in a factory town in south-western Pennsylvania wouldn't offer me the experiences of recent times. I also liked the Army life except for combat. Should I remain in the service as a career officer? Did I want to go to college? Recently graduated West Point Officers were arriving as replacements. They were assigned to the choice jobs. We "90-Day-Wonders" had served the purpose of the Army during combat and the early occupation of Korea, but we were no longer needed. White, Anglo-Saxon, university-educated men were the ones who would be permitted to climb the ladder of success. It gradually became clear to me that my time in the Army would end soon. I needed to go home and get on with my life.

■ ■ ■

Writing about my experiences in Korea has brought back so many plea-surable memories and reminds me of the significance of the fraternity that had developed among all of us. I wish that I had paid more attention to re-maining in contact with some of those former friends. I wonder where Jim Harkins is now or if he is still alive? He was best man at my wedding. Jean McClellan and I continued to see one another after the war when I attended Columbia. She also attended my wedding. Where might she be? Through distance, busy lives and neglect, I have lost touch with both of them. How could I have been so careless?

And, what about Sungja?

Part VI

The Trip from War

THE ORDER FOR ME TO report in two weeks to the Inchon port of debarkation came at just about the time I had expected. Sergeant Dick had staged a big Company "I" party for me back in Taejon. Upon flying to Taejon, I noted that an engineering battalion, staffed totally with black men, had replaced the former Kamikazes at the greatly improved and very busy airport. My former sergeant met me and commented that one whorehouse accommodated the black soldiers while several others were reserved exclusively for the white soldiers. The Japanese, before us, had established all of these houses and had recruited the women for the sexual gratification of their troops. The horny men of the 17th Infantry followed right after the Japanese to enjoy the women. The Japanese General asked me if I wanted a woman while I lived in Korea. An ample supply awaited.

Dick drove me out to the camp where I wanted to see Taka, who had sired a foal with the one mare among the 40 horses we inherited from the Japanese. Taka still pranced around and showed off to anyone who paid attention. The sergeant would be able to handle him. I took one last ride up in the hills but missed having my dog running along with us.

Few of my combat buddies remained in Company "I," now made up of mainly new recruits arriving daily from the States. A very poignant moment came the following day when I stood for one last formal troop review, then rode past them all lined up, on either side of the road; standing at attention and saluting me as I rode out of that special town for the last time. Most of these soldiers had never served with me in combat, but nevertheless I went through with the formalities for the sake of the few of us who knew one another well. Sungja and I spent that last night together out at the inn. No Lieutenant Ioto and his girl this time. Just Sungja and me. It turned out to be anything but a loving experience for either of us. She, filled with anger at my not remaining with her or taking her home; and me, all mixed up about my own feelings for her. Making love that last time turned into something like a wrestling match between deadly combatants. I can still see the fury in her eyes as we both experienced a convulsion of tears. She screamed, "Damn you! Damn you! Damn you! Baby Lew-Ten-Nut!" Shaking with anguish that I did not fully understand, I turned to leave the house.

We were, in fact, not alone. All of a sudden the old woman appeared and put her arms around Sungja in an attempt to quiet her down. It didn't work. Sungja stomped out of the room screaming at me. The old woman seemed to have anticipated this, and quietly led me to the door where she presented me with a silk-covered box containing two Japanese kimonos that Sungja and I had worn during our many times together.

Dick drove me away from Taejon the next morning after the ceremonies with the Company "I" men. "Cricket, did you ever consider taking Sungja home with you as your wife?"

"No, I couldn't do that. My parents would probably understand over time, our town in Pennsylvania allows only white people to remain in the village overnight. Sungja and I couldn't live there. I don't know where we would go. I might even lose my family if I attempted that. They are understanding but that would really push them."

"Do you love Sungja, Cricket?"

"No, I really don't think that I do now or ever did. I just loved being with her. To be honest, she is the first woman who I've ever been with since my teens who loved to fuck. She is a master professional at it and has taught me a lot about having sex with a woman that I never knew before leaving home. When I first met her back at Kimpo, I didn't realize that she did this for a living. That dawned on me when you guys threw that great party at the inn up in Chongju. After that, I paid her well for her services and have no regrets, but I really didn't have feelings of love towards her such as I remember my father's expression of love to my mother. I hope I will be as fortunate as my Dad in finding and loving a wife. Sergeant, I used Sungja, felt fond of her and enjoyed our times together, but never felt deeply in love with her. How do you suppose we will ever know when we really are in love with a woman? I've asked my parents that question a number of times. Do you know what they say? A little bird will tell you. You just wait until you hear it. Your time will come. Sounds silly, doesn't it? I guess I haven't yet heard the right chirp."

"Cricket, I need to tell you that I have been banging Sungja during your absence. You spoke the truth when you described her as a real pro in bed. I'll take care of her, as well as Taka. She is just like a spirited animal sometimes. And, I don't know what I will eventually do about her. I'll tell you one thing for damn certain. She can't go home with me to Akron, Ohio."

"Well, I'm not exactly surprised with your news about enjoying sex with her. I realized that she was laying other guys. I guess we both are lucky men to be alive after what we went through down on that bloody island, and also fortunate to have enjoyed Sungja. Do you ever wonder what she gets out of all of this fucking? She seems to really enjoy it. I really don't know what she expected of me. I never once spoke with her about our remaining together as man and wife. I just hope that what I learned with her in bed will last me a lifetime. Do you think we'll remember?"

"Cricket, I think we are both naturals at sex. Don't worry. You will hear that bird chirp one of these days and it will all come back to you. You might even have some great stories to tell your future wife."

"Dick, here is a present of kimonos given to me last night that I really don't want to take home. You should keep and use them. The old woman gave me others to take back. Enjoy them when you are with Sungja but take care. Perhaps you shouldn't show them to her?"

We drove along those dusty roads back to Chongju. I pondered what all this meant to me and my future. The period in combat didn't offer much of an opportunity to expand my knowledge about my developing sexuality. Masturbation, while fully dressed in combat fatigues lying or crouching at the bottom of a fox hole with bullets flying overhead, presents certain limitations. I learned that masturbation, aside from feeling good, could also be a reliable way to deal with fear and reduce stress when you thought you might get killed at any moment.

My association with Sungja, the Geisha, however, turned out to be very significant. As my sexual partner for a year and a half, she taught me about many things I didn't know beforehand. I previously mentioned my childlike fascination with her body. What an opportunity that was for me in my early twenties. We enjoyed recreational sex together. Love did not enter my mind, but apparently Sungja's fondness for me went further than I knew. Basically, I learned that I could get sex for money whenever and wherever I wanted it. My wallet had been badly depleted during that time.

I did not love Sungja. I used her, paid her well for her services and left her screaming at me. Not a happy ending. I doubt that I had fathered a Korean-American child with Sungja, but I don't really know for certain. I don't recall any man, among my World War II Army associates, who returned home committed to a Korean woman. There was still too much prejudice back home. The experience in later wars turned out to be very different.

The experience of loving between myself and another woman didn't happen to me until I met my wife. My sexual behavior in those earlier days in Korea focused upon the recreational and carnal aspects of sex. Some of those times, however, were filled with beauty and magic. I learned later on that sexual recreation, beauty and magic can also be present in a loving relationship.

In Korea, if I had been more mature, experienced and courageous, I might have been able to form that important link between physical and emotional loving. Perhaps I would have been strong enough to have brought Sungja home and withstood the criticism from a racist society, but I really doubt it. Justifiably furious with me, I can still see Sungja screaming and pounding me with her fists as I made my exit. "I hate you, I hate you . . . you . . . you . . . sumofabitch!"

My days as a "Storybook Soldier" came to an end as I looked forward to the real world back home in Youngwood, Pennsylvania and to seeing once again little old Ligonier and the Victorian house up on East Main Street. I learned that my Grandmother Egner had died while I was away.

Back in Chongju, my family of officers and Red Cross women busily prepared one last feast for us all to share before taking me over to the railroad station to catch a late night train to Seoul. Everyone kept busy during that last day to delay final good-byes until the evening. That we would ever be together again would be unlikely. We all felt the anxiety of separation.

Everybody piled into jeeps for the trip to the train station after the feast. Once there, I looked into the faces of Jim, Elaine, Jean, Betty and the others and didn't know what to say. It reminded me of my departure from my family at the Ligonier railroad station three and a half years earlier. Once again, I found myself leaning out of a train window waving one final good-bye to my friends. That earlier day seemed so long ago and had marked the beginning of my passage from boyhood to early manhood. Now, after sitting up all night and watching the Korean countryside slip by, it occurred to me how fortunate we were not to have fought in those barren mountains devoid of any kind of natural cover. As the train pulled into the Seoul station, I was on my way to the port of Inchon where I had landed as a storybook soldier a year and a half earlier. The Korean War loomed ahead.

I eventually made my way to the camp at Inchon where soldiers were being processed for the trip home. For several days prior to my own departure, I served as an inspector of baggage being carried by other G.I.s. We were well aware that many men were trying to take home souvenirs. I mailed my own collection home and it somehow made it all the way back. During these inspections of baggage, all guns and knives were to be confiscated. For hours on end, I would open duffel bags, spill out the contents and collect weapons that many were attempting to carry out of the country. I detected a box at the bottom of one bag. When I opened it, out spilled a skull with some black hair stuck to the top. I couldn't believe what I saw.

My last two days in Korea were spent with my dog, Taejon. We were reunited unexpectedly at the Port of Inchon just before I was to sail for home on the *Williams Victory.* He and the Red Cross woman had bonded. (Photo courtesy of Glenn family archives)

"Where in blazes did you find this?"

"Sir, that's all that remains from the head of one of the fuckin' Okinawa Japs."

"Well, how did you acquire it?"

"I cut it right off his fuckin' neck with this knife. Then I soaked it in lye to get rid of all the skin and brains. I'm takin' it home to give to my girlfriend. Don't ya think it will make one hell of a present for her?"

I felt sick with disgust as he put the skull back in his bag. I confiscated the knife. The image of the dead, headless Japanese soldier sitting sprawled along the path in Okinawa flashed again through my mind.

Reunion with King Taejon

I walked slowly back to my quarters along an army post street thinking that in just two days I would be boarding a ship to head home when I noticed a Red Cross girl walking down the other side of the street toward me leading a large dog on a leash. As they got closer, my eyes nearly popped out of my head. The dog looked just like Taejon. "Taejon! Here boy! Taejon! It's me!"

The dog froze in his tracks, looked at me for an instant, broke away from the girl and ran towards me. He jumped all over me as the girl screamed, "King! King! Come here, King!" She came running towards us while yelling for the dog. "Who are you? How do you know this dog? Where have you come from? What name did you call King?"

Taejon and I were so excited to find each other that I couldn't respond at first to the alarmed woman. It took us a few minutes to calm down. Taejon kissed the tears from my cheeks. I finally regained control of myself and got the dog calmed down. I told my side of the story and asked her to tell me how she had acquired the dog. As it turned out, Taejon had wandered away from the church that morning six months earlier. An officer from a military police unit billeted nearby picked him up. This officer went to Seoul soon after and gave Taejon to Lynn, the Red Cross girl. She had named him King.

The remaining day before boarding ship had us both walking the hills around Inchon with our dog. We had a picnic up on the hillside overlooking the harbor where we had landed. We looked out and saw the ship that would take me home. The brewery that my guys guarded that first night in Korea stretched out below where we sat. We talked and played with King Taejon. In my mind's eye I could visualize the cheering crowds, the waving flags, and hear the band strike up a Sousa march as it led the procession of storybook soldiers making our triumphal entrance into this now strange country.

It was too late to make arrangements to take King Taejon home, and I knew that it would also be impossible for me to attempt to take the dog away from his new mistress who loved him as much as I. She and the dog were as bonded as he and I once were in Taejon. I watched him as he nestled against her side as we sat there. What a beautiful sight. We walked down the hill and back to the camp. We ate together that evening and talked about our experiences in Korea and about our feelings of going home. Lynn would be stationed somewhere in the country and would take King Taejon with her. She snapped a picture of Taejon and me that I have retained all of these years. Whenever I see a German Shepherd anywhere, I think of Taejon.

They both came with me to the ship the next morning. I walked up the gangplank to the deck. No rope ladders to climb this time. Once again, an officer's stateroom awaited me shared with a few other officers whom I didn't know. Jim was still working in Chongju. Dick was probably wearing one of the kimonos with Sungja, or riding Taka over the mountains.

The *Williams Victory*

My dog wagged his tail and looked up at me. His mistress waved her hand in farewell. She looked beautiful to me, not as exotic as Sungja, more like my former girlfriends back home. Would I be able to find one like her when I got home?

The ship, named the *Williams Victory*, eased out of the harbor on the first leg of the voyage. Our next stop was Tokyo. The sky was filled with a mass of swirling birds, making a raucous noise, just as before when we arrived. There were no Koreans waving from the streets this time. Lynn and the dog had slipped out of sight as we sailed from shore.

Before dark that night, we rounded the southern tip of Korea and headed east on a course for Japan. Rising early the next morning, I went out on deck to see where we were. At dawn, the first rays of the eastern sun reflected against the land of Japan, now an occupied country. A mighty mountain filled the horizon. Mount Fuji rose there before me. What a sight! Its snow-covered tip blared red from the sun's reflections. I wondered if the Japanese general had found his wife alive, if Captain Isobe and his family had been reunited, and if the young Lieutenant Ioto Masayuki had married the woman in his photograph. Thank God, we didn't need to fight the battle of Japan. Thank God for the atomic bombs that saved so many lives. What a good start for home on this trip from war. What would it all mean to me in the future?

The *Williams Victory* sailed out of the crowded Tokyo harbor without fanfare passing every conceivable class of craft before reaching the open ocean. Mount Fuji loomed in the background as we sailed east for home. The defeated Japanese would eventually win the war of economics and reclaim the island of Okinawa, turning that sub-tropical paradise into a tourist destination. As we departed from Japan, I didn't recognize how deeply I'd been affected by the cultures and peoples of the Orient.

The first several blissful and warm days at sea on the calm Pacific were like going on a holiday cruise. We lounged around the decks getting our

The *Williams Victory* carried us from the Korean port of Inchon, to Japan where we gazed upon Mount Fuji before sailing across the north Pacific. It was like a vacation cruise. We worked on our tans and watched whales.

full share of rays. No urgent meetings or drills. The troops played cards, swapped war stories and spoke of their families. No grinding of knives as on the voyage to war. Tokyo Rose spent her days in prison while visions of our arrival at home danced in our heads.

This didn't last for long. The ship took a northerly course toward the Aleutian Islands. Five days out we began to see ice floes as the ship rolled in a more turbulent sea. One day, a pod of whales broke the surface. They reminded us of mini-submarines. We were all fascinated seeing them blow air and spray water into the sky above their heads while playing around our ship. The captain slowed the vessel so that we might all enjoy this natural spectacle. It was the first whale watching trip for just about everyone on board. Many years later I recalled that sight when I went whale-watching out of Provincetown, Massachusetts.

Our voyage across the Pacific took 12 days. We arrived in Seattle one foggy morning at a pier decked out in flags and banners that read:

> *"WELCOME HOME DEFENDERS OF LIBERTY"*

A band played while a large crowd waved and cheered. Many of us wiped away tears while we laughed, hollered and waved to the people waiting on the dock where Red Cross girls prepared to serve coffee to the troops coming down the gangplank. I spotted Bill Gilbert among the crowd who had arrived home earlier. He had watched the daily ship arrival notices so that he would be able to meet his returning friends. Beside him were the three young women whom Bill, Jim and I had dated before our departure for combat two years earlier. Everyone was shouting out names and running to meet soldiers in a madhouse of activity. Suddenly the realization that, finally, I stood on the soil of the United States really hit me. Many in the crowd were crying with happiness and hugging soldiers who they didn't even know.

Bill's parents opened their home to us once again. I called my family in Youngwood, Pennsylvania to let them know that I had landed safely and would soon head for home. Everyone tried to talk at once on the phone. My little sister, Doris, sounded grown up. Dad said, "Cappy, I knew that you'd make it." I called Peter's Mom and Dad in Georgia who were glad to hear from me. They, however, needed to tell me about his funeral and that made me keenly feel his loss all over again. I retold the story about the beautiful Easter sunrise service that Peter conducted on Saipan just before we boarded the ship for Okinawa, and what strong support he gave to the frightened men in the hold of the ship as we steamed toward war. They needed to hear, firsthand, how bravely he withstood combat and that he didn't suffer, that he didn't even know what hit him. I didn't think they needed to know that he had lasted less than 20 minutes in combat before being killed. They invited me to come and see them, but I never did, thinking that it would be too painful for us all. My good-byes to Peter were said at his first grave back on Okinawa.

Bill took me salmon fishing on Puget Sound several mornings before the sun rose. There before us stood spectacular Mount Rainier reminding me of Mount Fuji. Bill began to talk about what he wanted to do with his life. He seemed very sure of his direction and had already begun classes at the University of Washington. He intended to go to Alaska following graduation and become a commercial fisherman. That is exactly what he did. "Cricket, you should see the mountains of British Columbia just north of

As the *Williams Victory* eased toward the dock in Seattle, Washington, we were welcomed home by waving crowds and band music. I stood, with tears in my eyes, realizing that we were home. Our buddy, Bill Gilbert, met us at the dock and took us to his home. Bill's parents greeted us and urged us to call our parents. What a moment it was to hear their voices. (Photo courtesy of Glenn family archives)

here. I want my own fishing boat. Maybe I'll have one built just the way I want it. Every year from spring to fall, a number of small vessels with tall poles stretched out on either side of them appear, like large birds, all over these coastal waters. They seem to sit motionless on the surface, but they are moving gently. They're trawlers, like my boat will be—with a lacework of lines and hooks hanging into the sea from their poles—searching for the salmon. There's nothing more beautiful than one of our sunsets on the water. I really feel at peace there. Fishing for salmon is going to be a very big business in this part of the world. I'm going to buy me a piece of land and build me a little cabin right by the water's edge and have these mountains and waters all around me. I want to feel the sun, wind and rain on my back." Then this handsome young man, who knew exactly where he intended to go caught one fish and then another, and still another. I didn't catch a thing.

Bill's certainty about his future direction contrasted with my not having the faintest idea about what I wanted to do with my life. We corresponded for a time and then, through neglect on my part, lost contact with one another as our lives turned in radically different directions. Years later, I did attempt to locate him when I was visiting the Cancer Center in Seattle as a representative of the Cancer Center at Yale University. Even more recently, I made several telephone calls to various William Gilberts, but none of them turned out to be my war buddy. The occupants of his parent's home didn't even know that a Gilbert family had ever occupied the place. I am still attempting to reach him through the Alumni Office of the University of Washington.

Those few days fishing with Bill went by rapidly. His non-stop storytelling about the beauty of the northwest and of the many opportunities that were available to returning veterans were tempting me to follow a deeply-held instinct to remain close to nature, but I needed to get home first.

The Train Ride

One morning the Army loaded hundreds of us onto a troop train for the trip across the country. The train's coaches were converted boxcars equipped with row upon row of bunk beds. The very crowded conditions didn't seem to bother us one bit and a jolly mood prevailed as the train moved slowly through the magnificent northwest territory stopping on sidings to allow us to get out and exercise. The ride through Washington, Idaho and North Dakota took us along rushing rivers banked with taller pines than seen back home. There were mesa formations followed by vast prairies that were nothing short of spectacular. "Oh give me a home where the buffalo roam, where the skies are not cloudy all day. . . ."

We stopped at little towns along the way and noticed that the fronts of the wooden buildings along the main streets were built like the facades of houses that we saw in western movies. Most of the streets were unpaved. The citizens were accustomed to welcoming the homecoming G.I.s. High school bands would greet our train as it pulled into the flag-bedecked stations. Young majorettes would toss their batons high into the air and wiggle their behinds to our cheers and whistles. The townspeople set up sandwich stands in the little stations and offered us free food, coffee and cigarettes. They greeted us as if we were their own boys. Mothers and fathers rushed up to us as we stepped down from the train and threw their arms around us and hugged us so many times that I lost count. "We are so proud of you boys. Why, you look just like my son who was killed in France. Where is your home? Would you like to send this postcard to your Mom and Dad? We'll mail it for you. Here, take this sandwich along with you. I baked the bread this morning." At one town after another we experienced this expression of instantaneous joy at our arrival. They felt like members of our own families. I still think of them that way.

Our troop train moved on eastward and paused in Chicago, Cleveland and Pittsburgh where the celebrations grew larger and louder. The American Legion and Veterans of Foreign Wars were out in full force at these major stops. The mayor of Pittsburgh gave a rousing welcome home speech as little kids waved American flags. Getting this close to home, I could almost smell my Mom's cooking. As the train neared the Greensburg, Pennsylvania station, I went to the door of the car so that I could watch us pass the clock tower under which my dad and I stood and said goodbye several years earlier as I began the trip to war. I heard him say, "Get one for me, Cappy." My battered wallet still contained the little slip of paper with the copy of the 23rd psalm that Dad gave me just before I departed.

The train moved on slowly toward Johnstown and the famous curve at Altoona. My family would still be asleep and wouldn't realize how close I was to them during that night. I blew kisses out the train window to my cousin, Cubbie, to Nappy Fyock and to all the members of the Glenn clan who I would see again soon. I remembered the St. Christopher medal given to me by Cubbie to wear in combat and felt sorry that I had lost it.

We arrived the following morning just outside of Washington, D.C. at a rail depot that overlooked both the Capital and Pentagon buildings. Trucks waited to take us to Fort Meade, Maryland, the first Army camp I had arrived at in 1943 after being drafted. It was now the fall of 1946 and young men were still being drafted and trained at Meade for occupation duty in Europe and Asia. These boys were to become the replacements for the returning troops. At sunset one afternoon, we combat veterans were invited to review the retreat ceremony standing smartly dressed with medals on our chests beside the camp's Commanding General where Joan Blondell had stood three years earlier.

The men who have since returned from fighting in the Vietnam War didn't have that kind of experience. I've talked with some of these war veterans and found that in far too many cases, they were treated like lepers upon their arrival home. One man told me that he was hissed and spit at. Another soldier related his experience upon arrival at the Seattle dock. Nothing was extended free of charge, not even a cup of coffee. No bands were present at the village railroad stations. Instead, in some towns, the members of the local constabularies guarded the edges of the station platforms to prevent the "dirty, long-haired, ugly, wounded men" from wandering into the villages where citizens might be molested and shops looted. The people who did show up often greeted the confused combat veterans with peace signs and antiwar chants of "Two, Four, Six, Eight—It's that war we really hate!" Sometimes the American flag burned before the unbelieving eyes of these men who fought a lost-cause battle for their country.

The wounded Vietnam veterans weren't sent to rehabilitation centers at Miami's luxury hotels that were once converted to accommodate the wounded men who fought in W.W. II. In far too many cases, these wounded were shipped to filthy, sub-standard, under-equipped, inadequately staffed and poorly-financed hospitals. The movie *Born on the Fourth of July* portrays this period of our history well.

Going Home

A PROMOTION CEREMONY RESULTED in conflict within our group the morning we were discharged and ready to head home. We were all Infantry First Lieutenants and were given the choice of becoming Captains if we agreed to join the U. S. Army Reserve Corps. Accepting that deal carried with it an agreement that we could be called back into active service anytime the Army required us. I wanted to go home as a Captain with two silver bars. Dad Glenn called me "Cappy" all my life and I wanted it to become official. The thought that there would ever be another war requiring my services didn't seem possible. Most of my buddies, however, weren't so certain.

"Cricket, you're crazy. You're home free now. You've survived. What the hell are you thinking of? Who the hell will care if you're a First Lieutenant or a Captain? Shit, most of them won't even know what you've been through. Don't be a fool. Resign now and protect your ass. Who the hell knows what's goin' to happen next?

"Listen, guys. Don't you realize that we just won World War II and have delivered peace to every corner of the planet. I almost signed on to stay in the Army back in Korea. I'm steppin' up that ladder of success one rung after another. I'm ready. I've been trained all my life for this. I will never, never be out of a job as my Dad was during the Depression. We survived then as a result of the neighbor's donations of food and the game we shot in the woods. Mom kept tellin' me to just keep climbin' to the next rung and that's for damn sure what I'm goin' to do. I'm proud to have served my country. Yeah, even in combat. Just you wait and see. This Cricket will be president of something. I can feel it in my bones."

"OK, Cricket, go for it!" my comrades yelled.

So, I did. By standing there with many other officers and raising my arm high, swearing to serve my country at any calling, I became Captain Roland M. Glenn. My buddies pinned the two silver bars on my shoulders while shaking their heads and patting me on the back just before we were released to go home. Except for Jim, all the other guys became memories and I even lost track of him through neglect after he served at my wedding as Best Man. The only thing left is my memory of those associations. I did have brief meetings with two former officers of Company "I" in New York City and in Albany but even lost touch with those comrades as each of our busy lives propelled us in different directions.

The parents of one officer drove from Pittsburgh to meet their son and bring him home and they generously invited me to ride along with them across Pennsylvania from Fort Meade. I was surprised to see that the Pennsylvania Turnpike had been completed during the war years. New cars zoomed by at unheard speeds of forty-five miles per hour. The ride lasted well into the night before we pulled into my new hometown of Youngwood, Pennsylvania.

I asked my friend's father if he would stop the car a block before we reached our house so that I could adjust my uniform, see that my medals were pinned properly to my chest, and get my hat adjusted so that those silver bars on it would show. Then the car pulled up before the not very impressive frame house on Third Street. While stepping out of the car, a police officer ran out of the house towards me. It was my father, who suddenly stood at attention and saluted me! I saluted back and then he threw his arms around me. Dad must have been looking out the living room window waiting for my arrival. Mom ran down the steps with her arms raised in whirling circles right behind Dad and joined us in a long hug. She wept and laughed at the same time.

"Where is Doris? Is she awake?" They pointed me toward a rear room on the first floor of the house while inviting the family who had driven me to come in for a cup of coffee. My little sister slept soundly on a cot. I looked down at her silently for a moment. She looked just like Shirley Temple with all those red curls. Kneeling beside her while Mom and Dad watched, I whispered in her ear, "Sunny-Girl, it's Rollie. I'm home." Her eyes opened and she threw her arms around me as I picked her up hardly believing how tall she'd grown during my three years away.

We thanked the other family as they left for their own celebration in Pittsburgh. I can't begin to remember everything we said to one another that night, talking until dawn, eating Mom's freshly baked cookies, trying to relax, but really too keyed up.

Grandfather Egner, then eighty-nine, had lived with my parents and Doris after the death of my beloved grandmother a year earlier. He had sold the old Victorian house on East Main Street in Ligonier for $9,000. Grandpap also sold, for fifty bucks, his carefully maintained, Model T Ford sedan. My cocker spaniel, Chien, had died several months before my return. Dad had sold the old Chevy to a man at the factory where he proudly served his country as a guard. Dad looked a tad older. He wore his uniform with a pistol strapped to his belt, clearly enjoying his life and liking the idea that he could wear a firearm. It struck me odd that this gentle man could ever use a gun. After all those years of being out of work, he'd found a role to serve his country. I remembered the years of my childhood, while living in the McColly apartments in Greensburg, Pennsylvania. Dad would put on his W.W. I uniform and tell me stories about his own years of service in the Signal Corps. His route to independence, through joining the service, gave him the opportunity to get away from his very strict parents who clearly wished that he would marry a beautiful woman from Greensburg's high society. His smile never seemed to stop, his personality making his life rich with many friends.

Mom looked just the same as when I had departed, a rather short, stocky woman who always wore an apron ready for any job to be done on a moment's notice. Her graying curly hair never seemed to change. Her rather stocky legs made me think of the roots of a strong plant, hardy enough to bear the weight of the world. Hugging my mother always made me feel as if I had embraced the warmth of the entire sun.

She was also a leader, found following difficult, and succeeded in climbing her own ladder of success. She knew how to get what she wanted. She wanted my father most of all and knew how to love him even during his weakest times during the Depression.

My parents and little sister provided me with all the love and support needed to help me through the terrible combat on Okinawa. Their hundreds of letters, now preserved, are astonishing and reveal how they managed to get through it all. After exhausting ourselves with talk, I fell into a strange bed in a room that I never knew in a house also unknown to me. The family had moved into this house so that Dad could secure his job at the Robertshaw factory. In spite of my fatigue, sleep didn't come easily that night. Mom kept peeking into the room.

"Rollie, I just can't believe you're safely home. We prayed to God every day and night to look over and protect you and here you're safely back to us."

"I know, Mom, I prayed too." She said goodnight and then lit a candle and went upstairs to the second floor bedrooms that weren't wired for electricity. Sometime during the night, my little sister crept into bed with me and kissed me awake. I put my arms around her and we both went back to sleep.

Mom served what could only be described as a proper American breakfast the next morning. She prepared various dishes of eggs, potatoes, and ham using all four burners on her stove, plus serving us fresh baked bread. We sat around the table in our pajamas eating and chatting away. No one spoke of the war nor asked me to tell them what it felt like to kill other human beings. I wanted to talk about my experiences, but this opportunity with my dad didn't happen until several years later.

My Uncle Ford Wilt, Aunt Lucy and Corky came to visit and wish me well. The conversation never touched on the war. Corky and I took a walk together that evening while our parents visited. The two of us were able to share briefly what we went through in combat, he in the Navy and me in the Infantry. We also bragged about our sexual experiences with women. Corky provided vivid details of his encounters in bed while I avoided mentioning my relationship with Sungja. I'm not certain to this day why our parents and aunts and uncles avoided discussion of the war with us. With the war ended we all moved to other safer topics. We had helped to deliver peace to the world. There would never be another war. As my Dad would say, using one of his favorite expressions, "That's it, Fort Pitt!"

Before the war, I had switched from Ligonier's public high school to attend Kiski School. Kiski's headmaster, Dr. Monty Clark, had called my parents before I returned home to extend an invitation for me to return to the campus and live with him and his wife, Billie. I could take some refresher courses until I could get into college and figure out what I wanted to do. Monty and Billie had followed my progress during the war and had written supportive letters to me during those three years. They were like a second set of parents. Mom and Dad and the Clarks must have anticipated that I would need to do something other than sit around Youngwood, a town with a population of 2,500, none of whom I knew.

Uncertain of my objectives, I readily accepted the invitation from Dr. Clark to return to Kiski School. This would enable me to spend some time on a rural, sprawling campus located in Saltsburg, Pennsylvania. The school was known for its bright student body and talented teachers. Memories of Kiski were positive. I'd worked the Kiski farm, taking care of 40 sheep, three hogs and two horses to pay for my room and board before that senior year.

My grades were good during that year. The classic method of study, still in effect when I returned, allowed me to spend the better part of a day with the instructor, really delving into a subject. I had always done well with that kind of studying. Jake Ziegler and Carl Arnold were two of my favorites on the faculty. Spending uninterrupted hours studying chemistry or math with them will remain in my memory forever.

Experiences at Kiski, however, didn't come close to the daily routine I had followed as an Infantry Officer in the Orient while living in my own Japanese-style house and enjoying time with my geisha. I was finding it very difficult to forget those experiences and to surrender my sharp looking uniform with the medals to mothballs.

How to reach the next rung on the ladder of success wasn't clear to me. I thought about my options for specializing in something, anything to become rich, because I wanted to achieve a success that had eluded my father. I had sworn to never allow myself to get into a situation where groceries would have to be donated to my family by friends as was the case during the Great Depression. The pain of those stressful days was seared into my memory.

After accepting the invitation to return to Kiski, I first wanted to visit my former friends in my real home town of Ligonier. My former girlfriend had let me down gently with a letter informing me that she had met someone special while away at college but would always remember the fun times we shared. So much for that. She didn't have the sophistication of the Red Cross girls back in Korea anyway. I never found out if she liked sex because she never would go all the way with me. None of the "good" girls did in those days.

Getting back to Ligonier felt great, especially having the time with Corky to share memories. Some of my other male friends, who were servicemen, were also willing to talk about combat. Corky had married Joan Wiley during my time in Korea and worked as a house painter with his Dad, Uncle Ford. He had joined the Ligonier National Guard unit after the Navy, more for comradeship with other men rather than contemplating being called into active service once again. I sat with Corky and Uncle Ford one night and related the story of how I believed that the lessons learned during those hunting expeditions in the Allegheny Mountains probably had saved my life during combat.

Corky and I got together with some of the other guys to celebrate at one of the town's beer halls. Everyone seemed impressed with me all dressed up in my Officer's uniform sporting those silver bars of an Infantry Captain. Bob Myers remarked, "Roland, I can't believe that it's really you. You were such a skinny little kid." We all missed Steve Wuchina, another good friend, who had died suddenly a few months earlier. Most of the girls we had all dated were still around town. Some were in college. It took about a day to make the rounds and it didn't seem as exciting to be back as I had anticipated. It felt very strange to pass the old family house on East Main Street and to see Grandmother Egner's garden filled with weeds.

Mom and Dad realized that I needed to move on. I did return to Kiski and studied French while living on the top floor of the Clark's house with three other G.I.s who had returned to school for the same purpose. Monty Clark did want to know about our war experiences. We would meet in his living room before dinner in the evenings and talk about the war. He urged us to open up and share our war stories with him. The four of us also formed a swimming team representing Clark Hall but never won anything significant. Our hearts weren't into being students at this isolated location overlooking the Kiskiminatas River. Life couldn't have been duller. Swimming and telling each other war stories late into the night bored the hell out of us.

A back terrace overlooking Saltsburg became a place where we retreated and allowed our feelings of depression and confusion to surface. While I thanked God for having looked over me and for getting me home safely, what a let down this life had become in contrast to all that exotic experience back in Korea. I felt sort of crazy with boredom and anger at the situation even though I recognized the generosity of the school in welcoming me back. The Clarks seemed to realize what we were going through and tried their damndest to think up things that would put some excitement back into our lives.

One evening, dear Billie Clark urged us to attend a lecture on human sexuality. What a laugh! Another time we drove into Pittsburgh for the day to see a show. Big deal! The Andrew sisters and Frank Sinatra no longer performed at the Stanley Theater. Pittsburgh didn't cut it for the major artists of the day. We settled for a John Wayne movie, went out to dinner in town and plotted how to secure women. Pittsburgh, however, was a different city, now partially cleaned up and with the sky clear and unclouded without the black smoke from the steel mills as we remembered it before the war.

None of this activity helped me out of my depression and boredom. I didn't have my horse, Taka, to ride or my German Shepherd, running happily at my side. I would awaken in the middle of the night covered with sweat and shouting incoherent words. My G.I. buddies would shake me awake. My dreams about combat and killing never seemed to let up and allow me to rest. How could I ever share with anyone the experiences of my sexual relationship with Sungja, the geisha, and give voice to those terrible times on Okinawa and the exotic period in the Orient? I seemed to be caught in a web of confusion. Where would I go to college? What did I want to study? Where could I find a woman to really love and with whom to enjoy sex? There must be someone out there who could offer me more love than my romps with Sungja.

There were no parades, no one to salute, temples to explore, starving priests to feed, tigers to hunt down or vast stretches of rice paddies to look upon. The horse and dog were gone. I could no longer summon my private jeep driver nor have staff to supervise. The trips to explore those mountain tops were not so far in the past that the memory had faded. Sungja and the Japanese were far away. My war buddies were long gone back to their own homes far across the country, some already married and having children. My officer's uniform with those two silver bars hung with mothballs in a closet back in Youngwood.

Was I being selfish in seeking a more exciting life? Did I not fully appreciate the support of family, friends and Kiski? My leadership accomplishments while in combat saved the lives of other men and helped to win the war. My efforts while in Korea contributed to this now peaceful world. How could I use those proven skills and continue to lead? What could I possibly do with my life?

Where had that cocky young man called Cricket gone?

On the Boardwalk
in Atlantic City

WHILE FEELING VERY DEPRESSED and trying to make plans for college, my 85-year-old Grandfather Egner came to the rescue with an invitation to take our family to Atlantic City for a few days of holiday. I departed temporarily from the Kiski campus and went back home to join the family for the long train ride from Greensburg to the resort where both sets of my grandparents had vacationed many years earlier. Very excited to be taking such a long train ride to see the Atlantic Ocean for the first time, my little sister Doris, sat beside me and chattered away.

As the train moved around the Horseshoe Curve heading East, a young woman noticed me, dressed in my Captain's uniform, and asked if she might talk to me about her brother who had perished in the Normandy invasion. She took a letter, folded many times, from her pocketbook and asked that I read it. The letter, written by the young soldier's company commander, spoke about how bravely her brother had fought and died. I wondered about the truth behind the words, thinking back to the days when I composed such letters for soldiers killed in action, some almost unknown to me, who'd died minutes after entering combat. Reinforcing as best I could the image of her brother as described in the letter, she sat there quietly wiping tears from her eyes. The incident brought up memories that I preferred to set aside on this vacation jaunt to the Atlantic. We made it to Philadelphia, switched trains and an hour later arrived in the city by the sea on the Jersey coast.

Grandpap called ahead for rooms in what turned out to be a run-down hotel across from the Atlantic City railroad station, not the best location in town. Upon entering one of the bedrooms, lit by one light-bulb hanging from the ceiling, mother pulled up a mattress and we all saw roaches running for cover in all directions. She wasted no time in getting us out of that place while giving her father a very annoyed look. Grandpap, a tall, elderly man, dressed in a blue suit, high button shoes and wearing a straw hat didn't seem to notice or wasn't bothered. Securing another reservation at this late hour might be a problem. Dad remembered the name of the Albemarle Hotel, located one block from the boardwalk, where he and his older sister, my Aunt Maude, were taken on vacations as children by my Glenn grandparents. Amazingly, it still operated as a low-cost but clean hotel and was a palace compared to the dreary rooms at our first stop.

We dropped our bags, delayed unpacking and walked up to the boardwalk. Doris held tightly to my hand and became very excited when the Atlantic came into view. I remembered the first time I had seen the Atlantic and knew how she felt. As we stared out over the broad expanse of beach and waves, behind us stretched the city's huge, art-deco hotels utilized during the war as rehab centers for wounded G.I.s. A kind of moldering antiquity permeated these grand old buildings. Atlantic City still reflected some of the glamour of the previous years but reminded me somehow of a spinster never taken to the altar. No one had asked for her hand except the grateful wounded.

It was Columbus Day weekend of 1946 and there were still servicemen recovering on the brick verandahs overlooking the ocean. Dad took my elbow and nodded at an amputee soldier being pushed in one of the rolling chairs by a man and woman, probably his parents. I preferred to look the other way at the water. Dad spoke up. "Cappy, that might have been you. Mother and I prayed on our knees every night and asked God to save you and bring you back to us."

"I know, Dad. I prayed too."

Relaxing together on the beach and swimming in the ocean appealed to everyone except Grandpap Egner who took strolls down the boardwalk and said very little except at meal times. It seemed clear to all that he was enjoying giving us this present of time together. We rented beach chairs in the mornings and spent the day talking in an attempt to get caught up on events of the past few years. I heard about the passing of my Grandmother Egner, selling the old Chevy, and all about the litter of puppies my dog had before she went to live with another family on a farm where she could roam unleashed. Doris and I played together and made sand castles while Mom and Dad relished having their family together. Again, any mention of my combat experiences resulted in a change of subject. Monty Clark and Corky remained the two people I could talk to.

I looked back up at the beach from water's edge one afternoon and noticed that Dad had engaged a very attractive woman in conversation. Even from a distance I could see this woman, with blond hair piled high, pointing to someone on the beach. My father couldn't be anywhere for longer than five minutes without meeting and chatting with someone. He waved for me to come up. After I walked up, he introduced his new friend, Mrs. Taylor. It didn't take me long to understand what they were up to. While Doris and I swam, she had bragged about her daughter, recently graduated from the Columbia University Presbyterian Hospital School of Nursing after undergoing rigorous training to become a registered nurse, while Dad tossed out stories of his son, wounded and just returned from the war. They were two of a kind, very animated people, proud of their children and wanting everybody to know it.

Mrs. Taylor introduced me to Carol, her daughter, a younger, blonde version of herself and better looking than any other woman on the beach. I couldn't believe my eyes. She reminded me of the Red Cross girl who had inherited Taejon. My kid sister apparently felt this introduction to be a bad idea and wedged herself between us trying to take my attention away from this beautiful stranger. I solved that problem by suggesting that the attractive blonde and I go for a swim. We ran down the beach and jumped into the waves.

"So, your name is Carol Taylor."

"I hear you've just returned from the war."

"You live in New Jersey?"

"My home is way out in western Pennsylvania."

"You're a nurse? There were lots of nurses on Okinawa and I met some of them in a field hospital getting my wounds patched up."

"You just graduated from college?"

"I haven't begun yet. I just applied to several schools but don't know where I'll wind up. One of the places is Columbia University. Isn't that where you graduated?"

And, so it went. Idle chatter while we sized one another up, jumping up and down in the waves.

I became aware that a number of people swimming nearby were staring at us. No, they were staring at Carol who was having a wonderful time frolicking in the waves. She jumped up and down, up and down, up and down. What a beautiful sight! A more careful look revealed that she appeared to be naked and her lovely breasts were being admired by all around as she jumped above the waves.

"You better get down in the waves, Carol. Just lower yourself a bit in the water."

After she realized that her bathing suit top had floated around her middle, she made a quick adjustment, and zoomed out of the water like she was being propelled by a jet. Upon relating the incident to her parents, her dad remarked, "Well, I guess that's just about all he'll want to see of you." Little did he know what I thought and it certainly didn't turn out to be the case.

I invited Carol to go horseback riding with me on a couple of rented nags. Neither came close to resembling my stallion back in Korea but they would do. We galloped down the beach together. She later confessed that she was curious about my body since I'd told her about my wounds. She couldn't see any scars anywhere and began to wonder if my wounds where inflicted to that part of my body covered by very brief swimming shorts? We got all that straightened out later.

A first date that evening couldn't have been more romantic. Dressed in my Army uniform, which had been taken out of moth balls for this trip, and sporting my Captain's silver bars, I asked Mom and Dad to wish me luck. "You look great, Cap. Have a wonderful evening. Mom and I are going out too."

I went over to Colton Manor, the hotel where the Taylors were staying, and spent about a half-hour enjoying a drink with Carol and her parents. The two of us took off to dinner at the Claridge Hotel. But before dining, while walking down the boardwalk, we noticed a group of little houses out on one of the piers. Something drew us to them. A sign indicated that the Levitt Company was preparing to build an entire community for returning veterans to be known as Levitt Town. Carol and I walked through the rooms commenting on them and talking about how each of us wanted to have a home of our own one day. It felt so natural to be together even though we'd only known one another for half a day.

We dined and danced until late that evening at the Brighton Hotel, drinking potent Brighton Punches, and then removed our shoes and walked in the moonlight together down the beach, until we found a lifeguard's station complete with a little porch that provided a very private spot for some necking. We sat quietly looking out at the ocean and then talked about our lives. We asked questions. "Have you ever been in love? How will we know when we're really in love? Do you want to have children?" I don't know if questions like that are unusual on a first date or not. We both just seemed to be in the mood for a discussion about love. I didn't know at the time that Carol had recently broken off an engagement with another man. Her parents brought her to Atlantic City to recover from the pain of that ending and as a graduation present.

We walked down the boardwalk some more until we came to the colonnades that stand in front of Atlantic City's great Convention Hall. While standing there, I related the story that a little bird will tell you—my parent's version of how I would know when I was in love.

We went to an all-night diner for breakfast at about 2 A.M. Then I took her back to Colton Manor not wanting the time together to end. After such a splendid evening, it wasn't easy to part. We agreed to write letters. I told her about Kiski and the fact that a formal dance was coming up. "Would you like to come?" "Yes, yes, yes." I returned to my hotel, just several blocks away but couldn't get to sleep. At about 3 A.M. a porter knocked on my door and said that I was wanted downstairs on the house telephone. It was Carol. "Can't you stay a few days longer? We had such a good time, shouldn't it last a little longer? How about it?"

I agreed. My parents were already packed for the return home in the morning. I went down to their rooms. "What's the matter? Are you sick?" Two typical questions for a mother to ask. "No, Mom, I'm really very OK but I think that I heard that little bird last evening. You folks go on back home. I'm going to stay here for a few more days." Love at first sight! That's the only explanation. Carol and I enjoyed the next four days and nights together. It felt so natural to be with her. We just clicked from the start. When the time came to depart, it was certain to both of us that something important was developing between us.

I returned to Kiski to await acceptance to a college, still not knowing what I really wanted to do with my life beyond getting more education and pursuing Carol. We spent the next several months at the end of 1946 commuting back and forth between Youngwood and New York City. We both liked each other's parents. This was getting serious.

Kiski was staging a pre-Christmas formal dance and Carol had agreed to come out for it. I met her in Greensburg and we drove over to the campus in Saltsburg. Monty and Billie Clark had made room for her in the Headmaster's house where three other G.I.s and I lived on the third floor. Billie suggested that I wear Monty's tuxedo and I must say that I looked quite good in it. The house was all decked out for the holidays and Billie had a nice spread of food and punch for the group of us. The other guys also invited their girlfriends for the event. I was standing in the kitchen when Monty came along and complimented me on my tux. He didn't know that Billie had given me his to wear. The dance was lovely. Carol and I danced together all evening and then returned to the Clark's home where we felt so welcome. Monty and Billie went upstairs to bed, the other guys disappeared and the two of us were left alone. It was a nice way to end a perfect evening, just enjoying each other's company. I felt that somehow we would remain together.

One time when Carol had made the trip to Youngwood, the movie playing in Greensburg was *On the Boardwalk in Atlantic City.* We enjoyed seeing it and spending time with Mom and Dad and Doris back home in Youngwood. Another get together was when the Taylors came for a visit. While the financial circumstances of the two families differed, it became apparent to both sets of parents that their kids were in love and wanted to marry.

We were engaged on Valentine's Day, 1947 in New York City. I put her ring in a little box and placed it in the bottom of a small cage containing a canary. The caged bird, placed behind a picture standing on the mantle of the fireplace in the tiny studio where Carol lived, could not remain hidden for long. I could hardly wait for her to find it when the little bird chirped. Carol went over and took the cage down and discovered the ring box all covered with bird droppings. This turned out to be quite an event in the famous Tenth Street Artist's Studio building where a gala reception was held soon after in our honor. We have pictures of ourselves and our parents with me on my knee proposing. The bird cage rested on Carol's lap.

Our marriage took place a month later at the Taylor home in Glen Rock, New Jersey. My war buddy, Jim Harkins, served as my best man. Mom and Dad and my Aunt Lucy Wilt and cousin Adel Wilt represented my family. Elaine, one of the Red Cross Girls from Korea, attended the wedding. Doris filled the role of flower girl and Betty Love served as the Carol's maid of honor. Carol's next door neighbor, Alan Beasley, recorded the ceremony and comments by guests. Carol's music teacher played selections on the piano given to Carol by her grandmother, a piano still in our possession. Plenty of good food and drink added to the enjoyment.

We made our way in the family Buick back down the pike to the Boardwalk in Atlantic City and to the Colton Manor Hotel. The city by the sea became the town where we returned every time we could manage. Bosky (named Roland Montgomery after Monty Clark) and Robin arrived and we took them along with us on several return trips. This all took place before the city became the Las Vegas of the East. We haven't been back for some time now. Maybe we'll make it for one of our wedding anniversaries.

The little Tenth Street Studio became our first home with a rent of $30 per month. The only heat we needed came from a small pot-belly stove and we walked to the floor above and way down a hall to the toilet. Rumors of a ghost made middle of the night trips sorta scary. Fortunately our bladders held out longer in those days of our youth.

Columbia College accepted me for the winter term beginning that February. Carol earned slightly less than $300 per month nursing at the Columbia Presbyterian Hospital at 168th Street. That first semester at Columbia, I failed four out of five courses and needed to repeat them all the second semester, except Sex Education, the only course I passed. I found it very difficult to study and make love at the same time, both being urgent goals. I kept practicing.

We remained close friends with Monty and Billie Clark for the remainder of their lives. They would visit us on their summer trips north from their retirement home in Clearwater Beach, Florida and Bosky (Monty, Jr.) and I visited them once and went canoeing with Monty. They brought together several Kiski boys one evening and we chatted about our days together on campus. Both of the Clarks continued to be strong influences in my life and supported my decision to become a teacher. Monty urged me to consider returning to the Kiski School in a teaching position, but that never worked out. My focus was the East Coast. I still wanted to be rich and Monty assisted me in securing an advertising job in New York City, but fortunately, that didn't last. My lifetime career in education was soon to begin and I relentlessly began the climb up the ladder of success.

In this picture, the Glenn family is reunited in Atlantic City in October, 1947. Myrtle Egner Glenn (mother) and Raymond McCrea Glenn (father) sit behind their son, Roland, and daughter (Doris).

Part VII

After the War

The Tenth Street
Studio Building

THE TENTH STREET STUDIO BUILDING, built in 1856 on the north side of the street just east of Sixth Avenue became one of the earliest buildings to house artists in Greenwich Village. In the book *Greenwich Village and How It Got That Way* by Terry Miller, the historic structure is described "as the brainchild of art collector John Taylor Johnson who felt that artists would create greater works in well-designed surroundings. The three floors of the building featured eight studios each around a central atrium providing light. Winslow Homer called this "an atmosphere of comradeship" when he moved into the building in 1872. John La Farge certainly agreed because he remained in residence for more than 50 years. Emanuel Leutz, the painter of *Washington Crossing the Delaware*, lived in the studio building for a time, as did painter Eastman Johnson and sculptor Augustus Saint-Gaudens. Here actor Edwin Booth posed in 1863 as Hamlet for a life-sized bronze bust executed by his friend, Launt Thompson. The Studio was also the boyhood home of Alexander Calder, the inventor of the mobile, whose sculptor father, A. Stirling Calder created the *Washington in Peace* sculpture that has graced the west pedestal of the Washington Square Arch since 1918.

It took me a while to learn of this building's illustrious past after Carol and I began our life together in one small room during the late 1940s. Carol's mother, Zillah Taylor, became the Building Manager before our marriage and would regale us with stories about those early resident artists as we dined with her and Carol's father, Amos, in front of the warm coals of a Franklin stove, sipping sherry wine from cranberry

glasses, still in our possession. Mom Taylor prepared steak dinners to for-
tify us. We were poor but very happy kids without too much responsibility, enjoying just being together and doing whatever we felt like. On the
spur of the moment, we would take the subway to Times Square and see
some wonderful Broadway shows for a couple of bucks by going to the
box offices just after the curtains rose. Victor Borge, Ethel Merman, John
Raitt, Beatrice Lilly, Lunt and Fontaine. Or we would hop a Fifth Avenue
bus and ride the full length of Manhattan on the open-air top. The Studio Building, now past its prime, was a bit dusty but our lives were enriched by coming to know the artists who lived there. It was a cast of
colorful characters.

The arrangement of the studios around a central exhibition hall on
the first floor allowed the artists to open their doors when receptions were
held. The prospective customers could walk from studio to studio to ad-
mire the works of art and hopefully make their purchases. The unique design fostered both the creative and commercial needs of the artists.
Thankfully for us, Carol's mother always kept an eye out for a bargain.
Some of them still hang on our walls today.

Fabulous parties were held in the Studios while we lived there in tiny
Number 7, the smallest of nearly 25 working studios. George Barkinton,
Sr., famous for his restorations of classical paintings at the Metropolitan
Museum, and his son, George, Jr., a noted fashion photographer and his
wife, Jessica, a leading model, hosted an elite group of Broadway stars, art
critics, and supporters of the arts at their frequent parties. On New Year's
Eve, in the massive central studio, tables filled with delicacies would be
surrounded by clusters of beautifully dressed people in formal attire or
flamboyant costumes. David Wayne, appearing in *Finian's Rainbow*, would
captivate audiences in one corner while a ballet group performed in another, accompanied by live musicians. Occasionally, Joe DiMaggio, accompanied by Marilyn Monroe, came for a visit with the Barkintons. And
it was common to meet the then-president of Columbia University, Ike
Eisenhower, walking up to the third-floor studio of Tommy Stevens, who
gave the General painting lessons. Ike became president of Columbia the
year I entered and I joked that we were both freshmen. Not everyone at
Columbia liked the idea of a war hero becoming the president, but I
thought it to be nothing short of great. Carol and I became his strong supporters during the "I Like Ike" presidential campaign. The Taylors were
staunch Republicans. That campaign stands out in my memory as the real
beginning of my interest in politics. We wouldn't appreciate the intellec-
tual abilities of Adlai Stevenson until much later on.

No recollection of the culture of the Tenth Street Studio Building would be complete without the Building Superintendent, Larry Montelioni, who resided in the building's cellar. The cellar had served as a gathering place for artists to eat, and Larry carried on this tradition. He kept a large coal stove going at all times, usually with a pot of tomato sauce bubbling on the top and fresh bread baking in the oven. Larry had a large personality in a wiry, small body and he had adopted many of the residents, who would sit around his table drinking glass after glass of red wine and eating platters of his spaghetti. Larry liked to prepare meals for Carol and me, sensing that we needed plenty of nourishment. We did.

We spent hours down in that basement with Larry and Percy "The Horse" Ivory, a cowboy from California turned artist who was one of the last owners of the building. Percy knocked out paintings on short notice for the *Saturday Evening Post* magazine covers, sometimes with a deadline of less than a week. There were about 20 artists in Manhattan who gladly took on this job and generated paintings that now are representative of the ashcan period of early twentieth century painting. Fortunately, he gave Carol's mother two of these fine works of art, now in our possession. We value them. One oil painting is of Columbus Circle at Christmas, painted by Percy Ivory, and the other is of a lovely, shady Greenwich Village garden on West 11th Street, painted by Lou Brown's husband. I can still see Percy dressed in jeans, and a western style shirt with a bandanna around his neck, pulling himself up to full height and telling us stories about his life on his horse in the Wild West. He gave Carol a small oil of a cowboy on a horse that we like to believe is a self portrait. His own studio, known as "The Black Hole of Calcutta," barely provided enough space to walk, with its horde of overstuffed furniture, stuffed animal heads, easels, stacked paintings and bric-a-brac of every description along with heavy drapes on the windows. On New Year's Day, Percy's hot rum punch burbled away on a table draped with tapestry, with roasts of ham and slices of rare beef. We retreated to this den to recover from the Barkinton party of the night before.

On the building's second floor, in another large studio with a balcony for sleeping, lived flamboyant Russian painter, Feador Rimsky. His room, with museum quality armor, a candelabra, massive furniture, a brass samovar and a stage at one end, enabled him to paint models who posed in various stages of undress. He hired me to pose for a massive triptych to glorify World War II combat veterans. I bought a combat uniform and other gear to wear for these painting sessions that went on for hours. Fortunately, the hourly pay helped out. Feador aspired to have these three huge paintings hang in the National Gallery in Washington, D.C., a goal never realized. Feador, considered a master painter to those who knew him, never received the notoriety he coveted. Possibly his greatest accomplishment turned out to be an infant son. Sadly, Carol and I lost contact with this wonderful, loving man and we haven't a clue what happened to the painting of me in steel helmet, combat fatigues, and ammunition belt, with an M-1 rifle.

Down the hall from the Rimsky studio, Stow Wengenroth produced his delicate lithographs, four of which now hang on our walls. How fortunate we were to get to know Stow and his wife, Edith Flack Ackley, who hand-crafted dolls, one of which we own. Carol's mother had befriended the Wengenroths and their studio became one of our frequent places to visit.

Next to the Wengenroth studio lived dear Cliff Saber, an accomplished commercial photographer and painter. We didn't appreciate him as much when a fire swept through his studio one night, ignited from a cigarette on a couch where he had been reclining with one of his models. Young Barkinton and I were able to enter the burning room and save a whole cabinet with over 100 photographs. We didn't know what we'd saved until we laid them all out on the floor of Barkinton's ground floor studio. It turned out to be the first large exhibit of pornography I'd ever seen. Barkinton quickly closed the studio doors so that the police wouldn't find the photographs, and gave the two of us more time to casually appreciate the prints. Barkington and I dried the photos discreetly and after careful inspection, filed them away for safekeeping. Carol and I do own a watercolor painted by Cliff, depicting a deed to an acre of land in Redding, Connecticut. It was given to us by Carol's parents.

The Italian sculptor, Leo Lentelli and his tiny wife, Mimi, had a dusty studio containing a giant sculpted horse. Leo thought big and created massive sculptures for public squares. He gave us a wedding present of a horse that now stands on Carol's piano. We also have one of his wall plaques depicting Lincoln on a horse. Leo and Mimi were lovable people and we were always warmly welcomed at their studio.

Lou Brown and her friend, Mame, often invited us to a formal English tea seated at the window of their studio that overlooked the 11th street garden, painted by Percy. Lou was the wife of James Francis Brown, whose famous painting of George Washington hung on one wall of the studio. Lou and Mame went to their country place on weekends much to Mame's objections. She didn't like the country. On a typical Monday morning, when they pulled up in Lou's old car, Mame could be heard to remark, "Oh, that wonderful smell of carbon monoxide."

While we still lived in tiny Studio Number 7, our canary "Poppa Bird" sang away in his cage on a windowsill overlooking an air shaft. We dined on a small, drop-leaf table by candlelight most evenings when we weren't down in the cellar sponging off Larry. Our nesting instincts took hold and we bought a mate for "Poppa Bird". The two birds fell in love, built a nest and before long took turns sitting on the tiny eggs. The promising development didn't happen. "Momma Bird" didn't take to domestic living and refused to sit on the eggs. She finally kicked them out of the nest and our efforts to breed canaries ended abruptly. I've often thought about trying again. I still love birds.

Just inside the front door to the Tenth Street Studio building, a small office served as the nerve center where my mother-in-law, Zillah, presided. She filled the role of Queen Bee of the building and kept financial records for many of the artists. Just as Larry's basement had become the eating hub of the building, Zillah's little office became the building's communication center. Many transactions took place under "Zilch's" supervision. Percy Ivory always referred to her as "Zilch," a nickname she didn't appreciate but withstood because of her affection for Percy. They were both story-tellers and connivers ready to score the next deal.

A very small front porch stoop graced the entrance to the studio building. Two benches on opposite sides were adequate for about four people to sit and chat and bid good day to neighbors passing by, some of whom would pause for a rest and an exchange of local gossip. One of the infamous Greenwich Village regulars, Romany Marie, visited frequently.

One day, a very large crate arrived at the front office. Mother Taylor thought it must contain a large canvas for one of the artists until she saw the addressee listed as Carol. She called us down and opened the lid and we all stared at a gigantic stuffed sailfish. This monster had cost us $100 to have stuffed and shipped up from West Palm Beach, Florida where we had spent our honeymoon. The fish traveled with us from home to home and always took up an entire wall wherever we hung it. Its final destination in Westport, Connecticut ended that fish story when someone broke into our studio and stole the monster. Now, whenever we dine in a seafood place that displays a sailfish, we claim that it must be our fish.

The strength of Zillah Taylor's relationship with Percy Ivory didn't stop Percy from finally and sadly engineering the sale of the historic building after some years. Many of the artists were co-owners of the property and all of them needed the cash more than the work space. That co-ownership hardly seems possible now. The prospect of turning their shares into money became too enticing to them and a vote was passed to sell the building. The sale would terminate the building's rich history when the wrecking ball arrived before New York City had passed a law preserving historic structures. A garish, mediocre and uninspired brick apartment building now stands in the spot once occupied by the Tenth Street Studio building.

Our lives were filled with interesting people during this period of the late 1940s. The Goodmans, who lived across the street at Number 52, became lifelong friends. We started to have kids at the same time and watched our kids grow year after year until they began to have their own children. The days spent visiting together on Tenth Street, out at their summer home in Sag Harbor, and in Boston have kept us close and enriched our friendship. Two other friends of that period, Ruth and Max Lunan, lived near the Columbia University campus. Ruth Lunan and Carol were nurses and Dr. Max became an ear specialist. Entertaining one another was one the joys of those days when none of us had much of an income, yet all of us felt rich. Life couldn't have been better.

Then something happened that would take my life on a very different course for a number of years.

Reliving the War
on a Couch

I FIRST MET WILLIAM F. MARVIN one evening in 1947 at the Cooper Union in New York City. Zillah had invited Carol and me to a lecture on the subject of early childhood education. At that time, I'd been accepted as an undergraduate majoring in anthropology at Columbia College. Teaching young children was the furthermost thing from my list of goals. My vision was to become a scientist and explore ancient cultures with my wife in far flung corners of the earth. The exotic experiences of my time in Korea were not that far in the past. Attending a lecture by an unknown child psychologist was more to humor Mom Taylor than to stimulate my interest in kids. However, she wasn't too keen on my plan to take her daughter off to foreign lands.

As Mr. Marvin began to talk about his views on teaching young children, I found myself becoming interested in his theory and firmly held belief that every child wants to learn. All you needed to do in helping a child become excited about learning was to custom make an educational program based upon that individual child's personal interests. This struck me as being a very novel approach. It certainly wasn't like that when I went to school. Marvin advocated individualized approaches rather than forcing children to conform to classroom standards geared to all students learning the same things and at the same time, often by rote memory drills. By the end of his lecture I felt that I wanted to talk with him privately about his theories. He agreed to see me a few days later at his office.

In my mind, I hadn't connected the dots between the fact that I was waking up screaming in a cold sweat from nightmares of combat and my

William F. Marvin became my first psychologist in late 1947. I worked with him for five years at his office on West 9th Street in New York City. Bill was the first person to really listen to my war stories. He helped me to better understand and come to terms with the massive killing of human beings that I experienced during the battle for Okinawa. (Photo courtesy of Glenn Family archives)

interest to talking with Bill Marvin about teaching. He quickly detected that my mind held more to talk about than exploring his educational philosophy. Before I recognized or admitted to myself the hidden agenda, I found that Bill Marvin's interest in my army experience drew me into telling stories about my life during the years 1943–1947. On one occasion when telling him about the Okinawa battles, I broke out into a sweat. He placed a thermometer into my mouth and got a reading of 104 degrees. The following morning, waking drenched in sweat and trembling, Carol took me over to a medical clinic for blood tests that revealed I carried malaria. While being treated for this war-related illness, I began to see William Marvin on a regular three times a week schedule, paying his fee of $5 an hour which was pretty steep for me as an unemployed college student. My sessions were increased to 5 times a week during that first year of therapy. For the next five years of my life, Bill Marvin became the first person to hear my war stories. My family preferred not to hear about the horrors that I'd experienced.

Bill Marvin's excitement about teaching young children eventually influenced me to switch my college major from Anthropology at Columbia College to Early Childhood Education at New York University for my Masters Degree. The period of the early 1950s, saw my career as an educator take off. I became employed teaching at St. Bernard's School on East 98th Street in New York City and immediately found success working with young children. Over the years, I progressed from classroom teaching to teaching teachers at New York University and Bank Street College of Education. That led to my directing the Antheil School in Ewing, New Jersey and eventually entering the early childhood industry at Creative Playthings, Inc. in Princeton, New Jersey as Vice President, Director of Research and head of The Learning Center. These professional moves dramatically increased my income, enabling me to pay for my therapy sessions in the mid 1950s at $75 per hour. Bill Marvin and I relived the war several times during that five year period while I became a specialist in early childhood education.

My success as an educator, however, didn't mask my experiences in combat. Sometimes, during therapy, my throat would tend to close as I related incidents of killing Japanese on Okinawa. I simply couldn't speak about the lingering horrors. Bill encouraged me to draw pictures of my experiences in combat. I produced drawings at home and brought them to my therapy sessions with Bill. When I looked at a picture that I'd drawn of a dead Japanese, I could tell the story of what happened on the battlefield.

My biggest hurdle dealt with guilt stemming from my killing the young, severely wounded Japanese soldier behind a boulder on the top of a cliff. This incident, close to the end of combat, differed from the massive killings that had taken place during the many attacks on enemy positions. In those battles, I blazed away with my men, cutting down whole groups of the enemy. This case was different. I'd felt the boy's heart stop beating, and covered his body with ferns. Bill and I struggled long and hard in dealing with the guilt I felt from this one incident. Finally, agony partially lifted through my educational work with a young Japanese boy who attended the Heathcote School in Scarsdale, New York, where I worked to craft individualized programs for special children. His father, a diplomat at the United Nations, brought him to me for tutoring. Bill enabled me to see that my efforts at helping this one Japanese boy could release me from the guilt that I carried from the earlier incident. That technique only partially worked. I'm still haunted by the face of the man I killed.

Through therapy I'd come to deal with what today is called Post Traumatic Stress Disorder. That term didn't exist in 1950. The relationship, however, between the working of my brain and the rest of my body became clear to me during therapy. What was buried in my psyche also affected the workings of the rest of my body. The malaria came out in full force as I relived the war. My guts went into an upheaval often during that period and still are a problem. That I escaped having a stomach ulcer is a miracle. My heart eventually partially died. A cardiac episode once occurred during a therapy session landing me in the hospital for three angioplasty procedures. I survived once again.

The other major aspect of my therapy with Bill Marvin was dealing with my sexuality. I couldn't get Sungja out of my head. I dreamt about the times I spent with her. All that fucking was different than what I was experiencing sexually with my wife. Fortunately, I came to understand that the recreational sex I enjoyed with Sungja actually helped me to become a better lover with my wife. My relationship with Carol helped me to make the mental/physical connection between sex and love. I'd found a woman with deep feelings toward me, an entirely different experience than what I enjoyed with Sungja.

But there were all those memories of the exotic times spent with Sungja in Korea. What to do with those sexy feelings for a prostitute on the other side of the earth? I don't know exactly how this happened but I invented a fictitious character that I called Captain Conway. While making love to my wife, I told fantasy stories to her about the exploits of this daring young Captain. The technique worked. I found it possible to share those sexual adventures with my wife to our mutual enjoyment. That Captain Conway was quite a guy. He became our friend in bed.

By the time I returned home from Korea in 1947 as a decorated officer, I'd become a young adult ready for college, marriage and parenthood. But first I needed to relive the war on a therapy couch by not being afraid to tell these stories, not glossing over what was terrifying about World War II, and not forgetting what was good in my relationships with family, fellow soldiers and the young Korean woman.

Marriage, raising children and climbing the ladder of success consumed my successful adult life until I retired, now an old man, first to a seaside wilderness on Cape Cod and then to the coast of southern Maine. Finally I'd found a place where the beauty of nature replaced scenes of killing. We lived in a glass house called Umimatsu, located within the Cape Cod National Seashore in Wellfleet. A knarled pine tree reminded me of the one at my Japanese house in Taejon. One room, heated by a Korean fireplace, had a sunken tub in the brick floor. A huge greenhouse room called the Japanese Pavilion was planted with blooming camellia trees. At night we'd sit by a log fire while a mist from the ceiling fell upon the trees. The goldfish and frogs swam from outside our breakfast room to our feet inside through a figure eight pool that ran beneath the massive glass walls. Here at this very special place, I relived my exotic times of Korea. Only this time I shared the beauty with a woman I loved. It is impossible for me to describe a more peaceful setting.

Climbing the Ladder
of Success

IF I HAVE HEARD THE WORDS "climbing the ladder of success" once, I have heard them a thousand times. Sometimes I suddenly wake up believing my mother has said to me, "Keep your eye on the next rung of the ladder." At age 16, when I got my first job as a cashier at Idlewild Park that paid $12.50 per week, Mom Glenn patted me on the back, "Work hard now and you will be able to reach the next rung." I hadn't even collected my first weekly check when she pointed out that by working harder in collecting all those tickets I would impress my boss and probably get a raise. And, she was right. I did.

Every time I got a raise, I focused on the next rung and kept climbing and climbing. When I became a Private in the Army, I sought to become a Corporal. After being commissioned as a Second Lieutenant, the next rung would be a promotion to First Lieutenant, and then to Captain. As a classroom teacher, I sought to become a school principal. The logical next step was to become a Professor of Education at a leading university. I made that with ease. And, the next rung of the ladder led me from being vice president of a company to becoming president. My office was on the 30th floor of a New York City skyscraper overlooking the East River and the United Nations buildings.

Mom was sitting out in the garden when I returned home that night with news of my promotion. After I had described the office and the view, she said, "That is wonderful news, Roland. Do you suppose that there is a better office on the 31st floor? You should go up there and take a look. And you should go and buy yourself a new suit if you are going to be president." I told her that I was not going to be President of the United States but just of a small company. She replied, "It doesn't matter, you should look like the President. Go and buy a new suit." I did. My repeated successes were recognized but I felt unable to satisfy her.

Years later, when she lay dying and was no longer able to communicate, I whispered into her ear, "Mom, this is Rollie. We are all here with you. I love you, Mom." She gave a flicker of recognition. I imagine that her reply might have been, "I love you too and remember when I am gone, keep climbing the ladder of success." She still lives inside of me and always will. She speaks to me through dreams. I still carry out some of the family rituals that she taught me over the years.

From the time I was a little kid, and then an adolescent, and a young adult, my life had been controlled by a set of myths which had been drummed into my head by the culture of the times. Work hard! Get ahead! Make money! Seek a promotion! Get married! Have children! Build a house! Build another! Build! Build! Build! Become famous by the time you are 40 or at least become a doctor!

I didn't become famous or decide on medicine as a career. However, I did accomplish all of those other objectives. There was just one thing missing. I didn't work hard enough to provide the time, early on, to find out who I really was. I lived out several lives before this insight struck home. The bright student. The heroic soldier. The natural-born teacher. The sharp dresser. The hard-drinking business executive. The public service expert. The understanding advisor to so many. The very busy and loving husband and father. In all of these roles, I worked from dawn to dusk. And, I must admit that I had a very, very good time. I did some powerfully good work in those various roles. I now consider myself a fortunate man to have had such diverse experiences.

Psychoanalysis helped me to identify all of those myths which were controlling my existence. It probably saved my life. I was able to discard some of those grand objectives that had been doing me more harm than good. Other healthier objectives have replaced them. But even those can cause me to act out old patterns of behavior. Work hard at planting flowers. Look ahead to plan the next renovation project on the house. Get up early to avoid wasting time by sleeping my life away. Count my money to make certain that I have enough. Write fast before it is too late to tell all the stories. Work actively on community projects because I am so good at it. Participate! Participate! Participate! Visit more old and new friends than I have the time for, lest they forget that I am here. Assume more and more responsibility because I feel compelled to take it on.

It wasn't easy to break old habits even when the culture had shifted. The 1960s and 1970s attacked most of what I had been taught as a child. The work ethic was out. Being yourself was in. Making huge amounts of money was seen as a sin. Living like a vagabond became acceptable. Having large families was not considered desirable or necessary. One kid or no kid meant assuming less responsibility. Patriotism sucked. Ridiculing the government was the "in" thing to do.

Was it possible to strike a compromise between burning myself out versus putting all of the emphasis on self-gratification? Could I live by a set of rules that are more nourishing to the body and soul while still making a contribution to my community? Could I be true to myself? Could I be honest about who I really am? Being somewhat of an incurable optimist, I said, "Yes, it can be done." But it required that I get in touch with my own cultural history.

This is one of the reasons I am writing. I need to recognize and deal with all of the principles that were taught to me during the early years within my family and the society in which I functioned. I need to find comfort with my true identity. Others won't really care, but I will for the balance of my life.

Working on community projects often leads to new associations. Some of those associations lead to valuable new friendships. The ability to reach out and form friendships has provided me with love. Love fosters more energy. And so, the cycle continues. Hard work is not necessarily bad for me. To be making a contribution to my community is an act of creative giving. Those of us who are fortunate enough to have the capacity to do that should rejoice in the fact that we have those abilities. But we should know what we are doing with our lives. It should be a conscious act. The adopted roles we assume should be based upon our own decisions, not those imposed by our society. That is not always easy to do.

My mother's ambition for me to succeed probably stemmed out of her fear of poverty. That precept of being considered worthless put more mental stress on me for accomplishment. She wanted to help me to make a break from the circumstances of the depression. She didn't want to see her son immobilized like his father by being unable to make a good living. The fact that she always kept that damn ladder directly in front of me is something that I can now understand and appreciate. I no longer foster that myth as a controlling dynamic in my life. I am able to substitute another.

My love for Mom Glenn has become even stronger as I grasp more fully what that loving woman was really about during her lifetime. I am at peace concerning my relationship with her.

The decisions that I currently make for myself may not be right for members of my family and friends. I can observe them climbing to higher levels and enjoying all of the benefits. But I believe that they are smarter than I was in discovering earlier in their lives that the air at the top can get a bit thin. Nevertheless, just as I was molded by the myths which prevailed years ago, my children, grandchildren and younger friends are now being affected by the myths of their own early lives. They need to figure out what to discard and what to retain. I trust them to make their own decisions. We each have our own set of half-memories. There is still time to talk, compare notes, learn from past experience, experiment, and be supportive of one another. I may have difficulty with some of their decisions and enthusiastically applaud others. But if we all don't take some risks, nothing will happen.

When one approaches the later years of one's life, there's a tendency to take stock and ask yourself this question, how did I do? In my case the answer is, pretty well. I soared to rarified heights, sunk to some regrettable lows, learned to love, and became more comfortable inside my own skin. I am still reaching out to others, not knowing just when I might meet my best friend ever. There are others who were dear to me who took with them their own half-memories of our times together, leaving me with my own half-loaf while remembering how sweet it was when the cup remained full.

Window On My Soul

JUST BEFORE DAWN I pulled my feet out of bed and touched them down on the small hooked rug that my daughter, Heather, had made for me a number of years ago. The marvel of being alive in this seaside wilderness struck me. Framed by the large window at the foot of the bed, I saw a translucent oblong of blue light with the faintest hairline separating sea and sky. I'm a morning person. Those early minutes of each day are a special time for me. Carol encourages me to keep moving so that we lose no time in getting down by the sea where we walk with our golden retrievers, Beau and Salt Water Taffy. This early morning walk by the water is part of my recovery program following my heart attack. It is Carol who is gently pushing me to get going and do the exercising the doctors have recommended. Walk, walk, walk. That is the route to my recovery.

A huge boulder rising out of the water helps me to measure the distance of these walks. Once I was so weak that I could not even walk to it. Now I am able to go a considerable distance past it. The dogs and Carol are my support. They urge me to go a bit further each morning. I'm feeling stronger every day, beginning to recognize who I really am and what is important. My body is healing. All of those past titles have been cast aside, captain, teacher, vice president, president, director. I'm now recognizing who Roland Glenn is without those official designations. The love coming from my family, friends, and the dogs helps me to see through the fog.

We carry breakfast in a shoulder bag and eventually stop and sit on a large log that has been washed up to shore. That first taste of hot tea and an English muffin satisfies all the needs of the moment. We bring a biscuit or two for the dogs. There is so much to see at this special place. We sit quietly and take it all in. The rest of the world lies at our back as the sun rises before us. This space is ours. I think of my friend, Wil Wimberg, who has taken early morning walks with me in years past. He is, no doubt, up early and walking or riding his bike somewhere in Egypt where he is teaching. I have missed him this past year. I miss others who were a part of my life. But they will wait for me while I heal myself in this beautiful, isolated place. Right now I need the solitude. I need to be alone with Carol and the dogs. The future will take care of itself. There will be new experiences and people in the future if I just get well.

A light fog shrouds this area where we walk, sit, and think. The sand is firm under our feet as we go about collecting stones and beach glass to place among the flowers in a new little garden we are creating outside our kitchen door. The two of us are enjoying doing things together and being alone. We have been given more precious time to enjoy and love one another.

We train the dogs as we take these walks practicing stops, starts, right and left turns, and more. Beau is entering a more advanced stage of his training and now obeys the commands with a big grin on his face. Taffy is still acting like a baby who doesn't want to settle down to any serious business. We have decided to move both dogs into obedience work and field training. Beau looks like a great working dog and should be allowed to follow the hunting and retrieving instincts of his breed. He learns very fast but Taffy is still distracted by bugs and blowing paper.

The powerful North Atlantic is my muse. As I walk, I begin to compose in my head and sometimes come up with a few lines of poetry. Or, I suddenly remember something that has happened in the distant past. The breeze is fresh but without a chill as we walk close to the waves. Our glasses become blurred. Our hair becomes wet from the heavy mist and looks like grass covered with dew. Suddenly, the whole beach is bathed in the yellow warmth of the summer sun as it burns through the fog and is reflected against the high dune cliffs. It feels like the first day of the Creation.

We watch the high waves as they approach. The sun shines right through them. All of a sudden we see large fish swimming within the waves. It is like a gigantic aquarium has been created before our eyes. There are hundreds of these fish. Beau leaps into the water, dives under the surface, and comes up with a bluefish in his mouth. He is so proud of himself. The great hunter, he settles down on the sand and eats every bit of it. Taffy doesn't get a single bite.

The cliffs along this stretch of Wellfleet beach are taller than at any other point in the Cape Cod National Seashore. But even these giants have been crumbled and eroded by harsh winter storms. The sea pounds at their base and undermines their gigantic formations. Tons of sand has been swept away by the tremendous force to other locations along the shore.

The valley behind the dunes has a special trail that we like to follow on our return walk from the water. This path passes between the gorse and heather among the twisting brambles and stunted pines. In some places it dwindles to a thin thread of sand. At one secret spot there is a log bench which was built by an old man so that he and others might rest for a moment or two while looking out at the sea. This wild shore area is a perfect environment for both sea and land birds. The habits of these creatures are of greater interest to me than some of the larger issues of the day. I have isolated myself and withdrawn from the concerns of society like a wounded animal seeking seclusion deep in the forest. Healing is my major concern.

As we finished our early morning walk and headed back to our house in the pines on a hillside overlooking the ocean, there was still a haze on the horizon which could be either sky or sea. I found myself thinking of another walk which I took years ago with my father. My muse, the sea, began to work with me as lines began to take form in my head.

A Walk In the
Woods with Dad

I.

I would like to walk in the woods with you
Along a twisting path.
And, climb over huge boulders and scale steep cliffs,
To see the view at last.
I want to smell our evening meal
Cooked over a fire by a tent,
From things we have collected ourselves
Before our energy was spent.
The spot ahead we might enjoy the most
Is difficult to find.
The map is wrinkled and parts of it gone,
But maybe it's left in our mind.
Your quiet grace, I enjoy the most.
It offsets the rattle in me.
But, maybe as we come to the end of the trail,
We will chop away at the same tree.
If suddenly you get the urge to walk,
And would rather not go alone,
I would like to be there,
And jointly share the space we both feel in our bones.

II.

I walked awhile with someone I loved
Along a forest path.
He was old and grey and hungry
To share in a belly laugh.
We nearly didn't take the walk,
But just before the end
We found ourselves together
At the opening of a glen.

The species and sounds that he revealed to me
Had been there for many a year.
But I hadn't even noticed
Nor hardly opened my ear.
I was startled at first by this discovery,
Of what lay deep inside
This quiet, gentle fellow
Who helped make up my own hide.
The walk was short, we started late.
And at the very end,
We both knew we had made it,
And could now rest hand in hand.

III.

You caused me to think of this brief walk,
In the shadows, under trees, and by brooks,
With a man who was gentle and tender to touch,
And who lived like the inside of books.
He had covers around the guts of the tale,
Not saying whatever he thought,
For fear he might be stricken down,
By someone else's looks.
I wonder why it took so long
To understand his plight.
But it didn't seem to matter,
Once the trail came into light.

IV.

The briefness of the encounter
Didn't concern him nor me,
For the feelings we had for each other
As we lay there were given quite free . . .
On the moss, by the logs, along the twisting path,
Where we saw the view at last.
While we relished all the memories of the evening meals,
Cooked in those years so rapidly gone past.
But, I think that he felt, if only he could
Extend the time at the last.
There was more to reveal, that those covers concealed,
Which, for me, he wished to unclasp.
I often wish that I had taken the time, and the moments as they came by,
To look into that glen so near to me, and spend the time so dear to me,
With the fellow who gave this ear to me
And opened up as those final moments flashed by.

V.

The spot ahead you might enjoy the most, can be difficult to find.
The time is short and parts of it gone,
But the roots are still there and will continue to bear
When the birds start up their Spring song.
Your quiet grace I enjoy the most.
It offsets the rattle in me.
I hope you will continue to walk the trail,
A stong woodsman still chopping his tree.
But, if you ever get the urge to share
And would rather not go it alone,
I would like to be there
To jointly share the feelings that stem from our bones.

The Hawk
and the Dove

EVERY DAY, FOR an hour or two, I go to my special, private place where I do not concern myself with anything important. Bills to be paid and checks to be written are set aside and not permitted to enter into my consciousness. These transactions of daily life are less important to dwell upon than the realization that I'm still alive, having survived a war and a severe heart attack, both of which might have taken me. I've been provided with more time to think about my life and what I'm doing with it. Sitting at my writing desk makes me feel at peace, like when I walk along a deserted beach or through a forest.

What I'm trying to find is a personal peace. The only intrusions that I permit are of my own or nature's choosing. I have decided to lean toward the light rather than the dark. But even when alone at my special spot, I can't totally protect myself from pain. There are times when I still fear death. The horrible memories of being in combat return to haunt me. The frightening experience of lying immobilized in the emergency room following my heart attack in 1985 sends shivers up and down my spine.

As best I can, I try to put these thoughts out of my mind. The scene, which is now before my eyes on this extraordinary spring day, is not of a bloody battlefield or a sterile hospital room filled with electronic equipment. It looks much more like my imagined view of heaven than of hell. Even when surrounded by all this beauty, God seems to sit on one side of me and the Devil on the other. Both tempt me with what they have to offer during this remaining period of my life.

On this early spring day, the tips of the bulbs are beginning to show. The buds are beginning to swell with a hint that blossoms will soon follow. Male doves can be easily distinguished from the females that they follow. They all have been touched by Eros. This is also true of the jays, the finches that have already begun to build their nests, the woodpeckers that chase insects in the crevices of tree trunks, and the red-wing blackbirds that have just arrived only a day or two behind the robins. A covey of quail and several doves scratch the ground for seeds. Copulation and the quest for food appear to drive these beautiful birds.

How soon will the mild weather arrive? It's only a matter of days, even hours now that the ice will have melted and the winds will have died down and gone away. The air is warming us all. It's about to lure us into a frenzy of activity that we have been dreaming about while our bodies and our souls hunkered down and rested during the cold period of winter.

Suddenly, a very large red-tailed hawk descends from the sky and rests upon a branch just a few feet before me. Pictures of such a bird aren't nearly as beautiful as this splendid living creature. The bird's eyes sparkle with an intense purpose. The red and bronze spotted plumage reflects the rays of the early morning sun rising over the ocean horizon. The sharp talons and curved beak are clearly outlined against the dark branches of the tree. It's a privilege to be so close to this great bird that usually rides the currents of air high in the sky as it soars over pine forests and crashing waves of the North Atlantic.

Before I have time to think or react, the hawk suddenly turns from me, looks at the ground, and dives toward a dove. In an instant this defenseless dove takes flight directly toward where I sit. I scream and wave my arms in a desperate effort to try and save the dove. It crashes into the window inches from my eyes and drops dead to the ground. An impression of its living self is left on the glass. It's as if an artist has carefully etched every feather of the outstretched wings and outlined the head, neck and feet. In an instant, art has been created out of tragedy.

In a flash, my mind races and takes me back in time. *I must save the young soldier who is trapped.* The hawk screams defiantly. *The Japanese continue to fire upon the boy.* I run from my spot in an attempt to rescue something that is already dead. *I reach him and hold him in my arms. His face is ashen, body is limp.* The hawk flies over the bank and is gone. *The enemy has retreated.* The ground, which a second ago was covered with doves, quail, jays, woodpeckers, finches, and robins, is now suddenly barren. *Blood is running from the boy's nose. I put my mouth over his in an at-*

tempt to breathe life back into him. It feels like a dark cloud has risen to block out all life from my special place. *The dove is dead as is the boy.* Has the Devil made a move and God retreated?

I jump from my writing desk and run outside the house. The dead bird is sprawled on the ground beneath the window. Blood flows from its mouth. I kneel and pick it up feeling the warmth coming from its limp body. *I pick up the dead boy and carry his slack body to a protected spot.* The shock of death has left me trembling. This abrupt end of life has brought back horrible scenes, interrupting my moments of seeking peace.

What shall I do now? The dead dove is still in my hand. I take a moment to gaze upon its beauty even in death. I walk to the edge of the bank and fling the dove high into the air as if to give it one more opportunity to fly. The feathers flutter as it glides in an ark through space.

The hawk, which has hidden itself in a bush, takes flight and attacks the dead dove as it falls to the ground. It screams at me as it flies off with the dove's body held firmly in its talons. In an instant both are gone. *I stand over the boy's body noticing how handsome he was. I pick him up in my arms again and carry him to a waiting jeep and watch as the jeep carries him away. Two of his close friends and I stand together shedding tears as we watch him disappear over a hill.*

The ground is again covered with other doves. The impression of the dead bird remains on the window glass before me as a reminder of itself before its savage death. I will never forget that boy or that bird.

Epilogue:
Okinawa Revisited

I OFTEN HAVE FANTASIES about returning to Okinawa, wondering just what I might find on that semi-tropical island, now serving as a vacation resort for the Japanese. There certainly would be the cemetery to visit where lay the remains of Peter, Harry, David, Ben and other men who served with me during the battle. A total of 12,281 American service men, 110,071 Japanese, and approximately 150,000 Okinawan civilians were killed during the battle, more than the losses of Hiroshima and Nagasaki combined. This last battle of World War II was a great human tragedy.

The burial site of the two commanding generals of the Japanese forces is now a stop on the agendas of tourists. I understand that there is a Memorial Garden dedicated to all the men who were killed during the battle, both American and Japanese.

The giant boulder behind which I killed the Japanese soldier might still be in place. And there are the numerous installations of our armed forces located around the island.

In his book, *Sorrows of Empire*, (Metropolitan Books, Henry Wolf) Chalmers Johnson provides an overview of what the United States has established on twenty percent of the island's choicest real estate. "Like most other Americans who are not actively involved with the armed forces, I paid little attention to our empire of military bases until February 1996, when I made my first visit to our de facto American military colony of Okinawa, a small Japanese island that we have continuously occupied since 1945. My last encounter with the military had ended forty years earlier—when, in the summer of 1955, I left active duty as a naval officer in the western Pacific. In 1996, in the wake of the rape of a twelve-year old Okinawa girl by two American marines and a sailor, I was invited by the island's governor, Masahide Ota, to speak about the problem of our bases.'"

"I visited Kin village—almost totally swallowed by the marines' massive Camp Hansen, where the abduction and rape had occurred - and interviewed local officials. I came away deeply disturbed both by the Okinawan hostility and by the fact that no serious American strategy could explain the deployment of thirty-eight separate bases on the choicest 20 percent of the island."

"It was apparent from the numerous beaches, golf courses, and other recreational facilities reserved for the use of our military and the duplication involved in separate Air Force, Navy, and Marine Corps airfields that the bases had simply sprouted willy-nilly with the advent of the Cold War. No consideration had been given to equitable land use or the lives of the 1.3 million Okinawans. The military's situation in Okinawa struck me as similar to that of the Soviet troops in East Germany after the Berlin Wall came down. In both cases the troops preferred to stay on because the pleasures of life as a legionnaire in an imperial garrison far outstripped those of life back in the 'homeland.'"

"The troops and their families were happy with their clubs, apartments, gyms, swimming pools, and shopping malls (known in military argot as 'base exchanges' and undoubtedly preferred Okinawa to being stuck in small stateside towns like Oceanside, California, adjacent to the Marine Corps base at Camp Pendleton. If nothing else, the penalty for a rape conviction in California is considerably more onerous than for servicemen convicted of the same felony in Okinawa by the Japanese. Under the terms of the Status of Forces Agreement the United States imposed on Japan in 1953, the Japanese are even required to provide special meals for those few American servicemen turned over to Japanese authorities and actually imprisoned. On average there were 2,800 calories in the meals served to Japanese prisoners but 4,000 in those served to the twelve Americans jailed at the end of 2001."

"Only slowly did I come to understand that Okinawa was typical, not unique. The conditions there—expropriation of the island's most valuable land for bases, extraterritorial status for American troops who committed crimes against local civilians, bars, brothels crowding around the main gates of bases, endless accidents, noise, sexual violence, drunk-driving crashes, drug use, and environmental pollution—are replicated anywhere there are American garrisons. Compared with the numerous bases on the Japanese mainland, the more than one hundred installations in South Korea, and the huge deployments in Germany, Britain, Italy, the Balkans, the Persian Gulf, Latin America, and elsewhere, Okinawa is not unusual except in the number of bases, given the size of the island. America's military proconsuls being publicity-averse, the American press seldom visits, or reports on, its empire of bases. I had been given a glimpse into an aspect of contemporary American life that most Americans never see."

So, what's it to be, readers? We fought that last battle of World War II believing that peace had finally been achieved for the entire world for the rest of time. We really believed that the United States stood for a set of noble values. After our short, almost vacation tour of duty in Korea, many of us returned to our homes as decorated veterans. It took but a few years for the Korean War to begin, resulting in another 50,000 + American lives lost.

No sooner had the country recovered from that disaster when the Vietnam War initiated the first really gigantic American defeat on the battlefield. A few of those returning veterans became my friends while I lived on Cape Cod. One committed suicide. Another returned home an alcoholic and was never cured. He died a miserable death from liver cancer.

So now I look back on my experiences on Okinawa as a small moment in time, following a long history of American imperialism that began long before my birth in 1924 and continues to this day. The military-industrial complex is so entrenched in our economy that the survival of our democratic society is being threatened. And, sadly most Americans are not aware of what our country has done and is doing to the rest of the world.

I often have fantasies about returning to Okinawa, wondering just what I might find on that semi-tropical island, now serving as a vacation resort for the Japanese. Perhaps it is best for that trip to remain a fantasy.

Author's Notes

From *Respite and Loss*

The earlier drafts of *The Hawk and the Dove* were written as the 50th anniversary of the start of World War II was being observed. Sixty one out of 67 countries were involved. Fighting took place everywhere on earth except for Antarctica. World War II clarified where race hatred could really lead.

Six million Jews had their lives snatched from them as Hitler attempted to eliminate all Jews from the face of the earth. I'm still trying to figure out how this atrocity could have happened. We were supposedly fighting against what Hitler stood for, but in our own country, black soldiers were segregated into separate battalions and the Navy didn't even accept them at all, except as mess boys. Few recognized the irony. We were content to blame Hitler's Germany without facing the hatred being bred in our own country.

Separate whorehouses were set aside just to service black soldiers. It was un-thinkable that white guys would fuck the same whores messed over by blacks or, rather, that black soldiers would fuck the same whores used by whites.

Over 50 million people were killed before the Japanese surrendered. It was a romanticized war that put an end to a maniacal Hitler. It didn't put an end to ra-cial hatred in the United States.

The continental United States never came under attack. Our losses were only military. London, Paris, Berlin, Munich, Stalingrad, Manila, and Tokyo suffered differently than New York, Boston, Chicago, and Los Angeles. We heard a lot about how many children from England were sent to Canada and the United States to protect them from the devastation taking place in their own county. Very little has been related about what was happening to the children in Germany, the Soviet Union, Japan, or Italy. I wish that some of those now grown children would write their own stories.

I have often been asked, did you see your friends get killed? Did you ever think that it would happen to you? Did you ever kill anyone yourself?

I don't find it pleasant or easy to write about the answers to those questions. I do feel a strong need to put down exactly what happened to me and to the men who were there with me. This seems to be an appropriate time for me to get the job done.

Aside from the full reports submitted by Edward R. Murrow and Eric Severeid, it has been my feeling, until recently, that truthful reporting on the war was the exception rather than the rule. We now have the true accounts in *The Greatest Generation* and *The Greatest Generation Speaks* written by veterans and compiled by Tom Brokaw to add to the literature of personal histories. Studs Terkel's *Coming of Age* also adds to the literature of the war. Most recently a beautiful love story, *My War*, written by Tracy Sugarman provides a compelling history, in his drawings and letters to his wife, of the D-Day landing in Normandy. This precious book is not only a love story to his wife, but a gift to all of us who lived through that period.

"Follow Me" was the motto of The Infantry School at Fort Benning, Georgia. We officer candidates wore a small blue and white pin engraved with those words. I am reminded of this song which we sang mock-reverently to the tune of *Far Above Cayuga's Waters*:

> High above the Chattahoochee, And the Upatoi,
> Stands our noble Alma Mater, Benning School for Boys.
> Salt in tablets, scorching sun, Touch your toes on count of one,
> Expert, bolo, school solutions, Phoenix City institutions
> Hail to Benning, Hail to Benning, Follow Me's the cry.
> You must use the school solution. Follow me, or die.

It didn't always turn out that way.

From *A City Called Hiroshima*

The details of the feast served to Generals Ushijima and Cho, the statistics of war dead and wounded, and the photograph of the group of Okinawans were taken from *W.W.II*, a recent reissue of Time Life Book's history of the Second World War.

John Garcia and I corresponded with one another for several years following the end of the war. Eventually we lost touch. Unfortunately I do not have a picture or drawing of John to supplement his image that is etched forever in my brain, a huge man built along the lines of a sumo wrestler, his manner always easy going. Quite a character! I now regret not having his set of "half memories" to add to my own. In *The Good War, An Oral History of World War II*, Studs Terkel writes of a John Garcia from Hawaii who participated in the Okinawa campaign and includes the above description of him. I attempted to track John down with the assistance of Mr. Terkel who has since died. It is possible that John Garcia is still alive and lives somewhere in the Los Angeles area managing an apartment building. What a discovery it will be if I am able to locate him!

Lieutenant General Simon Bolivar Buckner, Jr. was one of those hard-luck generals found in every war. Just as he was ready to realize his life's ambition to walk through the rubble of Tokyo, he climbed to an observation post to watch his troops seize the last of Okinawa's ridgelines. As he gazed over the battlefield, he remarked, "Things are going so well here that I think I will move on to another unit." Five Japanese shells then struck Mezado Ridge. They exploded and filled the air with flying coral. A shard pierced General Buckner's chest and he died within a few minutes, knowing, at least, that his Tenth Army was winning. Not one of the officers surrounding him was so much as scratched.

For a number of years, while living on Cape Cod, I would stand silently with a group of people in front of the Town Hall in Wellfleet remembering the holocaust caused by the dropping of the atomic bombs on Japan. This was an annual ritual in the town. Admiral Chester Nimitz lived in Wellfleet at that time but unfortunately I never made an effort to meet and talk with him.

In 1995, while hospitalized following my heart attack, I met a nurse and her husband who had just returned from a tour of duty on Okinawa. We talked about the island. Okinawa is now a holiday retreat for the Japanese. It is like their Florida. The memorial to the two Japanese generals still stands in the same spot and is one of the tourist attractions on the island. The native Okinawans are still referred to as "gooks" by the Japanese. They treated them very badly during the war and apparently nothing has changed much since the island has been returned to their government.

In the 1960s, while I was a Professor of Education and Principal of the Antheil School in Ewing Township, New Jersey, my wife and I met Bob and Gladys Flemming. Bob was my mentor at New York University and became the Associate Commissioner of Education for the state. Gladys was still teaching as a Professor of Education at New York University. We became very good friends with the Flemmings.

One night, at dinner, the conversation turned to our experiences during World War II. I mentioned that I had gone through the Okinawa campaign. Gladys spoke up saying, "Isn't that interesting. I was a Colonel and Commanding Officer of all the nurses during that entire campaign. We had our headquarters on a hillside."

"I know, I was there."

From *The Inn at Chongju*

Many years later, my son, Woody, and I were driving around the Cape Cod National Seashore looking for a summer "Sweep-out Cottage." We looked over many properties. None seemed to catch our fancy. As a last resort, the real estate agent told us about a property whose previous owner had collected and cared for up to 1,500 orchids in his greenhouse. That's all it took. We rushed to the place and found an abandoned house of many rooms with soaring glass windows stretching along a knoll overlooking the North Atlantic.

This would become "Umimatsu," our fantasy escape home for the next fifteen years.

One of the rooms had twenty-foot walls of glass facing a gigantic, gnarled pine tree shaped like a bonsai. A water garden filled with Japanese Koi stretched to one side of the tree. A sunken tub in the room's floor, big enough for two and located beside a Korean fireplace became a favorite bathing pool for me and the woman I loved so well. When the moon shone down upon the tree and pond, however, I could easily imagine a return to the Inn at Chongju.

■ ■ ■

October, 1945
Kimpo Airport
Seoul, Korea

Dear Folks:

This is just an early morning short note to let you know that we are about to take off to Taejon, a city far south of here. It will probably take us several days of driving to get there. I want to get this into the mail before we take off. One of my sergeants has gone ahead with a couple of the men to find places for us to spend the nights along the way. I don't know where that will be and it isn't likely that I will have time to write another letter when I get there.

Guess what?

A little spotted dog wandered into our quarters last evening. We named her "Kimpo" and she has already become the company mascot. I will never forget the little village of Kimpo and the friendly people who were so glad to welcome us. This appears to be a wonderful country and I am so glad to be part of the history of helping these people after their bad experiences with Japan's harsh imperial occupation.

The Kimpo villagers threw a wonderful dinner for us. It was something like a church supper. I made a speech. We drank a warm wine called saki. I think you would like it once you became used to the special taste. These folks treated us like heroes.

It is hard to predict what we will encounter when we arrive in Taejon. The only thing we know is that an entire Japanese army is based there. It will be our job to get them out of there and on their way back to Japan. Colonel Packler tells me that we will be plenty busy. It is hard for me to imagine working with the Japanese after all the killing down at Okinawa. I will need God's assistance in the days ahead to make good decisions. I am to be a Liaison Officer with the Japanese Army. A Japanese officer will be appointed to work with me but I don't know who he will be.

I'll have lots of stories to tell you when I get home. In the meantime, we have another job to do and it already feels much better than combat. A Korean winter lies just ahead. We'll miss the warm sun and beaches of Okinawa but not the fighting and killing.

Stay well now. Keep the letters coming. Give my doggie a pat for me. Tell "Sunny Girl" that I love her and have her picture in my wallet where I keep precious items.

Your loving son, Rollie

From *The Hawk and the Dove*

My first loss of innocence took place when, as a young country boy, the war transported me from a quiet and safe rural village in western Pennsylvania to a battlefield in Okinawa. Peter's body, still warm in my arms, made it perfectly clear that I, too, could die instantly. From that moment forward, a place of safety didn't exist for me, or so I believed. But on my return home from the war, it seemed that the shock of killing so many humans so far away from peaceful Ligonier Valley would fade, I would put behind me dangers to my life that would never return. The instant the dove crashed into the window inches from my face stripped away the psychological shield that protected me from remembering the constant shocks of witnessing death. It took this sudden instant to bring it all back threatening my stability in an otherwise beautiful seaside environment. Months and years would go by without such a dramatic reminder of my mortality. Living out days and years of tranquility led me to believe that once again a safe world resulted from the carnage of war. We were living in a safe dream world. There was no need to fear or remember. My psychiatrist and I put to rest the demons in my head resulting from fighting and killing in Okinawa.

On September 11, "as I watched the TV window to the world, the planes crashed into the World Trade Center in New York City and the Pentagon in Washington, D.C.," my body stiffened with fear as it became clear that the entire country instantly lost a sweeping and total innocence as real as did the country boy who went to war. Safety no longer existed for an entire population. It would never return. No place to hide. Ever again. This was a war without an end. It would go on forever. The hawk would always be there. The image of the dead bird etched on the window pane could not be erased. The warmth of the dead boy's body in my arms could still be felt even when the sun of the coming springs brought forth another season of fresh green leaves and beautiful flowers.

From *Epilogue*

Hyde Park, New York is the birthplace of Franklin Delano Roosevelt and the former home of his parents. The Roosevelt estate is located along the Hudson River in the village of Hyde Park, a few miles north of the city of Poughkeepsie. The first Presidential Library, established on the estate, now has a new wing devoted to honoring Eleanor Roosevelt.

The President built his wife a cottage, known as Val Kil, where she could go to have some privacy. Mrs. Roosevelt did not like the "Big House" as she referred to the mansion. The relationship between Eleanor Roosevelt and her mother-in-law was very difficult.

During the 1950s, while I was teaching at New York University, I had the privilege of meeting Mrs. Roosevelt. She invited several of us young college teachers to bring our students to visit with her at Val Kil. Our students were African Americans who came to NYU during the summers to secure their master's degrees, not available to them at southern universities during that period of racial strife in our history. We would all spread out on the lawn by the lake and listen to Mrs. Roosevelt tell stories about her world travels. Later on, my wife Carol and I were invited to appear with Mrs. Roosevelt on one of her weekly television shows.

I have added this note for the benefit of young readers who do not yet know about Hyde Park, the Roosevelt Family, or much about World War II.

References

Maps of Operation Iceburg published by The Center For Military History

Okinawa: The Last Battle by Roy E. Appleman, James M. Burns, Russel A. Gugler, John Stevens and published by The Center For Military History, The War Department

Okinawa: The Last Battle of World War II by Robert Leckie

Tennozan: The Battle of Okinawa And The Atomic Bomb by George Feifer

The Good War by Studs Terkel

Coming Of Age by Studs Terkel

With The Old Breed At Peleliu and Okinawa by E. B. Sledge

Wartime by Paul Fussell

The Victors by Stephen E. Ambrose

Double Victory, A Multicultural History of America In World War II by Ronald Takaki

My War by Andy Rooney

My War, A Love Story in Letters and Drawings by Tracy Sugarman

The Greatest Generation by Tom Brokaw

The Greatest Generation Speaks by Tom Brokaw

An Album of Memories by Tom Brokaw

My Father's War by Julia Collins

Goodbye Darkness by William Manchester

Luck Of The Draw by Charles Young

Sorrows of Empire by Chalmers Johnson

Index